fine Cooking
Cook Fresh

150 Recipes for Cooking and Eating Fresh Year-Round

Editors of *Fine Cooking*

The Taunton Press

The Taunton Press
Inspiration for hands-on living®

The Taunton Press, Inc.
63 South Main Street
PO Box 5506, Newtown, CT 06470-5506
e-mail: tp@taunton.com

Editor: Carolyn Mandarano
Copy editor: Valerie Cimino
Indexer: Heidi Blough
Jacket/Cover design: Kimberly Adis
Interior design: Kimberly Adis
Layout: Kerstin Fairbend
Cover photographer: Scott Phillips, © The Taunton Press, Inc.
Cover food stylist: Adrienne Anderson
Interior photographers: Scott Phillips, © The Taunton Press, Inc., except for
the following: p. iv, 6, 9, 11, 25, 52, 53, 60, 67, 72, 75, 80, 83, 86, 92, 96, 99, 109,
112, 117, 125, 130, 133, 134, 142, 154, 157, 163, 164, 171, 172, 174, 182, 185, 191,
194, 212, 217: Maren Caruso, © The Taunton Press, Inc.; p. 2, 10, 178 : Judi Rutz;
p. 5: Quentin Bacon; p. 12: John Kernick; p. 30, 168: Pernille Pendersen; p. 32:
Steve Hunter, © The Taunton Press, Inc.; p. 202: Mark Ferri; p. 207: Alexandra
Grablewski; p. 209: Kate Sears; p. 223 (top): Anna Williams

Fine Cooking® is a trademark of The Taunton Press, Inc., registered in the U.S.
Patent and Trademark Office.

The following names/manufacturers appearing in *Fine Cooking Cook Fresh* are
trademarks: Cholula®, Grand Marnier®, Grill Friends™, Heinz®, Hendrick's®,
Kitchen Friends™, Knob Creek®, Lee Kum Kee®, Mae Ploy®, Maker's Mark®,
Pepperidge Farm®, Pyrex®, Tabasco®, Woodford Reserve®

Library of Congress Cataloging-in-Publication Data in progress

ISBN: 978-1-60085-959-5

Printed in the United States of America
10 9 8 7 6 5 4 3 2 1

contents

asparagus, goat cheese &
bacon tart
(recipe on p. 10)

starters & drinks

toasted pita with black sesame seeds and sumac

MAKES ABOUT 36 PIECES

- 2 tsp. black sesame seeds
- 1 tsp. ground sumac
- ¼ tsp. cayenne; more to taste
  Kosher salt
- 6 whole-wheat or white pita breads
- ⅓ cup (approximately) extra-virgin olive oil
  Garlic-Yogurt Sauce (recipe below)

The pita chips keep well in a sealed bag. Look for black sesame seeds and sumac in specialty stores.

1. Position a rack in the center of the oven and heat the oven to 400°F.

2. In a small bowl, combine the black sesame seeds, sumac, cayenne, and ½ tsp. salt.

3. Split each pita horizontally into 2 rounds and tear each round into 3 rustic pieces. Brush a large rimmed baking sheet with a generous amount of olive oil, and spread 12 of the pita pieces in a single layer, inner side down, on the sheet. Brush the outer side of the pita with additional olive oil and sprinkle evenly with about a third of the spice mixture. Toast the pita in the oven until golden brown and crisp, about 8 minutes. Repeat with the remaining pita and spice mixture in 2 more batches. (The chips may be made 1 day ahead.) Serve with Garlic-Yogurt sauce on the side. *—Tasha DeSerio*

PER SERVING: 50 CALORIES | 1G PROTEIN | 6G CARB | 2.5G TOTAL FAT | 0G SAT FAT | 1.5G MONO FAT | 0G POLY FAT | 0MG CHOL | 105MG SODIUM | 1G FIBER

garlic-yogurt sauce

MAKES ABOUT 1 CUP

- 1 cup full-fat plain yogurt
- 2 Tbs. extra-virgin olive oil
- 1 medium clove garlic, minced and mashed to a paste with a pinch of salt
  Kosher salt

This very simple sauce makes a great dip for vegetables, too.

Combine the yogurt, oil, and garlic in a small bowl and season to taste with salt. Refrigerate until shortly before serving. (The sauce may be made 1 day ahead.)

PER SERVING: 25 CALORIES | 1G PROTEIN | 1G CARB | 2G TOTAL FAT | 0.5G SAT FAT | 1.5G MONO FAT | 0G POLY FAT | 0MG CHOL | 50MG SODIUM | 0G FIBER

creamy white bean and herb dip

SERVES 6 TO 8

2 15-oz. cans cannellini beans, rinsed and drained

4 oz. cream cheese (½ cup)

⅓ cup chopped yellow onion

2 Tbs. fresh lemon juice

1 anchovy fillet, rinsed and patted dry (optional)

Kosher salt and freshly ground black pepper

2 Tbs. extra-virgin olive oil

3 Tbs. thinly sliced fresh chives

1 Tbs. chopped fresh marjoram or oregano

Crudités, crusty sourdough bread, or crackers, for serving

This fresh take on bean dip is equally good served cold or at room temperature.

1. Put the beans, cream cheese, onion, lemon juice, anchovy (if using), 1 tsp. salt, and ½ tsp. pepper in a food processor and process until smooth. With the motor running, drizzle in the oil. Transfer the spread to a large bowl and fold in 2 Tbs. of the chives and the marjoram. Season to taste with salt and pepper.

2. Transfer the spread to a serving bowl, garnish with the remaining 1 Tbs. chives, and serve with crudités, bread, or crackers.
—*Liz Pearson*

PER SERVING: 170 CALORIES | 5G PROTEIN | 16G CARB | 9G TOTAL FAT | 3.5G SAT FAT | 4G MONO FAT | 1G POLY FAT | 15MG CHOL | 300MG SODIUM | 4G FIBER

chunky guacamole

- **1 medium tomato, finely diced (about 1 cup)**
- **½ small red onion, finely diced (about 3 Tbs.)**
- **½ cup coarsely chopped fresh cilantro**
- **3 Tbs. fresh lime juice**
- **¼ tsp. crushed red pepper flakes**
- **Kosher salt**
- **2 large Hass avocados (about 1 pound), cut into ½-inch dice**

There are few dishes as simple yet as easily varied as guacamole. This version lets the flavor and texture of the avocado shine through, amply reinforced with cilantro, red onion, and a splash of lime juice. It can be set out as a dip, used as a garnish for tacos or chili, or spread on sandwiches and burgers.

In a medium bowl, toss the tomatoes with the onion, cilantro, lime juice, red pepper flakes, and 1 tsp. salt, and let sit for about 5 minutes. Add the avocado and gently mash it into the tomato mixture with a fork. Serve immediately. —*Tony Rosenfeld*

PER SERVING: 70 CALORIES | 1G PROTEIN | 5G CARB | 6G TOTAL FAT | 1G SAT FAT | 4G MONO FAT | 0.5G POLY FAT | 0MG CHOL | 115MG SODIUM | 3G FIBER

Store avocados at room temperature until they become just soft and ripe, and then transfer them to the refrigerator, where they'll keep for up to 1 week. (Their skin darkens as the avocados become ripe.) If you want avocados to ripen quickly, put them in a brown paper bag and store them in a warm place (such as near the stove) for a day or two.

crostini with brie, dates & toasted walnuts

SERVES 8

- **1 medium baguette (about ½ lb.), sliced into ½-inch rounds (about 24 slices)**
- **2 Tbs. olive oil**
- **Kosher salt**
- **½ cup coarsely chopped toasted walnuts**
- **½ cup Medjool dates (6 to 8), pitted and coarsely chopped**
- **1 Tbs. honey**
- **1 Tbs. balsamic vinegar**
- **6 oz. Brie, rind trimmed and softened to room temperature**
- **2 Tbs. thinly sliced chives**

This nibble builds on the classic pairing of cheese, dried fruit, and nuts. A splash of balsamic vinegar helps bring together all the flavors. The crostini are best served right out of the oven, though they can also hold for an hour or two at room temperature.

1. Position a rack in the center of the oven and heat the oven to 425°F. Set the bread slices on a large baking sheet; dab both sides with the oil and sprinkle one side lightly with salt (about ¼ tsp. for all the bread). Bake until the bread starts to brown and crisp, about 8 minutes. Meanwhile, in a medium bowl, toss the walnuts with the dates, honey, and vinegar.

2. While the bread is still warm, spread with Brie and then top with the date and nut mixture. Sprinkle with the chives and serve.
—*Tony Rosenfeld*

how to toast nuts

There are two methods for toasting nuts. You can heat them in a skillet over medium-low heat on the stovetop until golden brown (tossing the nuts every 30 seconds or so to avoid scorching), 5 to 10 minutes. Or toast them on a baking sheet in a 350°F oven (with a rack positioned in the center of the oven) until golden brown, 7 to 10 minutes. The oven offers more even and gentle heat, though it's easier to watch the progress when toasting on the stovetop.

asparagus, goat cheese & bacon tart

SERVES 6 TO 8

- 5 slices bacon
- 1 shallot, finely chopped
- 1 bunch asparagus (about 1 lb.), tough ends trimmed, cut into 1-inch pieces
- ½ lb. puff pastry, defrosted if frozen
- ½ lb. soft goat cheese
- Kosher salt and freshly ground black pepper
- 1 large egg yolk mixed with ½ tsp. water

Be sure to cook the pastry fully to get it light and crisp.

1. Heat the oven to 450°F. Cook the bacon in a medium frying pan over medium heat until crisp, about 8 minutes. Transfer to paper towels. Pour off all but 1 Tbs. of the bacon fat from the pan. Add the shallot to the pan and sauté for about 1 minute. Add the asparagus and cook over medium-high heat until the asparagus is crisp-tender, about 5 minutes. Remove the pan from the heat. Crumble the bacon into tiny pieces and mix it with the asparagus and shallot.

2. On a lightly floured piece of parchment, roll out the pastry to a 10x16-inch rectangle. Transfer the pastry and the parchment to a baking sheet.

3. Using your fingers, pat the goat cheese onto the pastry, spreading it as evenly as you can and leaving a 1-inch border around the edge. Sprinkle the asparagus, bacon, and shallot mixture evenly over the goat cheese. Season with salt and pepper. Brush the edge of the tart with the egg wash.

4. Bake until the pastry is golden brown, 20 to 25 minutes. Let cool slightly and serve warm. —*Jan Newberry*

PER SERVING: 580 CALORIES | 20G PROTEIN | 32G CARB | 42G TOTAL FAT | 17G SAT FAT | 19G MONO FAT | 4G POLY FAT | 90MG CHOL | 630MG SODIUM | 3G FIBER

buying and storing asparagus

Look for firm spears with tightly closed buds at the tip. Asparagus begins to lose sweetness the moment it's cut, so check the stem ends for freshness: The best asparagus is not dried out. Many people think thin asparagus is the most tender, but tenderness depends more on freshness.

Submerge the stem ends in water and refrigerate. For best flavor, cook within 2 days.

vegetable crudités with jalapeño dipping sauce

SERVES 8 TO 10

2 cups plain yogurt (preferably not fat-free)

⅓ cup jarred jalapeño slices, drained well

1 small clove garlic, minced and mashed to a paste

Kosher salt and freshly ground black pepper

¼ cup chopped fresh cilantro

2 tsp. chopped fresh thyme

3 lb. fresh vegetables, trimmed, for dipping

The heat of a jalapeño spices up this refreshing vegetable dip. For a tangy alternative with less heat, substitute a teaspoon of lime juice for the jalapeño. Dig in with any of your favorite vegetables, like carrots, asparagus, red pepper slices, cherry tomatoes, broccoli, celery, or fennel.

In a food processor, pulse the yogurt, jalapeños, garlic, ½ tsp. salt, and ½ tsp. pepper until uniform but slightly chunky, 1 or 2 pulses. Transfer to a medium bowl and stir in the cilantro and thyme. Taste and season with more salt and pepper if needed. (You can refrigerate for up to 1 day before serving.) Serve with the vegetables. —*Tony Rosenfeld*

marinated olives

MAKES 2 CUPS

- ½ cup extra-virgin olive oil
- 4 medium cloves garlic, peeled and smashed
- 4 3x1-inch strips orange zest
- 3 3x1-inch strips lemon zest
- 1 Tbs. fresh rosemary leaves
- 1 large or 2 small dried Turkish bay leaves
-   Pinch of crushed red pepper flakes
-   Generous pinch of ground allspice
- 1 cup pitted brined green olives, preferably Picholine
- 1 cup pitted brined black olives, preferably Kalamata

Turkish bay leaves have a more complex, well-rounded flavor than the domestic variety. Here, they add a subtle, sweet astringency to a combination of green and black olives.

1. Heat the oil and garlic in a 2-quart saucepan over medium-low heat until the garlic turns golden, about 3 minutes. Add the orange and lemon zests, the rosemary, bay leaves, red pepper flakes, and allspice and sizzle for another 2 minutes, stirring occasionally. Add the olives and toss to coat. Transfer to a bowl and let cool. Cover and refrigerate, stirring occasionally, for at least 2 days and up to 1 week.

2. Just before serving, gently reheat the olive mixture in a small saucepan over low heat until warmed through, 2 to 3 minutes. Scoop the olives and aromatics into a serving bowl and pour a bit of the oil on top. Serve warm or cool. —*David Leite*

PER SERVING: 130 CALORIES | 0G PROTEIN | 4G CARB | 13G TOTAL FAT | 1.5G SAT FAT | 9G MONO FAT | 1.5G POLY FAT | 0MG CHOL | 410MG SODIUM | 1G FIBER

fresh cherry and jícama relish with goat cheese crostini

SERVES 6

1   cup fresh sweet cherries (about 5½ oz.), pitted and finely chopped

½   cup finely diced jícama

1   medium scallion (white and green parts), very thinly sliced

1   tsp. chopped fresh mint

½   tsp. red-wine vinegar

    Pinch of cayenne; more to taste

    Kosher salt and freshly ground black pepper

2½ oz. (⅓ cup) soft fresh goat cheese

2½ oz. (⅓ cup) ricotta cheese

18 ½-inch-thick baguette slices, toasted

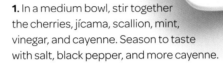

This relish is also delicious spooned over grilled chicken breasts, tossed into a chilled couscous or rice salad, or served as a salsa with tortilla chips.

1. In a medium bowl, stir together the cherries, jícama, scallion, mint, vinegar, and cayenne. Season to taste with salt, black pepper, and more cayenne.

2. In a small bowl, mix the goat and ricotta cheeses with a pinch each of salt and black pepper. Lightly spread the cheese over each baguette toast and top with the cherry relish. *—Joanne Weir*

PER SERVING: 25 CALORIES | 1G PROTEIN | 2G CARB | 1.5G TOTAL FAT | 1G SAT FAT | 0G MONO FAT | 0G POLY FAT | 5MG CHOL | 70MG SODIUM | 0G FIBER

More about Jícama

Part of the legume family, the jícama plant is a vine that can grow 20 feet or longer. The plant's edible tuberous roots (also known as Mexican potatoes or yam beans) weigh between 4 ounces and 6 pounds and are turnip-shaped, with thin skin that requires peeling. Jícama's ivory-colored flesh is a good source of vitamin C and potassium.

Buying and storing

Jícama is available year-round, but its peak season is between November and June. Choose firm roots that seem heavy for their size; blemishes, wrinkled skin, or dark spots indicate overripeness. Store whole jícama in the fridge for up to 1 month; wrap cut jícama in plastic and refrigerate for up to a week.

Prepping and using

Remove jícama's thin, fibrous peel with a vegetable peeler or paring knife, as you would for a potato. Peeled jícama can be sliced, diced, julienned, or shredded and prepared many ways. In Mexico, it's commonly served raw with a squeeze of lime juice, a sprinkle of salt, and a touch of chile powder for a snack. Uncooked, it adds crunch to salads, condiments, and slaws; cut into large sticks, it can be dunked in guacamole and other dips. Try it sautéed with chicken or shrimp, add it to savory stews, or glaze and broil it. Jícama can also be baked, boiled, steamed, and fried. It pairs well with fresh flavors like cilantro, ginger, lemon, and lime.

pink lemonade

**MAKES ABOUT 7 CUPS;
SERVES 6 TO 8**

1½ cups granulated sugar

1 cup coarsely chopped fresh
   strawberries (about 6 oz.)

   Zest of 2 lemons, peeled off
   in strips with a vegetable
   peeler (avoid the white pith)

2 cups fresh lemon juice

*Strawberries are the secret to this lemonade's bold hue. They lend a
sweet berry contrast to the tart lemon flavor.*

1. In a medium saucepan, combine the sugar and strawberries with
2 cups water. Bring to a boil over medium-high heat, stirring occasionally. Reduce the heat to low and simmer until the berries begin to
release their color and soften slightly, about 3 minutes. Stir in the lemon zest. Set aside and let cool completely. The berries will continue to
soften and release their color while the syrup cools.

2. Pour the cooled syrup and berries into a fine-mesh sieve set over
a pitcher or bowl. With the back of a spoon or a rubber spatula, press
lightly on the berries to extract most of the syrup. Discard the solids.

3. Add the lemon juice and 2 ½ cups cold water to the syrup mixture
and stir until well blended. The lemonade can be served immediately
over ice or refrigerated for up to 2 days. *—Abigail Johnson Dodge*

PER SERVING: 170 CALORIES | 0G PROTEIN | 45G CARB | 0G TOTAL FAT | 0G SAT FAT |
0G MONO FAT | 0G POLY FAT | 0MG CHOL | 0MG SODIUM | 1G FIBER

fresh cherry margarita

SERVES 1

- **12** fresh sweet cherries, pitted
- **1¼** fl. oz. (2 ½ Tbs.) tequila, preferably blanco 100% agave
- **1** fl. oz. (2 Tbs.) fresh lime juice
- **¾** fl. oz. (1½ Tbs.) agave nectar, preferably dark
- **½** fl. oz. (1 Tbs.) maraschino liqueur
- **1** fresh sweet cherry with stem, for garnish

Look for agave nectar at the supermarket near the honey and maple syrup.

Put the pitted cherries in a cocktail shaker and mash them with a muddler or the end of a wooden spoon until well crushed, about 1 minute. Add the tequila, lime juice, agave nectar, maraschino liqueur, and 8 large ice cubes. Cover the shaker and shake vigorously for 30 seconds. Immediately strain into a rocks glass filled with fresh ice. Garnish with the cherry. *—Joanne Weir*

PER SERVING: 270 CALORIES | 1G PROTEIN | 46G CARB | 0G TOTAL FAT | 0G SAT FAT | 0G MONO FAT | 0G POLY FAT | 0MG CHOL | 0MG SODIUM | 0G FIBER

watermelon gin punch

SERVES 8

- **½** small round seedless watermelon (about 3½ lb.), peeled and cut into chunks
- **½** cup granulated sugar
- **½** cup fresh lemon juice, strained
- **8** sprigs fresh mint; more for garnish
- **2** cups gin, preferably Hendrick's®

Gin's herbal flavors are a natural match for melon in this summery cocktail.

1. Working in batches, purée the watermelon in a blender or food processor and press the purée through a strainer. You'll need about 4 cups juice—it's fine if there's some pulp in the juice. Chill.

2. Put the sugar in a small saucepan over medium heat and add ½ cup water. Cook, stirring, just until the sugar is dissolved. Cool.

3. Put the lemon juice, sugar syrup, and mint in a 3-quart serving pitcher or a punch bowl and mash the mint thoroughly with a muddler or the back of a wooden spoon. Add about 4 cups ice, the gin, and the watermelon juice and stir. Serve in rocks glasses over ice, garnished with mint sprigs. *—St. John Frizell*

PER SERVING: 190 CALORIES | 1G PROTEIN | 15G CARB | 0G TOTAL FAT | 0G SAT FAT | 0G MONO FAT | 0G POLY FAT | 0MG CHOL | 0MG SODIUM | 0G FIBER

mojito

SERVES 1

6 large fresh spearmint
   leaves, plus 1 nice sprig for
   garnish

4 tsp. superfine sugar; more
   to taste

1 lime

   Crushed ice as needed

2 fl. oz. (¼ cup) light rum

   Cold club soda as needed

This refreshing Cuban cocktail (it's pronounced moh-HEE-toh) makes the most of fresh mint and lime. If your barware is particularly fragile, muddle the mint and sugar together in a mortar or other vessel and then transfer it to the serving glass. This recipe doubles or quadruples easily.

If you have trouble finding superfine sugar, just make your own by grinding regular granulated sugar in a food processor or blender.

1. In a tall, narrow (Collins) glass, mash the mint leaves into the sugar with a muddler or a similar tool (like the handle of a wooden spoon) until the leaves look crushed and the sugar starts to turn light green, about 30 seconds. Cut the lime into quarters. Squeeze the juice from all 4 quarters into the glass, dropping 2 of the squeezed quarters into the glass as you go. Stir with a teaspoon until the sugar dissolves into the lime juice.

2. Fill the glass with crushed ice and pour the rum over the ice. Top off with club soda, stir well, garnish with the mint sprig, and serve right away. —*Jennifer Armentrout*

PER SERVING: 180 CALORIES | 1G PROTEIN | 13G CARB | 0G TOTAL FAT | 0G SAT FAT | 0G MONO FAT | 0G POLY FAT | 0MG CHOL | 35MG SODIUM | 0G FIBER

derby day mint julep cocktail

FOR THE MINT SYRUP

25	fresh spearmint or apple mint leaves
¾	cup granulated sugar

FOR THE JULEPS

3½	quarts crushed ice
3½	cups bourbon (such as Maker's Mark® or Knob Creek®)
14	thin lemon slices
14	sprigs fresh spearmint or apple mint

There are as many variations of the mint julep as there are thorough-breds that have run in the Kentucky Derby, which is when this sweet concoction is traditionally served. It's often stirred with ice in a silver cup; this version calls for shaking with a slice of lemon for a frothy, refreshing drink.

MAKE THE MINT SYRUP

In a small saucepan, stir the mint with the sugar and ¾ cup water, crushing the mint lightly with the spoon. Bring to a boil over medium-high heat and boil for 1 minute. Remove from the heat and let cool in the pan, about 30 minutes. Strain into a small container. Use immediately to make the cocktails or chill for up to 2 weeks.

FOR EACH COCKTAIL

Have a chilled 8- to 10-oz. cocktail or wine glass ready. In a cocktail shaker, combine 1 Tbs. of the mint syrup with 1 cup ice, ¼ cup bourbon, and a lemon slice. Shake for 30 seconds; pour into the chilled glass. Garnish with a mint sprig. —*Jessica Bard*

PER SERVING: 160 CALORIES | 0G PROTEIN | 8G CARB | 0G TOTAL FAT | 0G SAT FAT | 0G MONO FAT | 0G POLY FAT | 0MG CHOL | 0MG SODIUM | 0G FIBER

A Buyer's Guide to Mint

There are more than 200 mint varieties, all of which fall into one of two categories: spearmint or peppermint. They're similar in taste and aroma, but peppermints contain menthol, which gives them a stronger character and a cooling sensation. Here's a guide for some of the common varieties.

SPEARMINT

The most versatile of mints, spearmint has a natural affinity to fruits and spring vegetables (think peas, asparagus, and artichokes), herbs like basil and cilantro, and spices like ginger, cumin, and cardamom. Its relatively mild flavor makes it ideal for a variety of savory dishes, including grilled and roasted meats.

Spearmint varieties

Pineapple mint With a fruity scent reminiscent of pineapple and a flavor that's a bit sweeter than regular spearmint, pineapple mint complements other fresh, fruity flavors and livens up rich cheeses and meats.

Apple mint Its gentle spearmint flavor has a hint of green apple. It's lovely in iced tea.

Curly and smooth-leaf mint Both taste just like spearmint but have different textures. Curly mint is ruffled and a bit coarser, while smooth-leaf mint is soft and velvety. Use them to add textural variety to a dish.

PEPPERMINT

Peppermint is assertive enough to stand up to strong flavors, so it's ideal for chocolate desserts and boldly flavored dishes.

Peppermint varieties

Orange mint Overtones of orange and sometimes bergamot make it a good choice when you want to add a citrusy note.

Chocolate mint This peppermint has an unmistakable hint of chocolate that makes it ideal for desserts that feature chocolate and berries.

Ginger mint The ginger notes complement dishes that use fresh or ground ginger.

Grapefruit mint Hints of grapefruit set off anything with citrus zest.

tortellini soup with carrots,
peas & leeks
(recipe on p. 27)

soups

root vegetable and barley soup with bacon

**MAKES 13 CUPS;
SERVES 6 TO 8**

- **1 oz. dried porcini mushrooms**
- **2 medium cloves garlic**
- **Kosher salt**
- **4 slices bacon, halved crosswise**
- **2 medium red onions, chopped**
- **2 small bay leaves**
- **¾ tsp. caraway seeds**
- **½ tsp. dried thyme**
- **Freshly ground black pepper**
- **2 quarts homemade or lower-salt chicken broth**
- **5 medium carrots, peeled and cut into small dice**
- **2 medium purple-top turnips, peeled and cut into small dice**
- **2 medium Yukon Gold potatoes, peeled and cut into small dice**
- **¾ cup pearl barley, picked over, rinsed, and drained**
- **4 tsp. fresh lemon juice**

If you store this for more than a day, the barley will absorb some of the liquid and you'll need to thin the soup with a little water when you reheat it. Store leftovers in the refrigerator for up to 2 days.

1. In a small bowl, soak the mushrooms in 1 cup boiling water for 20 minutes. Remove the mushrooms and pour the liquid through a fine-mesh strainer to remove any grit. Reserve the liquid. Rinse the mushrooms, chop them, and set aside.

2. Chop the garlic, sprinkle it with ¾ tsp. salt, and then mash it to a paste with the side of a chef's knife. Set aside.

3. Cook the bacon in a 6-quart (or larger) Dutch oven over medium heat until crisp, about 8 minutes. Transfer to a paper-towel-lined plate, set aside, and crumble when cool.

4. Add the onion and 1 tsp. salt to the bacon fat and cook, stirring occasionally, until softened, 6 to 8 minutes. Stir in the garlic paste, bay leaves, caraway seeds, thyme, and ¼ tsp. pepper and cook, stirring constantly, until fragrant, about 1 minute. Add the chopped mushrooms, reserved mushroom liquid, chicken broth, carrots, turnips, potatoes, barley, and 1½ cups water. Bring to a boil over high heat; skim any foam as necessary. Reduce the heat, cover, and simmer, stirring occasionally, until the barley and vegetables are tender, 20 to 25 minutes. Discard the bay leaves, add the lemon juice, and season with salt and pepper. Serve garnished with the crumbled bacon.
—*Lori Longbotham*

PER SERVING: 210 CALORIES | 11G PROTEIN | 37G CARB | 3.5G TOTAL FAT | 1G SAT FAT | 1.5G MONO FAT | 0.5G POLY FAT | 5MG CHOL | 450MG SODIUM | 7G FIBER

chilled cucumber-buttermilk soup

SERVES 4

1½ **lb. cucumbers, peeled, seeded, and cut into chunks**

2 **medium celery ribs, coarsely chopped**

1 **small shallot, coarsely chopped**

¼ **cup extra-virgin olive oil; more for garnish**

Kosher salt

½ **cup sour cream**

½ **cup buttermilk**

Freshly ground black pepper

Chopped chives, for garnish

In this summery soup, sour cream bolsters the buttermilk's tang, which in turn plays up the cooling notes of cucumber; celery lends a savory undertone. You can make this soup up to 2 days ahead.

In a blender, purée the cucumber, celery, shallot, olive oil, and 1 tsp. salt until smooth. Strain through a medium-mesh sieve into a large bowl, pressing on the solids to extract as much liquid as possible. Whisk in the sour cream and buttermilk and season to taste with salt and pepper. Refrigerate until chilled, at least 1 hour. Serve drizzled with olive oil and garnished with chives. *—Maria Helm Sinskey*

PER SERVING: 200 CALORIES | 2G PROTEIN | 6G CARB | 19G TOTAL FAT | 5G SAT FAT | 11G MONO FAT | 1.5G POLY FAT | 15MG CHOL | 490MG SODIUM | 1G FIBER

chilled red pepper soup
with sautéed shrimp

MAKES 6 CUPS

- **1** **seedless English cucumber, peeled and coarsely chopped**
- **3** **jarred roasted red peppers, cut into ½-inch dice (about 1½ cups)**
- **3** **cups tomato juice**
- **2** **slices baguette, toasted and cut into 1-inch cubes (about 1 cup)**
- **½** **cup extra-virgin olive oil**
- **2** **Tbs. plus 1 tsp. sherry vinegar or cider vinegar**
- **1** **medium clove garlic, minced and mashed to a paste**
- **½** **tsp. ground cumin**
-    **Kosher salt and freshly ground black pepper**
- **¾** **lb. medium shrimp (36 to 40 per lb.), peeled and deveined**
- **1** **tsp. chopped fresh thyme**

This cold soup builds on the flavors of Spanish gazpacho, only roasted red peppers take the place of tomatoes in the lead role.

1. Cut three-quarters of the cucumber into 1-inch pieces and purée in a blender with the red peppers, tomato juice, toasted bread, 6 Tbs. olive oil, 2 Tbs. vinegar, garlic, cumin, and ½ tsp. each salt and pepper (you may have to purée the soup in batches, depending on the size of your blender). Taste and season with more salt and pepper if needed, and refrigerate until cold, at least 30 minutes and up to 1 day.

2. Heat 1 Tbs. of the olive oil in a large (12-inch) skillet over high heat until it's shimmering. Add the shrimp and cook, tossing, until it starts to brown and lose its raw color, about 2 minutes. Stir in the thyme, ½ tsp. pepper, and ¼ tsp. salt and cook until the shrimp are just cooked through, about 1 minute. Transfer to a plate to cool.

3. Just before serving, cut the remainder of the cucumber into ¼-inch dice (about ½ cup) and toss with the remaining 1 Tbs. olive oil, the remaining 1 tsp. vinegar, and ½ tsp. salt. Serve the soup cold in individual bowls, garnished with the cucumber and shrimp.

—*Tony Rosenfeld*

black bean soup with sweet potatoes

**MAKES ABOUT 14 CUPS;
SERVES 8**

- 2   Tbs. vegetable oil
- 2   medium yellow onions, chopped
- 3   medium cloves garlic, coarsely chopped
- 1½   tsp. ground coriander
- 1   tsp. ground cumin
- ¼   tsp. aniseed
-     Freshly ground black pepper
- 2   quarts lower-salt chicken broth or homemade vegetable broth
- 4   15½-oz. (or two 29-oz.) cans black beans, rinsed and drained
- 2   medium sweet potatoes, peeled and cut into medium dice
-     Kosher salt
- ½   cup plain yogurt
- 8   paper-thin lime slices

The sweet potatoes in this soup contrast nicely with the tang of the yogurt and the tartness of the lime. Aniseed lends an unusual hint of licorice flavor.

1. Heat the oil over medium heat in a 6-quart (or larger) Dutch oven. Add the onion and cook, stirring occasionally, until it starts to soften and brown slightly, about 8 minutes. Add the garlic, coriander, cumin, aniseed, and ¼ tsp. pepper and cook, stirring constantly, until fragrant, about 30 seconds. Add the broth, beans, sweet potatoes, and ¾ tsp. salt and bring to a boil over high heat; skim any foam as necessary. Reduce the heat and simmer, uncovered, stirring occasionally, until the sweet potatoes are tender, about 15 minutes.

2. Using a slotted spoon, set aside 3 cups of the beans and potatoes. Carefully purée the remaining soup in batches in a blender. Pour the puréed soup back into the pot and return the solids to the soup, reheat gently, and season to taste with salt and pepper. Serve topped with a dollop of the yogurt and a lime slice. Store leftovers in the refrigerator for up to 5 days.   *—Lori Longbotham*

PER SERVING: 310 CALORIES | 17G PROTEIN | 51G CARB | 6G TOTAL FAT | 1G SAT FAT | 2.5G MONO FAT | 2G POLY FAT | 0MG CHOL | 370MG SODIUM | 11G FIBER

tortellini soup with carrots, peas & leeks

SERVES 4

2 medium leeks
(¾ lb. untrimmed)

1 Tbs. unsalted butter

3 cloves garlic, finely chopped
(about 1 Tbs.)

½ medium carrot, peeled and
finely diced (2 Tbs.)

Kosher salt and freshly
ground black pepper

5 cups homemade or lower-
salt chicken broth

½ lb. frozen cheese tortellini

1 cup frozen peas

¼ cup freshly grated
Parmigiano-Reggiano or
Grana Padano

You can make most of the soup ahead, but don't add the tortellini until you're ready to eat or they'll become mushy.

1. Trim the roots and dark green leaves from the leeks. Slice the white and light green parts in half lengthwise and then thinly slice the halves crosswise. Rinse well and drain.

2. Melt the butter in a 4-quart saucepan over medium heat. Add the garlic, leeks, and carrots. Season with a couple of pinches of salt and cook, stirring occasionally, until tender, 5 to 7 minutes. (It's fine if the vegetables brown lightly.) Stir in ¼ tsp. pepper and cook for about 20 seconds, then add the chicken broth and bring to a boil.

3. Add the tortellini and cook for 3 minutes. Reduce the heat to a simmer and add the peas. Continue to simmer until the tortellini are cooked, 3 to 5 minutes. Season to taste with salt and pepper. Portion the soup into bowls, top each with some of the cheese, and serve.
—*Joanne Smart*

PER SERVING: 310 CALORIES | 17G PROTEIN | 43G CARB | 9G TOTAL FAT | 4.5G SAT FAT | 2.5G MONO FAT | 1G POLY FAT | 35MG CHOL | 540MG SODIUM | 4G FIBER

pea and mint soup with lemon cream

- **2 Tbs. unsalted butter**
- **½ cup coarsely chopped shallots**
- **1 tsp. minced garlic**
- **4 cups fresh shelled peas (3½ to 4 lb. unshelled) or frozen peas**
- **2 cups homemade vegetable broth**
- **½ cup chopped fresh mint**
- **Kosher salt and freshly ground black pepper**
- **Pinch of granulated sugar (optional)**
- **½ cup heavy cream**
- **Finely grated zest of ½ medium lemon**

You can serve this soup hot or cold. Its flavor is brighter if you use very fresh, young peas. The starchiness of mature peas can give the soup a split-pea flavor, so if you can't find young peas, use frozen instead.

1. Melt the butter in a 3- to 4-quart saucepan over medium heat. Add the shallot and garlic and cook, stirring frequently, until both are soft, 6 to 8 minutes. They shouldn't brown. If they're cooking too fast, reduce the heat to medium low.

2. Add the peas, broth, half of the mint, and 2 cups water. Season with salt and pepper. Bring to a boil, reduce the heat to medium low, and simmer vigorously until the peas are very tender, 8 to 10 minutes.

3. Purée the soup in a blender until smooth, working in batches and making sure to vent the blender by removing the pop-up center or lifting one edge of the top (drape a towel over the top to keep the soup from leaking).

4. Season to taste with salt and pepper. If the peas weren't very sweet, stir in the sugar.

5. Pour the heavy cream into a medium bowl and whip it to soft peaks with a whisk. Fold in the lemon zest and season to taste with salt and pepper.

6. Ladle the soup into serving bowls and top with a spoonful of the lemon cream. Scatter the remaining mint over the soup and serve. If you choose to serve the soup cold, chill it in the fridge but take it out 15 minutes before you serve. Adjust the seasonings if necessary.
—Annie Wayte

PER SERVING: 200 CALORIES | 7G PROTEIN | 17G CARB | 12G TOTAL FAT | 7G SAT FAT | 3.5G MONO FAT | 0.5G POLY FAT | 35MG CHOL | 240MG SODIUM | 5G FIBER

chicken noodle soup with lemongrass

2½ Tbs. canola oil

2 small boneless, skinless chicken breast halves (about ¾ lb. total), butterflied (cut horizontally almost all the way through and then opened like a book)

Kosher salt and freshly ground black pepper

3 medium shallots (about 4 oz.), peeled and thinly sliced into rings

2 stalks lemongrass, trimmed, outer layers discarded, halved lengthwise, and smashed with the side of a chef's knife

1 Tbs. minced fresh ginger

2 tsp. packed light brown sugar

5½ cups homemade or lower-salt chicken broth

3½ oz. fresh shiitake mushrooms, stemmed and quartered (1½ cups)

9 oz. fresh udon noodles

1 Thai bird chile (or 1 small serrano chile), sliced into thin rings

8 large fresh basil leaves, torn; plus sprigs for garnish

1 medium lime, ½ juiced and ½ cut into wedges

1 Tbs. soy sauce; more to taste

2 medium scallions, trimmed and sliced, for garnish (optional)

1 medium carrot, cut into matchsticks, for garnish (optional)

½ cup fresh cilantro leaves, for garnish (optional)

In this cross between Vietnamese pho and Japanese udon noodle soup, fresh udon noodles are the star. Fat and bouncy in texture, they cook faster and tend to be more delicate than dried.

1. Heat 1½ Tbs. of the oil in a 5- to 6-quart Dutch oven over medium-high heat until shimmering hot. Season the chicken with ½ tsp. each salt and pepper and cook without disturbing until it's browned and releases easily from the bottom of the pot, about 2 minutes. Flip and cook until the second side is browned and almost firm to the touch (just short of cooked through), another 1 to 2 minutes. Transfer the chicken to a cutting board to cool.

2. Add the remaining 1 Tbs. oil and the shallot to the pot. Sprinkle with ¼ tsp. salt, reduce the heat to medium, and cook, stirring, until the shallot starts to soften, about 2 minutes. Add the lemongrass, ginger, and brown sugar and cook, stirring, until the ginger and lemongrass sizzle and become fragrant, about 1 minute. Add the chicken broth, scraping up any browned bits from the bottom of the pot, and raise the heat to medium high. Bring the broth to a boil and then reduce to a simmer. Add the mushrooms and cook, stirring occasionally, until tender, 5 to 7 minutes.

3. Meanwhile, bring a medium pot of well-salted water to a boil and cook the noodles, stirring, until just tender, about 3 minutes. Transfer to a colander and run under cold water to cool slightly. Drain well.

4. Use your fingers or the tines of a fork to shred the chicken. Add the chicken and noodles to the broth and cook until the noodles are completely tender and the chicken is cooked through, about 2 minutes. Discard the lemongrass. Stir in the sliced chile, torn basil, lime juice, and soy sauce; season with more soy to taste. Portion the noodles among 4 large, deep bowls. Ladle the soup over the noodles and garnish with the basil sprigs and scallions, carrot, and cilantro, if using. Serve with the lime wedges for squeezing. *—Tony Rosenfeld*

PER SERVING: 500 CALORIES | 35G PROTEIN | 59G CARB | 15G TOTAL FAT | 2G SAT FAT | 7G MONO FAT | 3.5G POLY FAT | 45MG CHOL | 930MG SODIUM | 5G FIBER

More about Lemongrass

Evergreen in warm climates, lemongrass is a sharp-bladed, perennial, blue-green grass that grows in 3- to 6-foot-tall cascading clumps. In addition to its uses in the kitchen, it's valued medicinally as a remedy for a wide range of ailments, from stomach troubles and fever to depression.

The ethereal aroma of lemongrass—redolent of tropical flowers, ginger, and all things citrus—is like a delicate perfume for food. Lemongrass pairs well with just about anything, although it's particularly good with seafood, chicken, and pork. It also has an affinity to coconut milk. Its most iconic use is in Thai curry pastes, where it's puréed with chiles, shallots, ginger, garlic, and spices to become an aromatic flavor base for all types of curries.

Buying and storing
Much of lemongrass's flavor is concentrated in its lower, cane-like stalks, which is why most markets sell them already trimmed of their leafy tops, leaving just a few short, spiky blades still attached. Look for firm, pale green stalks with fat, bulbous bottoms and reasonably fresh-looking tops (they may be a little dry but shouldn't be desiccated or yellowed). To store, wrap in plastic and refrigerate for 2 to 3 weeks, or freeze for up to 6 months.

Cooking
There are two main ways to cook with lemongrass, and each determines how you handle it. To infuse teas, broths, soups, and braising liquids, trim off the spiky tops and the bases, crush the stalks with the side of a knife to release their aromatic oils, and then cut them into 1- or 2-inch pieces. Remove the pieces before eating (they tend to be woody) or eat around them.

To use lemongrass in marinades, stir-fries, salads, spice rubs, and curry pastes, trim the top and base of the stalks—you want to use only the bottom 4 inches or so. Then peel off any dry or tough outer layers before finely chopping or mincing. Lemongrass holds up to long cooking and gains intensity the longer it's cooked. If you'd like a strong lemongrass flavor, add minced lemongrass at the start of cooking, browning it along with the other aromatics. For a lighter, fresher lemongrass flavor, add it near the end of cooking.

escarole and white bean soup with rustic croutons

SERVES 4

- ¼ cup extra-virgin olive oil
- 1 medium onion (about 6 oz.), diced
- 1 Tbs. minced garlic
- 1 medium to large head escarole (about 14 oz.), trimmed of outer leaves, 2 inches of root end cut off, leaves sliced across into ¾-inch wide strips (to yield about 9 to 10 cups), and thoroughly washed

  Kosher salt and freshly ground black pepper
- 2 cups homemade or lower-salt vegetable broth
- 1 cup cooked small white beans (if canned, drained)
- 1 Tbs. fresh lemon juice
- ¼ cup grated Parmigiano-Reggiano

  Rustic Croutons (recipe below)

This is a variation on a classic Italian soup that traditionally has more escarole and beans than broth. Escarole is one of the easiest greens to prepare since you don't need to stem it; just slice the whole head across into ribbons before washing.

1. Heat the olive oil in a 4-quart low-sided soup pot or Dutch oven over medium to medium-high heat. Add the onion and sauté until softened and browned, about 12 minutes. Add the garlic, stir, and sauté until fragrant, about 1 minute. Add the escarole and stir thoroughly to coat the leaves (and to deglaze the pan slightly with their moisture). Season with ½ tsp. salt and a few grinds of pepper. Add the broth, stir well, and bring to a boil; cover the pot, lower to a simmer, and cook for 8 to 10 minutes. Uncover the pot, add the beans, and simmer for another 2 to 3 minutes. Add the lemon juice and turn off the heat.

2. Ladle the soup into 4 shallow soup bowls and top each with 1 Tbs. of the cheese and a quarter of the croutons. *—Susie Middleton*

PER SERVING: 390 CALORIES | 14G PROTEIN | 30G CARB | 25G TOTAL FAT | 5G SAT FAT | 16G MONO FAT | 2G POLY FAT | 15MG CHOL | 1080MG SODIUM | 9G FIBER

rustic croutons

MAKES 2 CUPS

- 2 Tbs. extra-virgin olive oil
- 2 cups lightly packed ¾-inch cubes of bread from a good airy loaf like ciabatta

  Kosher salt

Heat the olive oil in a nonstick skillet over medium-high heat. Add the bread cubes and stir to coat with the oil. Season with salt and sauté, stirring constantly, until crisp and browned on most sides, 2 to 4 minutes.

summer vegetable soup with dill

SERVES 8 AS A FIRST COURSE

- 3 cups buttermilk, chilled and well shaken
- 1 cup plain Greek yogurt, chilled
- 2 cups seeded medium-diced ripe tomatoes
- 2 cups fresh corn kernels
- ½ cup small-diced fresh fennel, plus chopped fronds if available
- ½ cup peeled, seeded, and small-diced cucumber
- 3 Tbs. finely chopped fresh dill; more for garnish

  Kosher salt and freshly ground black pepper

Showcase summer's delicious bounty with a chilled buttermilk soup loaded with in-season vegetables and flavored with aromatic dill. This soup makes a great starter for just about anything you're putting on the grill for dinner. If you have sweet, tender farm-fresh corn, use it raw. If your corn is a little starchy, blanch the ears in boiling water before cutting off the kernels.

Try adding other herbs to the soup—basil or flat-leaf parsley would be particularly nice.

1. Whisk the buttermilk and yogurt in a large bowl. Stir in the tomatoes, corn, fennel, cucumber, dill, 1 tsp. salt, and ¼ tsp. pepper. Season to taste with more salt and pepper. Serve immediately or cover and refrigerate for up to 24 hours.

2. Serve the soup in chilled bowls, garnished with dill.
—*Lori Longbotham*

PER SERVING: 120 CALORIES | 6G PROTEIN | 16G CARB | 4G TOTAL FAT | 3G SAT FAT | 1G MONO FAT | 0G POLY FAT | 10MG CHOL | 250MG SODIUM | 2G FIBER

curried carrot soup with cilantro

2 Tbs. vegetable oil

1½ lb. carrots, cut into 1-inch chunks (about 4 cups)

1 large yellow onion, cut into 1-inch chunks

3 large cloves garlic, thinly sliced

1 tsp. curry powder

3 cups lower-salt chicken broth

Kosher salt

1½ cups carrot juice; more as needed

¼ cup packed fresh cilantro leaves

Freshly ground black pepper

Chopped peanuts, for garnish (optional)

The sweetness of the carrots is the perfect foil to spicy curry and the fresh citrus flavor of cilantro.

1. Heat the oil in a 10- or 11-inch straight-sided sauté pan over medium-high heat until hot. Add the carrots and then the onion. Cook, stirring very little at first and more frequently toward the end, until the vegetables are golden brown, 6 to 8 minutes.

2. Add the garlic and curry powder and cook, stirring, for about 30 seconds. Add the broth and ½ tsp. salt and bring to a simmer over medium-high heat. Reduce the heat to low, cover, and simmer until the vegetables are very tender, 10 to 15 minutes. Add the carrot juice and cilantro.

3. Purée the soup in a blender, working in two batches and making sure to vent the blender by removing the pop-up center or lifting one edge of the top (drape a towel over the top to keep the soup from leaking).

4. Return the soup to the pan, heat through, and season to taste with salt and pepper. If necessary, add more carrot juice to thin to your liking. Ladle into bowls and serve, sprinkled with the peanuts, if using.
—Pam Anderson

PER SERVING: 140 CALORIES | 4G PROTEIN | 21G CARB | 6G TOTAL FAT | 1G SAT FAT | 2.5G MONO FAT | 2.5G POLY FAT | 0MG CHOL | 230MG SODIUM | 4G FIBER

noodle soup with kale and white beans

SERVES 6 TO 8

- 2 Tbs. extra-virgin olive oil
- 3 medium carrots, peeled and chopped
- 1 medium red onion, chopped
- 1 cup broken (2- to 3-inch pieces) dried capellini
- 2 quarts lower-salt chicken broth
- 1 small bunch kale, ribs removed and leaves coarsely chopped (about 6 cups)
- 1 15-oz. can cannellini beans, rinsed and drained
- 3 Tbs. fresh lime juice; more to taste

  Kosher salt and freshly ground black pepper

- ¼ cup coarsely chopped fresh cilantro

If you can find fideo noodles in the Latin section of your supermarket, try them in place of the capellini.

1. Heat 1 Tbs. of oil in a large pot over medium-high heat. Add the carrots and onion and cook, stirring occasionally, until the onion is soft and just golden brown, about 10 minutes. With a rubber spatula, scrape the vegetables into a medium bowl and set aside. If necessary, wipe the pot clean.

2. Heat the remaining 1 Tbs. oil in the pot over medium-high heat. Add the pasta and cook, stirring often, until dark golden brown, 3 to 4 minutes. Add the broth and stir, scraping the bottom of the pot to release any stuck-on pasta. Add the carrot and onion, kale, beans, lime juice, ½ tsp. salt, and ¼ tsp. pepper and bring to a boil. Reduce the heat to medium low and simmer until the kale, carrot, and pasta are tender, 8 to 10 minutes.

3. Remove the pot from the heat, stir in the cilantro, and season to taste with lime juice, salt, and pepper before serving. *—Liz Pearson*

PER SERVING: 200 CALORIES | 11G PROTEIN | 29G CARB | 6G TOTAL FAT | 1G SAT FAT | 3G MONO FAT | 1G POLY FAT | 0MG CHOL | 230MG SODIUM | 4G FIBER

spiced tomato and red lentil soup

MAKES ABOUT 14 CUPS;
SERVES 8

- 3 Tbs. vegetable oil
- 2 medium yellow onions, chopped
  Kosher salt
- 2 tsp. Madras curry powder or garam masala
- 2 quarts lower-salt chicken broth or homemade vegetable broth
- 2 14½-oz. cans petite-diced tomatoes
- 1 lb. (2⅓ cups) dried red lentils, picked over, rinsed, and drained
- 2 medium celery ribs, cut into small dice
- 1 medium carrot, peeled and cut into small dice
- 2 medium cloves garlic, peeled and chopped
- ⅛ to ¼ tsp. cayenne

Curry powder and garam masala are both Indian spice blends, which vary in flavor from blend to blend. Experiment to find one you like. Store leftover soup in the refrigerator for up to 5 days.

1. Heat the oil in a 6-quart (or larger) Dutch oven over medium heat. Add the onion and a generous pinch of salt and cook, stirring occasionally, until the onion is softened and just starting to brown, 6 to 8 minutes. Add the curry powder or garam masala and cook, stirring constantly, until fragrant, 30 seconds to 1 minute.

2. Add the broth, tomatoes and their juices, lentils, celery, carrot, garlic, cayenne, ¾ tsp. salt, and 2 cups water. Bring to a boil over high heat, stirring frequently to keep the lentils from sticking; skim any foam as necessary. Reduce the heat and simmer uncovered, stirring occasionally, until the lentils, carrot, and celery are tender, 35 to 40 minutes. Season with salt to taste. —*Lori Longbotham*

PER SERVING: 320 CALORIES | 22G PROTEIN | 45G CARB | 8G TOTAL FAT | 1G SAT FAT | 3G MONO FAT | 2.5G POLY FAT | 0MG CHOL | 480MG SODIUM | 9G FIBER

summer corn soup with crisp prosciutto

**MAKES ABOUT 8 CUPS;
SERVES 8 AS A FIRST COURSE**

- **3** **very thin slices prosciutto**
- **3** **or 4 large ears fresh corn**
- **4** **Tbs. unsalted butter**
- **1** **medium yellow onion, chopped (about 1 ½ cups)**
- **Kosher salt**
- **2** **cups homemade or lower-salt chicken broth**
- **1½** **cups medium-diced peeled red potatoes (from 2 to 3 medium)**
- **Freshly ground black pepper**
- **2** **Tbs. coarsely chopped fresh basil**

Resist the temptation to remove corn husks at the store. The husks keep the corn fresh and moist.

1. Position a rack about 4 inches below the broiler and heat the broiler on high. Arrange the prosciutto in a single layer on a small baking sheet and broil until it begins to curl, 1 to 2 minutes. Flip the prosciutto and broil until it appears dry-crisp and has curled a bit more, about 1 minute. Let cool, then finely chop or crumble by hand; set aside.

2. Slice the kernels off the corncobs for a total of 3 cups corn. Reserve the cobs.

3. In a medium Dutch oven over medium heat, melt the butter. Add the onion and cook until softened and slightly golden, 5 to 7 minutes. Season with a generous pinch of salt.

4. Add 4 cups water, the broth, potatoes, 1½ cups of the corn, the cobs, and 2 tsp. salt. Bring to a boil. Reduce the heat to medium low and simmer until the potatoes are tender, 10 to 15 minutes. Remove from the heat and discard the cobs.

5. Working in batches, carefully purée the soup in a blender, transferring each batch to a large heatproof bowl or large liquid measuring cup.

6. Pour the puréed soup back into the pot. Add the remaining 1½ cups corn and bring to a boil over medium-high heat. Reduce the heat to medium low and simmer, stirring occasionally, until the corn kernels are tender, 3 to 5 minutes. Season to taste with salt and pepper. Garnish each serving with the crisped prosciutto and basil.
—Maryellen Driscoll

PER SERVING: 170 CALORIES | 5G PROTEIN | 24G CARB | 7G TOTAL FAT | 4G SAT FAT | 2G MONO FAT | 0.5G POLY FAT | 20MG CHOL | 440MG SODIUM | 3G FIBER

how to cut corn off the cob

Removing corn kernels from the cob can be messy—they like to bounce off the cutting board and end up scattered all over the counter and floor. To keep those kernels in their place, insert the tip of the ear of corn into the center hole of a Bundt pan. Cut the kernels away from the cob in long downward strokes, letting them fall into the pan.

tomatillo gazpacho

MAKES ABOUT 5 CUPS; SERVES 4 TO 6 AS A FIRST COURSE

- 1 **14-oz. can lower-salt chicken broth**
- 1 **lb. tomatillos (8 to 12 medium), husked, rinsed, and cut into medium dice (3 cups)**
- 1 **medium clove garlic, minced**
- 2 **Tbs. extra-virgin olive oil**
- 2 **ripe medium avocados, peeled, pitted, and cut into small dice (1½ cups)**
- ½ **seedless English cucumber, cut into small dice (2 cups)**
- ½ **large red bell pepper, cut into small dice (½ cup)**
- ¼ **small red onion, finely diced (¼ cup)**
- 2 **Tbs. chopped fresh cilantro**
- 1 **Tbs. fresh lime juice; more as needed**

  Kosher salt and freshly ground black pepper

This recipe is quick to prepare but needs to chill for at least an hour for the flavors to develop.

1. Heat the broth in a 3-quart saucepan over medium-high heat. Add the tomatillos and garlic, bring to a boil, reduce the heat, and let simmer until the tomatillos are cooked through but still hold their shape, about 1 minute. Let cool slightly, about 5 minutes, and then carefully purée the mixture in a blender along with the olive oil. Pour the purée into a nonreactive 9x13-inch pan and refrigerate to cool quickly.

2. When the purée has cooled, remove the pan from the refrigerator and stir in the avocado, cucumber, bell pepper, onion, cilantro, and lime juice. Season to taste with salt and pepper. Refrigerate for at least 1 hour and up to 4 hours.

3. Before serving, taste and adjust the seasoning with more lime juice, salt, and pepper, as needed. Ladle the gazpacho into individual bowls or mugs. —*Pam Anderson*

PER SERVING: 190 CALORIES | 4G PROTEIN | 12G CARB | 15G TOTAL FAT | 2.5G SAT FAT | 10G MONO FAT | 2G POLY FAT | 0MG CHOL | 170MG SODIUM | 6G FIBER

More about Tomatillos

Small, round fruits encased in a delicate, papery husk, tomatillos ripen to various colors, from yellow to red to purple. They're most flavorful if harvested just before ripening, when they're vibrant green. Indigenous to Mexico and Central America, tomatillos are also called husk tomatoes or *tomates verdes* (green tomatoes).

Tomatillos have a tangy, almost citrusy flavor, which turns slightly sweet with cooking. They are a perfect match for chile peppers, onions, and cilantro. Tomatillos are also good with avocados, corn, lime, and scallions.

Buying and storing

Look for firm fruits about the size of walnuts in their shells, without blemishes and with their papery husks firmly attached. When fresh, tomatillos are a vibrant green color. Don't buy ones that have turned a yellowish green. Store tomatillos in their husks in a paper bag and refrigerate for up to a week.

Cooking

To prep tomatillos, peel the husk and rinse off the sticky residue it leaves behind. You don't need to remove the seeds. If eaten raw, tomatillos can be a little acidic and sharp-tasting. When cooked, their flavor mellows, letting their sweeter side shine. Toss raw chopped tomatillos in salads, or roast or grill them whole and add to salsas and dips. You can also cut them into wedges and stir into stews and braises.

cheddar and cauliflower soup

MAKES 8 CUPS; SERVES 6 TO 8

Kosher salt

½ **head cauliflower (about 1 lb.), cored and cut into 1½-inch florets**

2 **Tbs. unsalted butter**

1 **medium yellow onion, finely diced**

1 **medium clove garlic, minced**

2 **Tbs. unbleached all-purpose flour**

¼ **tsp. packed freshly grated nutmeg**

⅛ **tsp. cayenne**

2 **cups lower-salt chicken broth**

½ **cup heavy cream**

3 **sprigs fresh thyme**

4 **cups grated sharp or extra-sharp white Cheddar (about 14 oz.)**

Freshly ground black pepper

Depending on how much you enjoy the intense flavor of Cheddar, choose between a sharp or extra-sharp version of the cheese for this rustic soup. To dress it up for a special occasion, garnish with a combination of 3 Tbs. of chopped toasted walnuts, 1 Tbs. of chopped fresh flat-leaf parsley, and 1½ tsp. of finely grated lemon zest.

1. Bring a large pot of salted water to a boil. Boil the cauliflower until tender, about 4 minutes. Drain and let cool slightly. Trim the stems from 18 of the cauliflower pieces and cut the crowns into mini florets about ½ inch wide; set aside. Reserve the trimmed stems with the remaining larger pieces.

2. Melt the butter in a 4-quart saucepan over medium-low heat. Add the onion and ¼ tsp. salt and cook, stirring frequently, until the onion is soft, 10 to 12 minutes.

3. Add the garlic and cook until the aroma subsides, 2 to 3 minutes. Increase the heat to medium; add the flour, nutmeg, and cayenne and cook for 3 minutes, stirring constantly. Whisk in the broth, cream, and 2 cups water. Add the thyme and bring to a simmer. Stir in the cheese until melted and simmer for 5 minutes to develop the flavors.

4. Remove and discard the thyme stems and stir in the larger cauliflower pieces and reserved stems. Working in batches, purée the soup in a blender. Return the soup to the pot, and season with salt and pepper to taste. Add the mini cauliflower florets and reheat gently before serving. —*Allison Ehri Kreitler*

PER SERVING: 340 CALORIES | 17G PROTEIN | 7G CARB | 28G TOTAL FAT | 17G SAT FAT | 8G MONO FAT | 1G POLY FAT | 90MG CHOL | 540MG SODIUM | 2G FIBER

beet salad with oregano,
pecans & goat cheese
(recipe on p. 45)

salads

avocado, mango & pineapple salad with pistachios and pickled shallots

SERVES 4 TO 6

- **1** medium shallot (1 to 2 oz.), sliced into very thin rings
- **2** Tbs. Champagne vinegar or rice vinegar

  Kosher salt
- **3** Tbs. extra-virgin olive oil
- **1** tsp. red-wine vinegar
- **2** cups baby arugula or watercress
- **¼** cup roasted, salted pistachios, coarsely chopped
- **1** Tbs. thinly sliced fresh mint
- **1** Tbs. thinly sliced fresh basil

  Freshly ground black pepper
- **3** medium firm-ripe avocados (6 to 7 oz. each), peeled, pitted, and sliced lengthwise ¼ inch thick
- **2** kiwis, peeled, halved, and sliced ¼ inch thick
- **1** medium mango, pitted, peeled, and sliced lengthwise ¼ inch thick
- **½** medium pineapple, peeled, cored, and cut into ½-inch dice (about 2 cups)

A shower of peppery greens balances the sweetness of the mango and lets the avocado shine through.

1. In a small bowl, toss the shallot with the Champagne vinegar and a pinch of salt and set aside for 10 minutes, stirring once. Drain the shallot into a small bowl and reserve the vinegar. Whisk the olive oil and red-wine vinegar into the shallot vinegar.

2. In a medium bowl, toss 1 Tbs. of the vinaigrette with the pickled shallot, arugula, pistachios, mint, basil, ¼ tsp. salt, and a few grinds of pepper. Arrange the avocado, kiwi, mango, and pineapple on a platter. Drizzle with the remaining vinaigrette and season to taste with salt and pepper. Top with the arugula mixture and serve immediately.
—*Deborah Madison*

PER SERVING: 330 CALORIES | 4G PROTEIN | 30G CARB | 24G TOTAL FAT | 3.5G SAT FAT | 16G MONO FAT | 3.5G POLY FAT | 0MG CHOL | 80MG SODIUM | 10G FIBER

beet salad with oregano, pecans & goat cheese

SERVES 6 TO 8

- **8** to 10 medium beets (red, golden, or a combination)
- **3** Tbs. extra-virgin olive oil
- **3** Tbs. aged balsamic vinegar

  Sea salt or kosher salt and freshly ground black pepper
- **4** oz. soft goat cheese, crumbled
- **2** Tbs. chopped fresh oregano
- **¼** cup chopped pecans, lightly toasted

Beets and goat cheese are a classic pairing, but for a twist, try substituting blue cheese for the goat cheese and walnuts for the pecans. You can cook, peel, and cut the beets up to 6 hours ahead. Refrigerate, then return to room temperature before finishing.

1. If the beets have leaves and stems, trim off the leaves and all but ¼ inch of the stems. Wash the beets. In a large saucepan or stockpot fit with a steamer basket, steam the beets until a paring knife enters them easily, 30 to 45 minutes, depending on their size. Set aside until cool enough to handle but still warm.

2. Peel the beets; the skin will rub right off. Trim and discard the tops and tails and cut the beets into thick wedges. Transfer the beets to a large serving bowl and drizzle with the olive oil and vinegar. Season with a generous pinch of salt and pepper. Sprinkle the goat cheese, oregano, and pecans over the beets and serve. —*Melissa Speck*

PER SERVING: 140 CALORIES | 4G PROTEIN | 7G CARB | 11G TOTAL FAT | 3G SAT FAT | 6G MONO FAT | 1.5G POLY FAT | 5MG CHOL | 110MG SODIUM | 1G FIBER

Buying and Storing Beets

At the market, you may find more than red beets—give yellow or striped beets a try. Their flavors differ in sweetness by variety. Look for smooth skins and tails that aren't too shaggy. If the greens are attached, that's a good sign of freshness in general, but look specifically for the bunch with the brightest and greenest leaves.

Kept in a cool place, beets will last for weeks. Store both roots and leaves in a loosely closed bag in the crisper drawer of the refrigerator.

heirloom tomato napoleon with parmesan crisps and herb salad

SERVES 4

FOR THE PARMESAN CRISPS

2½ cups grated Parmigiano-Reggiano

FOR THE VINAIGRETTE

1 small shallot, minced (about 1½ Tbs.)

4 tsp. Champagne vinegar

1 tsp. Dijon mustard

Kosher or sea salt and freshly ground black pepper

2 Tbs. extra-virgin olive oil

2 Tbs. grapeseed oil or canola oil

1 cup baby arugula leaves

1 cup fresh flat-leaf parsley leaves

1 cup fresh basil leaves, torn into bite-size pieces if large

½ cup fresh tarragon leaves

½ cup 1-inch-long fresh chive pieces

20 small nasturtium leaves (optional)

Kosher or sea salt and freshly ground black pepper

16 ⅓-inch-thick heirloom tomato slices, preferably of different colors, sizes, and shapes (2 to 3 lb.)

About 20 various heirloom cherry tomatoes, halved or quartered

Here's an impressive and delicious way to show off a variety of colors and styles of heirloom tomatoes. The heirlooms available in supermarkets aren't necessarily grown locally. Check their origin—the farther they travel, the less flavor they'll have. It's worth going out of your way for the taste of a just-picked tomato from a farmstand or farmer's market.

MAKE THE PARMESAN CRISPS

Position a rack in the center of the oven and heat it to 375°F. Line a rimmed baking sheet with a nonstick baking liner or parchment. Spread the grated cheese over the entire surface of the liner. Bake until the cheese is amber brown, about 18 minutes. Remove from the oven and cool. Break into irregular pieces (each about 3 inches across). You'll need 12 pieces for the Napoleons, but this batch makes extra to cover the inevitable breaking (and snacking).

MAKE THE VINAIGRETTE

Put the shallot, vinegar, mustard, and a pinch each of salt and pepper in a small bowl or dressing cruet. Allow the shallot to sit in the vinegar for at least 20 minutes and up to 1 hour. Whisk or shake in both oils. Season to taste with more salt and pepper.

TO SERVE

1. In a large bowl, mix the arugula, parsley, basil, tarragon, chives, and nasturtium leaves (if using). Lightly dress with some of the vinaigrette. Season to taste with salt and pepper.

2. Divide the salad evenly among 4 salad plates. Arrange a large tomato slice on each salad, sprinkle lightly with salt, and top with a piece of Parmesan crisp. Continue to alternate the lightly salted tomatoes and cheese pieces until you have used 3 pieces of the Parmesan crisp in each Napoleon. Finish off the top of each Napoleon with an unsalted tomato slice. Arrange the cherry tomatoes around the Napoleons and drizzle any remaining vinaigrette around the plates. Sprinkle everything with salt and pepper. Serve immediately. —*Eric Rupert*

PER SERVING: 230 CALORIES | 8G PROTEIN | 16G CARB | 17G TOTAL FAT | 3.5G SAT FAT | 6G MONO FAT | 6G POLY FAT | 5MG CHOL | 390MG SODIUM | 5G FIBER

Buying and Storing Tomatoes

- **Never mind their looks:** Heirlooms are often misshapen and mottled, but this has no bearing on taste. And don't be put off by cracked skins, as long as they aren't leaking juice.
- **Go for heft:** Pick one up—it should feel heavy for its size.
- **Take a whiff:** Ripe heirlooms will have an earthy, green scent; avoid those that smell musty.
- **Treat gently:** Don't pile them in a bag; the weight of one will squash another.
- **Don't refrigerate:** Temperatures colder than 50°F will destroy their flavor and texture.

blood orange and radicchio salad with hazelnuts and shaved parmigiano

SERVES 6

- 5 medium blood oranges
- ¼ cup extra-virgin olive oil
- 1 Tbs. white-wine vinegar

  Kosher salt and freshly ground black pepper
- 1 medium head radicchio (¾ lb.), washed, cored, and cut into 1- to 2-inch pieces (about 5 loosely packed cups)
- 1 medium head butter lettuce (6-oz.), washed, cored, and cut into 1- to 2-inch pieces (about 4 loosely packed cups)
- ¾ cup blanched hazelnuts, toasted and coarsely chopped
- 1 1½-oz. chunk Parmigiano-Reggiano or aged goat cheese

The bitter radicchio is tempered by the sweet orange flavor and salty cheese.

1. Finely grate 1 tsp. zest from one of the oranges and then squeeze 2 Tbs. juice from it. In a medium bowl, whisk the zest and juice with the olive oil, vinegar, ½ tsp. salt, and a few grinds of pepper.

2. Using a sharp knife, trim off the peel and white pith from the remaining 4 oranges and cut crosswise into ¼-inch slices; remove any seeds.

3. In a large bowl, toss the radicchio and butter lettuce with the hazelnuts and just enough dressing to lightly coat (about ¼ cup). Season to taste with salt and pepper. Portion the salad among 6 serving plates and top each with 3 or 4 blood orange slices. With a vegetable peeler, shave a few shards of cheese over the top.   —*Deborah Madison*

PER SERVING: 250 CALORIES | 5G PROTEIN | 19G CARB | 19G TOTAL FAT | 2.5G SAT FAT | 13G MONO FAT | 2G POLY FAT | 0MG CHOL | 120MG SODIUM | 5G FIBER

vegetables and tofu with spicy peanut sauce

SERVES 2 OR 3

- **4** medium red potatoes (¾ lb.), cut into ⅓-inch-thick slices
- **2** medium carrots (4 oz.), peeled and cut on the diagonal into ⅓-inch-thick slices
- **1** 7-oz. package pressed, baked tofu (regular or Thai flavor), sliced into 1-inch-square pieces, ½ inch thick
- **1** small crown broccoli (7 oz.), cut into 1-inch florets
- **3** oz. green beans, trimmed and halved crosswise on the diagonal
- **½** cup natural unsalted peanut butter (smooth or chunky)
- **1** Tbs. soy sauce
- **1½** tsp. Asian chile paste, such as sambal oelek; more to taste

  Kosher salt

On the Indonesian island of Java, this hearty, main-course salad—known as gado-gado—is sold by street vendors, who carry the ingredients on yoke-like poles, assembling each serving to order. It's surprisingly easy to make.

1. Put a steamer basket in a large pot and fill the pot with water to just reach the bottom of the basket.

2. Put the potatoes in a single layer in the steamer basket, set the pot over medium-high heat, and bring the water to a boil. Cover the pot and cook for 4 minutes, then carefully remove the lid, move the potatoes to one side of the pot, and add the carrots in a snug, slightly overlapping layer. Cover the pot and steam until the carrots and potatoes are just tender, another 6 to 7 minutes. Transfer the potatoes and carrots to a platter. Put the tofu, broccoli, and beans in the steamer; cover and cook until the tofu is hot and the broccoli and beans are just tender, about 4 minutes. Transfer to the platter with the other vegetables.

3. In a medium bowl, combine the peanut butter, soy sauce, chile paste, and ½ cup hot water from the pot. Whisk to combine, adding more water as needed to create a thick but fluid sauce. Add more chile paste and salt to taste. Serve with the sauce on the side.
—Dabney Gough

PER SERVING: 530 CALORIES | 30G PROTEIN | 41G CARB | 29G TOTAL FAT | 4G SAT FAT | 0G MONO FAT | 0G POLY FAT | 0MG CHOL | 1070MG SODIUM | 10G FIBER

spinach and artichoke salad with couscous cakes and feta

SERVES 3

FOR THE DRESSING

- 2 Tbs. fresh lemon juice
- 1 Tbs. sour cream
- 1 tsp. finely chopped fresh mint
- 5 Tbs. extra-virgin olive oil

  Kosher salt and freshly ground black pepper

FOR THE COUSCOUS CAKES

- ¾ cup couscous

  Kosher salt
- 1 large clove garlic, peeled
- ¼ cup packed fresh flat-leaf parsley leaves
- ½ cup canned chickpeas, rinsed and drained
- 2 large eggs, lightly beaten

  Finely grated zest of 1 medium lemon (about 1½ tsp.)
- 3 Tbs. vegetable or canola oil

FOR THE SALAD

- ½ lb. baby spinach, washed and dried (about 6 lightly packed cups)
- 1 14-oz. can artichoke bottoms, rinsed, drained, and sliced
- 15 cherry tomatoes, halved

  Kosher salt and freshly ground black pepper
- 1 oz. crumbled feta (about ¼ cup)

Quick-to-cook couscous cakes make this meatless main-course salad satisfying.

MAKE THE DRESSING

In a small bowl, combine the lemon juice, sour cream, and mint. Whisk in the olive oil in a slow, steady stream. Season to taste with salt and pepper.

MAKE THE COUSCOUS CAKES

1. Put the couscous and 1 tsp. salt in a medium bowl. Add 1 cup boiling water to the couscous, cover the bowl with a pan lid or plate, and let sit for 4 to 5 minutes.

2. Coarsely chop the garlic in a food processor. Add the parsley and pulse until finely chopped. Add the chickpeas and 1 tsp. salt and pulse until coarsely chopped.

3. Uncover the couscous and fluff with a fork. Stir in the chickpea mixture, eggs, and lemon zest until well combined. Press the couscous mixture into a ¼-cup measure, smooth the top, and invert the measuring cup to release the cake onto a plate. Repeat with the remaining couscous mixture to make 9 cakes.

4. Heat 1½ Tbs. of the vegetable oil in a large skillet over medium heat until shimmering hot. Add 5 of the couscous cakes to the skillet and use a spatula to lightly flatten the cakes so they're about ¾ inch thick. Cook, flipping once, until crisp and golden brown on both sides, 2 to 3 minutes per side. Transfer to a paper-towel-lined plate. Add the remaining 1½ Tbs. vegetable oil to the skillet and cook the remaining cakes the same way.

ASSEMBLE THE SALAD

In a large bowl, toss the spinach, artichokes, and tomatoes with about three-quarters of the dressing. Season to taste with salt and pepper and portion among 3 large plates. Top each salad with 3 couscous cakes, sprinkle each salad with feta, and drizzle with the remaining dressing. —*Maryellen Driscoll*

PER SERVING: 710 CALORIES | 20G PROTEIN | 63G CARB | 44G TOTAL FAT | 8G SAT FAT | 24G MONO FAT | 9G POLY FAT | 155MG CHOL | 1580MG SODIUM | 9G FIBER

More about Couscous

Is couscous a grain or a pasta? Neither, really. A Middle Eastern and North African staple, couscous is simply durum semolina (the wheat flour from which most Italian pastas are made) that has been lightly moistened with salted water and rolled into little granules.

Traditionally, couscous is steamed and served with butter or with stewed vegetables or meats. But many recipes (like the one here) suggest simply mixing couscous into boiling liquid and setting it aside to swell and soften. Although this method sacrifices a certain degree of fluffiness for convenience, it does work quite well for medium and fine couscous. Larger-grained versions can be steamed in a couscoussière or simmered in broth or water until tender.

Most supermarkets carry several brands of medium (Moroccan) couscous, but if you want to choose from a full range of sizes, try Middle Eastern markets, natural-foods stores, or mail-order sources. Store couscous in sealed containers or bags to keep out moisture. At room temperature or cooler, it will keep well for a year.

grilled bread salad with basil and cherry tomatoes

SERVES 8

1 medium loaf (about ½ lb.) rustic white bread (like ciabatta), cut lengthwise into 1-inch-thick slices

½ cup extra-virgin olive oil

Kosher salt

1 clove garlic, halved lengthwise

1 pint cherry or grape tomatoes, halved

1 bunch scallions (about 8), trimmed and thinly sliced (both white and green parts)

12 large basil leaves, torn into small pieces

¼ cup red-wine vinegar

½ lb. fresh bocconcini, halved

A trip to the grill gives the makings of a classic Italian bread salad—a good crusty loaf of bread, ripe summer tomatoes, and basil—a little smokiness and crisp texture. Because this salad can sit out at room temperature for an hour or two, it's the perfect side for a picnic or barbecue. If you can't find bocconcini—small fresh mozzarella balls—substitute a large fresh mozzarella and cut into 1-inch pieces.

1. Prepare a medium-high fire on a gas or charcoal grill. Clean and oil the grates to prevent sticking. Using a pastry brush, dab both sides of the bread slices with 2 Tbs. oil and sprinkle with ½ tsp. salt. Grill the bread until it browns and gets good grill marks, about 2 minutes. Grill the other side until browned, about 2 minutes, and transfer to a large cutting board to cool. Rub the cut sides of the garlic over the bread and discard the garlic. Put the cherry tomatoes and scallions in a large serving bowl with the basil. Cut the bread into 1-inch pieces and add to the bowl.

2. In a small bowl, whisk the remaining oil with the red-wine vinegar, pour over the bread mixture, and toss well. Let the salad sit for up to 2 hours before serving. Just before serving, fold in the bocconcini and season with salt to taste. *—Tony Rosenfeld*

PER SERVING: 300 CALORIES | 10G PROTEIN | 16G CARB | 22G TOTAL FAT | 5G SAT FAT | 12G MONO FAT | 1.5G POLY FAT | 20MG CHOL | 270MG SODIUM | 1G FIBER

niçoise salad with haricots verts and yukon gold potatoes

2 lb. baby Yukon Gold potatoes, halved (or large Yukon Gold potatoes, cut into 1-inch pieces)

Kosher salt

1 lb. haricots verts, trimmed and cut in half

3 Tbs. red-wine vinegar

1 Tbs. whole-grain Dijon mustard

¾ cup extra-virgin olive oil

1 medium shallot, finely diced (about 3 Tbs.)

1 Tbs. chopped fresh thyme

Freshly ground black pepper

1 can tuna (12 oz., preferably oil-packed), drained well and flaked

2 Tbs. capers, rinsed and drained

1 pint cherry tomatoes, halved

¾ cup pitted Niçoise or Kalamata olives, coarsely chopped

trimming haricots verts

These small beans are more delicate than green beans, but you'll still want to trim the ends. It's slow to snap off the stems by hand; instead, grab a small handful of the beans, line up the stem ends, and trim them as a group with a chef's knife.

Tender green beans; tiny, buttery potatoes; and salty capers and olives are the highlights of this Niçoise salad. Try to use good-quality, oil-packed canned tuna to add another layer of flavor. Anchovies and hard-cooked eggs have been omitted to keep the dish light, but feel free to add them. If you have any fingerling potatoes on hand, substitute them for the Yukon Golds.

1. Set the potatoes in a large (6-quart) pot, cover them with cold water by a couple of inches, stir in 2 Tbs. salt, and bring to a boil. Reduce the heat to a gentle simmer, cover, and cook until the potatoes are tender when pierced with a fork, 10 to 12 minutes. Stir in the haricots verts and cook until they turn bright green and tender, 3 to 4 minutes. Drain well and cool under running water.

2. In a blender or food processor, blend the vinegar with the mustard. With the machine still running, add the oil in a slow, steady stream so the mixture comes together into a thick emulsion. Add the shallot, 2 tsp. thyme, 1 tsp. salt, and 1 tsp. pepper, and purée until incorporated. Taste and season the dressing with more salt and pepper if needed. Add 1 or 2 Tbs. water if needed to thin the dressing to a pourable consistency. Transfer the potatoes and beans to a large mixing bowl and toss well with half the vinaigrette. Taste and season with salt and pepper if needed and transfer to a large platter. In the same mixing bowl, toss the tuna with the capers and 2 or 3 Tbs. of the vinaigrette, and set the mixture over the potatoes in the center of the platter. Sprinkle the tomatoes and olives over the potatoes, around the perimeter of the tuna. Drizzle the salad with the remaining vinaigrette, sprinkle with the remaining 1 tsp. thyme, and serve.

3. To plate individually, lightly toss the potatoes, beans, tomatoes, and olives with half the vinaigrette and plate; top with the tuna, capers, and the remaining thyme; and serve the remaining dressing on the side.
—Tony Rosenfeld

PER SERVING: 420 CALORIES | 17G PROTEIN | 27G CARB | 28G TOTAL FAT | 4G SAT FAT
19G MONO FAT | 4G POLY FAT | 10MG CHOL | 1090MG SODIUM | 4G FIBER

cranberry-bean and salmon salad with spinach and radicchio

SERVES 4

9 oz. (1½ cups) dried cranberry beans

Kosher salt

1 medium lemon

¼ cup extra-virgin olive oil

1 large shallot, cut into small dice (½ cup)

1 small clove garlic, mashed to a paste

1 tsp. ground coriander

Freshly ground black pepper

½ lb. skin-on salmon fillet (½ to ¾ inch thick), preferably wild

2 cups (2 oz.) baby spinach

½ cup thinly sliced radicchio (from ½ a small head)

⅓ cup small sprigs fresh dill

Cranberry beans, with their soft texture and sweet, chestnut-like flavor, make a delicious addition to salads. To keep the cranberry beans intact and beautiful, let them boil for only a moment at the beginning of cooking and don't overcook them.

1. Spread the beans out and pick through them, discarding any rocks, bits of debris, and shriveled beans. Rinse the beans under cold water to remove any dust or dirt. Put the beans in a large metal bowl with enough cool water to cover by about 3 inches. Soak at room temperature for 6 to 8 hours, adding more water if the level gets low. To see if the beans have soaked long enough, cut one in half. It should be the same color at its center as it is at the edge. Drain and rinse.

2. Put the beans in a heavy-duty 4-quart saucepan. Add 6 cups cool water, or enough to cover the beans by about 1 inch. Bring just to a boil over medium-high heat, reduce the heat to maintain a gentle simmer, and cook, partially covered, stirring occasionally and adding hot water if necessary to keep the beans submerged, until they begin to soften, about 30 minutes.

3. Add ¼ tsp. salt and continue to cook, partially covered, until tender but still firm to the bite, another 15 to 20 minutes. Drain the beans in a colander and let cool to room temperature.

4. Finely grate the zest of the lemon to yield ¾ tsp. and then squeeze it to yield 3 Tbs. juice. In a large bowl, whisk the lemon zest and juice, oil, shallot, garlic, coriander, ¼ tsp. salt, and ¼ tsp. pepper. Add the beans, toss to combine, and let sit at room temperature for at least 15 minutes and up to 2 hours.

5. Put the salmon skin side down on a plate. Season with ¼ tsp. salt and ¼ tsp. pepper, turn the salmon over, and let sit at room temperature for 15 minutes.

6. Meanwhile, position an oven rack about 4 inches from the broiler and heat the broiler on high. Cover the top of a broiler pan with aluminum foil.

A long soak is the best way to ensure even cooking of the beans, but if you're short on time, you can do a quick soak instead: Put the beans in a large pot with enough cool water to cover by about 3 inches. Bring to a boil; boil for 2 minutes. Remove from the heat, cover, and let stand for 1 to 2 hours. Drain and rinse.

7. Broil the salmon skin side up until just opaque throughout, 5 to 7 minutes. The skin will become blackened. Transfer to a cutting board and let cool to room temperature. Remove and discard the skin and break the flesh into 1-inch pieces with your hands.

8. Season the beans to taste with salt and pepper. Add the salmon, spinach, radicchio, and dill to the bean mixture, toss, and serve.
—Lori Longbotham

PER SERVING: 440 CALORIES | 28G PROTEIN | 42G CARB | 16G TOTAL FAT | 2G SAT FAT | 10G MONO FAT | 2.5G POLY FAT | 35MG CHOL | 270MG SODIUM | 17G FIBER

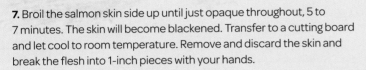

grilled steak and arugula salad with white beans and shiitake

SERVES 4 TO 6

FOR THE FLANK STEAK

1	cup coarsely chopped fresh flat-leaf parsley
⅓	cup coarsely chopped fresh mint
3	Tbs. coarsely chopped fresh rosemary
8	medium cloves garlic, peeled
¼	cup fresh lemon juice (from 2 medium lemons)
¼	cup soy sauce
	Kosher salt and freshly ground black pepper
½	cup extra-virgin olive oil
1	flank steak (1½ to 2 lb.), trimmed of excess fat

FOR THE BEANS AND MUSHROOMS

2	Tbs. extra-virgin olive oil
4	cups thinly sliced red onion
	Kosher salt and freshly ground black pepper
1	lb. fresh shiitake mushrooms, stemmed, caps sliced ½ inch thick (about 6 cups)
1	15 ½-oz. can cannellini or white beans, rinsed and drained
1½	Tbs. sherry vinegar
1	Tbs. finely chopped fresh thyme
¼	tsp. crushed red pepper flakes

Peppery arugula, earthy mushrooms, caramelized onions, and white beans make a luxurious bed for flank steak. Serve with garlic-rubbed grilled bread.

MARINATE THE STEAK

1. Set aside 2 Tbs. of the parsley. Combine the remaining parsley with the mint, rosemary, and garlic in a food processor and pulse until finely chopped. Add the lemon juice, soy sauce, 1 tsp. salt, and 1 tsp. pepper and process until smooth. With the motor running, add the olive oil in a thin stream.

2. Put the steak in a nonreactive baking dish. Pour the marinade over it and turn to coat. Cover and refrigerate for at least 4 hours or overnight, turning occasionally.

PREPARE THE BEANS AND MUSHROOMS

Heat the oil in a 12-inch skillet over medium-high heat until shimmering. Add the onion, season generously with salt and pepper, and reduce the heat to medium. Cook, stirring occasionally, until the onion is tender and caramel colored, 10 to 12 minutes. Add the shiitake and continue cooking, stirring occasionally, until wilted and soft, about 5 minutes. Off the heat, stir in the beans, vinegar, thyme, and pepper flakes. Season to taste with salt and pepper and let cool to room temperature. (You can prepare and refrigerate the bean mixture up to a day ahead.)

MAKE THE VINAIGRETTE

In a small bowl, combine the vinegar, shallot, and mustard. Whisk in the olive oil in a steady stream. Season to taste with salt and pepper. (You can make and refrigerate the vinaigrette up to a week ahead.)

GRILL THE STEAK

1. Remove the steak from the refrigerator 1 hour prior to cooking.

2. Prepare a medium-high gas or charcoal grill fire. Clean and oil the grill grates.

3. Remove the flank steak from the marinade, wipe off any excess, and season generously with salt and pepper. Grill the steak, covered, until grill marks form and the steak has a nice brown sear, 5 to 6 minutes. Flip the steak and continue grilling until grill marks form on the other side and the steak is cooked to medium rare (an instant-read thermometer inserted in the thickest part should read 135°F), 3 to 5 minutes more. Let rest for 10 to 15 minutes.

4. Cut the flank steak across the grain.

FOR THE VINAIGRETTE

- ¼ **cup sherry vinegar**
- 2 **Tbs. finely chopped shallots**
- 1 **Tbs. Dijon mustard**
- ½ **cup extra-virgin olive oil**
- **Kosher salt and freshly ground black pepper**

FOR THE SALAD

- ½ **lb. baby arugula (about 10 cups)**

ASSEMBLE THE SALAD

In a large bowl, gently toss the arugula with enough of the vinaigrette to lightly coat. Season to taste with salt and pepper. Arrange the arugula in a large serving bowl or platter and top with the bean and mushroom mixture and the sliced steak. Drizzle with some of the remaining vinaigrette (you may not need it all) and serve. —*Kate Hays*

PER SERVING: 420 CALORIES | 21G PROTEIN | 24G CARB | 26G TOTAL FAT | 5G SAT FAT | 18G MONO FAT | 2.5G POLY FAT | 30MG CHOL | 540MG SODIUM | 5G FIBER

cherry tomato, fennel & arugula salad with goat cheese dressing

SERVES 4

- **2** oz. soft goat cheese, at room temperature
- **⅓** cup buttermilk
- **2** Tbs. plus 1 tsp. extra-virgin olive oil
- **1** Tbs. mayonnaise
- **1** Tbs. fresh lemon juice
- **2** Tbs. thinly sliced chives

  Kosher salt and freshly ground black pepper

- **¼** lb. baby arugula leaves
- **1** large or 2 small fennel bulbs, stalks trimmed, outer layer removed, and cored
- **1** pint various heirloom cherry tomatoes, cut in half (or substitute 3 medium heirloom tomatoes cut into bite-size pieces, about 2 cups)

A tart goat cheese dressing and crisp fennel elevate this simple tossed salad.

1. In a food processor, blend the goat cheese, buttermilk, 2 Tbs. of the olive oil, mayonnaise, and lemon juice until smooth. Transfer to a medium bowl and stir in the chives. Season to taste with salt and pepper.

2. Put the arugula in a large bowl. Using a mandoline set at a very thin setting or a vegetable peeler, shave the fennel and add to the arugula. Toss with enough of the dressing to just coat the salad. Season to taste with salt and pepper. Portion the salad among 4 large salad plates and mound slightly. Toss the tomatoes in a bowl with the remaining 1 tsp. olive oil and a little salt and pepper; scatter on the salads. Serve immediately, passing the remaining dressing at the table. —*Eric Rupert*

PER SERVING: 180 CALORIES | 5G PROTEIN | 10G CARB | 14G TOTAL FAT | 3.5G SAT FAT | 7G MONO FAT | 1G POLY FAT | 10MG CHOL | 280MG SODIUM | 3G FIBER

frisée salad with oranges and pistachios

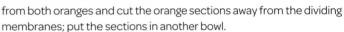

SERVES 4

- **1** **large or 2 small heads frisée, rinsed, dried, and torn into bite-size pieces (about 6 cups)**
- **2** **navel oranges or blood oranges**
- **2** **Tbs. sherry vinegar or red-wine vinegar**
- **1** **tsp. honey**
- **3** **Tbs. finely diced red onion**
- **⅓** **cup extra-virgin olive oil**
- **Kosher salt and freshly ground black pepper**
- **½** **cup pistachios, toasted**

The peppery taste of frisée combines well with sweet oranges and salty nuts in this light salad.

1. Put the frisée in a large salad or mixing bowl. Finely grate the zest of one of the oranges into a small bowl. Slice the skin from both oranges and cut the orange sections away from the dividing membranes; put the sections in another bowl.

2. Add the vinegar, honey, and onion to the zest, whisk in the oil, and season to taste with salt and pepper. Add just enough of the dressing to the frisée to coat it lightly. Mound the frisée on 4 salad plates, scraping any red onion remaining in the bowl over the frisée. Arrange the orange slices on top, scatter with the pistachios, and serve immediately. *—Eva Katz*

PER SERVING: 290 CALORIES | 5G PROTEIN | 16G CARB | 25G TOTAL FAT | 3G SAT FAT | 17G MONO FAT | 4G POLY FAT | 0MG CHOL | 250MG SODIUM | 4G FIBER

toasting pistachios

The simplest way to toast pistachios is in a medium oven (325° to 375°F). Spread them in a single layer on a rimmed baking sheet. Give the nuts a stir every few minutes. The nuts will be ready in 5 to 10 minutes.

You can also toast the nuts in a dry skillet over medium heat, but you'll need to shake and stir them constantly to avoid dark or burnt spots.

hoisin snap pea and carrot salad

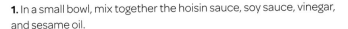

SERVES 6

- **2 Tbs.** hoisin sauce
- **1 Tbs.** reduced-sodium soy sauce
- **1 Tbs.** rice vinegar
- **2 tsp.** Asian sesame oil
- **3 Tbs.** canola oil
- **10 oz.** sugar snap peas, ends trimmed
- **3** medium carrots, peeled and thinly sliced on the diagonal (about 2 cups)
- **1** small red onion, thinly sliced

  Kosher salt
- **1 Tbs.** minced fresh ginger

Hoisin sauce is a Chinese dipping sauce that is often used with barbecued meats and in stir-fries. Salty, sweet, and spicy, hoisin sauce gives this simple side of snap peas and carrots distinctive flavor. The taste of the sauce can be strong; feel free to dilute it with a tablespoon of water or more depending on personal preference.

1. In a small bowl, mix together the hoisin sauce, soy sauce, vinegar, and sesame oil.

2. Heat the canola oil in a medium (10-inch), heavy-duty skillet over medium-high heat until shimmering. Add the vegetables, sprinkle with ½ tsp. salt, and cook, stirring, until the vegetables brown in places and start to soften, about 4 minutes. Add the ginger and cook for another 30 seconds. Add ½ cup water and cook, tossing, until the vegetables are crisp-tender and the water mostly cooks off, about 4 minutes. Toss with the hoisin mixture, then transfer to a large bowl and serve.
—Tony Rosenfeld

trimming snap peas

Though it's perfectly fine to eat snap peas without trimming the strings that run from end to end, you'll have a far nicer dining experience without them. To remove them, pinch off the stem and then, grasping the stringy seam between your thumb and a knife blade, pull it away.

grilled peach and buffalo mozzarella salad

SERVES 4

- ¾ cup balsamic vinegar
- 2 sprigs fresh thyme

  Kosher salt and freshly ground black pepper
- 2 firm-ripe peaches (¾ lb. total), halved and pitted
- 4½ tsp. extra-virgin olive oil
- 4 cups lightly packed baby arugula (about 2¼ oz.)
- 1 ball buffalo mozzarella (5 to 7 oz.), cut into ¾-inch chunks (about 1 cup)

Reduced balsamic vinegar adds a tangy kick to peaches that are grilled to bring out their inherent sweetness. Be sure to choose firm fruit; if the peaches are soft, they'll collapse on the grill.

1. Prepare a medium gas or charcoal grill fire.

2. Combine the vinegar and thyme in a 2-quart saucepan and bring to a boil over medium heat. Reduce the heat to a simmer and cook until the mixture is thick, syrupy, and reduced to ¼ cup, 6 to 9 minutes. Remove from the heat, discard the thyme sprigs, and season with a pinch of salt and a few grinds of pepper.

3. Rub the peaches all over with 2 tsp. of the oil and season lightly with salt and pepper. Grill cut side down until lightly charred, 3 to 4 minutes. Transfer to a cutting board and let cool slightly. Slice each half into thirds.

4. In a medium bowl, toss the arugula with the remaining 2½ tsp. oil and season to taste with salt and pepper. Arrange on a platter. Top with the mozzarella and peaches and drizzle with about 2 Tbs. of the reduced balsamic vinegar, adding more to taste. Season to taste with salt and pepper and serve.   *—Melissa Pelligrino*

PER SERVING: 210 CALORIES | 7G PROTEIN | 16G CARB | 14G TOTAL FAT | 6G SAT FAT | 6G MONO FAT | 1G POLY FAT | 30MG CHOL | 75MG SODIUM | 1G FIBER

spicy grilled corn salad with black beans and queso fresco

SERVES 6 TO 8 AS A SIDE DISH

- 3 ears fresh corn, husked
- 1 medium red onion, cut into disks about ⅓ inch thick
- 1 large red bell pepper
- ½ cup olive oil

  Kosher salt and freshly ground black pepper
- 1 small canned chipotle, seeded and minced, plus 1 Tbs. adobo sauce (from a can of chipotles in adobo)
- 2 Tbs. cider vinegar
- 1 15½-oz. can black beans, rinsed and drained
- 5 oz. queso fresco or feta, crumbled (1 cup)
- ¼ cup chopped fresh cilantro
- 1 Tbs. chopped fresh oregano

Queso fresco, a mild white cheese popular in Latin American cuisines, has a feta-like texture and flavor that pairs well with the starchy corn and beans in this recipe.

1. Prepare a medium charcoal or gas grill fire. Put the corn, onion, and pepper on a large rimmed baking sheet and brush with 2 Tbs. of the oil. Season with 1 tsp. salt and ½ tsp. pepper. Grill the corn and onion, flipping occasionally, until beginning to brown (the onions should still be a little crunchy), 6 to 10 minutes. Transfer to a cutting board to cool slightly. Grill the red pepper until charred on all sides, about 12 minutes. Put the pepper in a bowl, cover, and let cool slightly.

2. Meanwhile, in a small bowl, whisk the remaining 6 Tbs. oil, the chipotle and adobo sauce, vinegar, 1 tsp. salt, and ½ tsp. pepper.

3. Cut the corn from the cobs and coarsely chop the onion. Skin, seed, and coarsely chop the red pepper. Combine all the vegetables in a large bowl, along with the beans, cheese, cilantro, and oregano.

4. Rewhisk the dressing, add it to the salad, and toss well. Season to taste with salt and pepper. (The salad may be made up to 1 day ahead. Refrigerate and return to room temperature, adding the fresh herbs just before serving.) *—Tony Rosenfeld*

PER SERVING: 240 CALORIES | 7G PROTEIN | 20G CARB |
16G TOTAL FAT | 3G SAT FAT | 10G MONO FAT | 1.5G POLY FAT |
5MG CHOL | 420MG SODIUM | 4G FIBER

grilled lamb kebab salad with cucumber, tomatoes & pita

SERVES 4

- 6 Tbs. fresh lemon juice
- 2 large cloves garlic, mashed or crushed through a garlic press
- 1¼ tsp. ground allspice
- ¾ tsp. kosher salt; more as needed
- ¾ tsp. freshly ground black pepper
- ½ cup plus 2 Tbs. extra-virgin olive oil
- 2 lb. boneless lamb leg or shoulder meat, trimmed well and cut into 1½-inch cubes (to yield about 1½ to 1¾ lb.)
- 1 small head romaine lettuce, washed, dried, and torn or cut into large bite-size pieces (about 6 cups)
- 1 large cucumber, peeled, seeded, and cut into large dice
- 2 tomatoes, cut into large dice
- 1 cup packed mint leaves (from 2½ to 3 oz. mint sprigs), coarsely chopped
- 2 pita breads, 5 to 6 inches in diameter

Main-dish salads are summer's answer to the one-bowl weeknight meal. They're super easy to put together, and in this case, the lamb salad is light but complete. It's also a great alternative for those nights when you want a juicy, meaty salad but need a break from beef.

1. Heat a gas grill to medium. In a small bowl, whisk the lemon juice, garlic, allspice, salt, and pepper. Whisking constantly, drizzle in ½ cup of the oil. Toss the lamb pieces in a medium bowl with 2 Tbs. of the vinaigrette. Thread the lamb onto 3 or 4 metal skewers; sprinkle with salt.

2. Combine the lettuce, cucumber, tomatoes, and all but about 2 Tbs. of the mint in a large bowl. Using a knife, split the pitas and pull the sides apart. Brush the pita halves with the remaining 2 Tbs. oil. Grill until crisp and charred in places, 30 to 60 seconds per side, and transfer to a plate.

3. Grill the lamb, turning the skewers every 90 seconds or so, until cooked to medium, 6 to 8 minutes. Remove from the grill and let the lamb rest for 5 minutes. Meanwhile, rip the pitas into large bite-size pieces, add to the bowl with the vegetables, and toss. Slide the lamb off the skewers and cut each cube in half. In a medium bowl, toss the lamb with 3 Tbs. of the vinaigrette (whisk to recombine first).

4. Toss the vegetables with the remaining dressing and season to taste with salt and pepper. Portion the vegetables onto 4 plates. Top the salads with the lamb and sprinkle with the remaining mint. Serve immediately. —*Eva Katz*

PER SERVING: 657 CALORIES | 38G PROTEIN | 29G CARB | 44G TOTAL FAT | 8G SAT FAT | 30G MONO FAT | 4G POLY FAT | 100MG CHOL | 471MG SODIUM | 6G FIBER

kohlrabi-radish slaw
with cumin and cilantro

SERVES 8

- **3 Tbs. white-wine vinegar**
- **1 tsp. Dijon mustard**
- **1 tsp. clover honey**
- **¼ tsp. cumin seeds, toasted and coarsely ground in a mortar and pestle**
- **Kosher salt and freshly ground black pepper**
- **5 Tbs. canola oil**
- **2 small unpeeled kohlrabi bulbs (purple, green, or both), trimmed and cut into ⅛-inch-thick matchsticks (3 cups)**
- **5 radishes, grated (about 1 cup)**
- **3 medium carrots, grated (about 1½ cups)**
- **½ medium head green cabbage (about 1 lb.), thinly sliced (5 cups)**
- **⅓ cup chopped fresh cilantro**

To speed up the vegetable prep, use the grating and slicing blades on a food processor for the radishes, carrots, and cabbage, and the julienne cutter on a mandoline for the kohlrabi.

1. In a small bowl whisk the vinegar, mustard, honey, cumin, ¼ tsp. salt, and a pinch of pepper. Gradually whisk in the canola oil until combined.

2. Put the kohlrabi, radishes, carrots, cabbage, and cilantro in a large bowl. Pour in the dressing and gently toss to combine. Season to taste with salt and pepper. —*Melissa Pelligrino*

PER SERVING: 120 CALORIES | 2G PROTEIN | 10G CARB | 9G TOTAL FAT | 0.5G SAT FAT | 6G MONO FAT | 2.5G POLY FAT | 0MG CHOL | 90MG SODIUM | 4G FIBER

Buying and Storing Kohlrabi

It may look like a turnip, but kohlrabi is a type of cabbage related more to broccoli and cauliflower than to any kind of root vegetable. Both bulb and leaves are edible and are best cooked separately. You can find purple and green kohlrabi, although both are white inside and taste essentially the same. Look for bulbs 3 inches in diameter or less (about the size of a medium turnip). They're more tender and delicate in flavor than larger ones and usually don't require peeling. Large bulbs tend to be tough and woody, with a hard outer layer.

Cut the leafy stalks off the bulbs and refrigerate them separately in zip-top bags. If stored properly, the bulbs can last a few weeks. The leaves, however, should be eaten within 2 or 3 days.

grilled shrimp salad with feta, tomato & watermelon

SERVES 4

- 1½ lb. raw extra-jumbo shrimp (16 to 20 per lb.), peeled (leave tail segment intact) and deveined
- ¼ cup plus 2 Tbs. fresh lemon juice
- 1 tsp. smoked sweet paprika
  Kosher salt and freshly ground black pepper
- ¼ cup extra-virgin olive oil
- 1½ tsp. honey
  Vegetable oil, for the grill
- ½ medium head frisée, torn into bite-size pieces (4 cups)
- 3 cups small-diced seedless watermelon (about 1 lb.)
- 3 medium ripe red or yellow tomatoes, cored and cut into wedges
- 2 cups yellow cherry or pear tomatoes, halved
- 6 oz. feta, cut into small dice (1¼ cups)
- 30 fresh basil leaves, thinly sliced (½ cup)

Ripe, in-season ingredients are the key to this summery main-course salad, so use the best tomatoes and watermelon you can find.

1. Prepare a hot gas or charcoal grill fire.

2. In a medium bowl, toss the shrimp with 2 Tbs. of the lemon juice and the paprika; marinate at room temperature for 5 minutes. Thread the shrimp onto metal skewers or wooden skewers that have been soaked in water for at least 30 minutes. Season the shrimp on both sides with ½ tsp. salt and ¼ tsp. pepper.

3. In a small bowl, combine the remaining ¼ cup lemon juice with the olive oil, honey, and a pinch each of salt and pepper. Whisk well.

4. Clean and oil the grill grates. Grill the shrimp, flipping once, until firm and opaque throughout, 4 to 6 minutes total.

5. In a large bowl, gently toss the frisée with 3 Tbs. of the dressing. In a medium bowl, gently toss the watermelon, tomatoes, feta, basil, 2 Tbs. dressing, ¼ tsp. salt, and ⅛ tsp. pepper. Divide the frisée among 4 plates and spoon one-quarter of the watermelon mixture over each. Top with the shrimp skewers, drizzle with the remaining dressing, and serve. *—Dina Cheney*

PER SERVING: 430 CALORIES | 36G PROTEIN | 20G CARB | 24G TOTAL FAT | 9G SAT FAT | 12G MONO FAT | 2.5G POLY FAT | 290MG CHOL | 990 MG SODIUM | 3G FIBER

island-spiced chicken salad with mango and scallions

SERVES 6

Kosher salt and freshly ground black pepper

½ tsp. ground allspice

½ tsp. ground cinnamon

Heaping ¼ tsp. chipotle powder

2 lb. boneless, skinless chicken thighs (about 8), trimmed of fatty patches

2 Anaheim or poblano chiles, halved, cored, and seeded

6 scallions (both white and green parts), ends trimmed

3 Tbs. canola or peanut oil

2 mangos (about 1½ pounds), pitted and cut into ½-inch dice (about 2 cups)

1 Tbs. fresh lime juice; more as needed

This sweet and spicy salad is the perfect meal on a warm summer night. Serve in Boston lettuce leaf cups. This recipe makes plenty; put any leftovers on top of greens or in a tortilla for an easy lunch.

1. For a gas grill, light the front burner to medium high and the back burner(s) to medium. For a charcoal grill, light a medium-high fire (400°F) with two-thirds of the coals banked to one side. Clean and oil the grill grates.

2. In a small bowl, mix 1½ tsp. salt and 1 tsp. pepper with the allspice, cinnamon, and chipotle powder. Sprinkle the chicken all over with the spice rub. Sprinkle the chiles and scallions with 1 Tbs. oil, ½ tsp. salt, and ½ tsp. pepper.

3. Set the chicken over the hot zone of the fire, and the chiles and scallions over the cooler zone. Grill until the chicken, peppers, and scallions have good grill marks, 3 to 4 minutes. Continue to grill the peppers and scallions until they brown and become just tender, about 3 minutes more. Grill the chicken, flipping as needed, until it is firm to the touch and cooked through (slice into a thicker piece of the chicken with a knife to check), 6 to 8 more minutes. Transfer the chicken and vegetables to a large cutting board to cool. Coarsely chop the chicken, peppers, and scallions.

4. In a large serving bowl, toss the mango with the chicken, peppers, and scallions. Add the lime juice and the remaining 2 Tbs. oil and toss well. Season with more lime juice, salt, and pepper if needed. Serve immediately. —*Tony Rosenfeld*

> Store mangos at room temperature until they become just soft and ripe, and then transfer to the refrigerator, where they'll keep for up to a week. To ripen the fruit more quickly, store in a paper bag at room temperature. Mangos can also be sliced and the fruit frozen whole or as a purée.

white bean salad with mint and red onion

SERVES 4

- ½ cup small-diced red onion
- 3 Tbs. sherry vinegar
- 1 15-oz. can white beans, drained and rinsed (like Great Northern)
- ½ cup coarsely chopped fresh spearmint or smooth-leaf spearmint leaves
- ½ cup small-diced red bell pepper
- 2 Tbs. nonpareil (small) capers
- 2 Tbs. extra-virgin olive oil

  Kosher salt and freshly ground black pepper

This flavorful bean salad goes well with most meat and poultry, particularly roasted pork tenderloin or broiled lamb chops.

In a small bowl, mix the red onion and vinegar; let sit for 15 minutes. In a medium bowl, mix the onion and vinegar with the beans, mint, red pepper, capers, olive oil, and salt and black pepper to taste.
—*Jessica Bard*

PER SERVING: 160 CALORIES | 7G PROTEIN | 21G CARB | 7G TOTAL FAT | 1G SAT FAT | 5G MONO FAT | 1G POLY FAT | 0MG CHOL | 530MG SODIUM | 7G FIBER

southwestern grilled chicken salad with tomato and black bean salsa

SERVES 4

- **1** boneless, skinless chicken breast half (6 to 7 oz.), trimmed
- **1** tsp. chili powder
- **1** tsp. light or dark brown sugar
- **½** tsp. ground coriander
- **½** tsp. ground cumin
  Kosher salt
- **6** Tbs. extra-virgin olive oil; more for the grill
- **2** Tbs. plus 2 tsp. fresh lime juice
- **1** Tbs. plus 2 tsp. chopped fresh cilantro, plus leaves for garnish
- **2** tsp. honey
  Freshly ground black pepper
  Green Tabasco® (optional)
- **1** cup canned black beans, rinsed and drained
- **4** oz. small cherry (or grape) tomatoes, quartered or halved (about ¾ cup)
- **1** large scallion, thinly sliced
- **2** small heads Bibb lettuce, torn into bite-size pieces (about 9 cups)
- **1** medium firm-ripe avocado
- **¼** cup toasted pine nuts or pepitas

This quick dinner is heavy on the veggies and light on the meat. The salsa makes this salad filling; you won't even notice the smaller portion of chicken.

1. Prepare a medium-high gas or charcoal grill fire. Trim and then butterfly the chicken breast by slicing it horizontally almost but not entirely in half so you can open it like a book.

2. In a small bowl, combine the chili powder, brown sugar, coriander, cumin, and ¾ tsp. salt. Rub some of the spice mix over both sides of the butterflied chicken breast (you won't need it all) and let sit while the grill heats.

3. Clean and oil the grill grate. Grill the breast until the edges of the top side are white, about 3 minutes. Flip and cook until just done, another 1 to 2 minutes. Let the chicken rest for 5 to 10 minutes.

4. In a small bowl, combine the olive oil, lime juice, 1 Tbs. of the cilantro, the honey, ½ tsp. salt, a few grinds of pepper, and a few shakes of green Tabasco (if using). Whisk or shake well to combine.

5. Combine the black beans, tomatoes, scallion, the remaining 2 tsp. cilantro, and a pinch of salt in a small bowl. Add 2 Tbs. of the dressing and toss gently.

6. Put the lettuce in a bowl, season with a little salt, and toss with just enough of the dressing to lightly coat. (Reserve a little to drizzle on the chicken.) Arrange the lettuce on a platter or 4 dinner plates. Slice the chicken breast very thinly. Pit, peel, and slice the avocado. Arrange the chicken, avocado, and salsa on the lettuce. Drizzle a little of the remaining dressing over the chicken and avocado. Garnish with the pine nuts or pepitas and the cilantro leaves. —*Susie Middleton*

PER SERVING: 470 CALORIES | 18G PROTEIN | 28G CARB | 33G TOTAL FAT | 5G SAT FAT | 21G MONO FAT | 5G POLY FAT | 25MG CHOL | 510MG SODIUM | 9G FIBER

pan-seared salmon with baby greens and fennel

SERVES 4

FOR THE DRESSING

2½   Tbs. Champagne vinegar or white-wine vinegar

2   Tbs. fresh orange juice

1   tsp. finely grated orange zest

    Kosher salt and freshly ground black pepper

¼   cup dried cherries

½   cup extra-virgin olive oil

FOR THE SALMON

4   6-oz. skinless salmon fillets, preferably center cut

1   tsp. kosher salt

¼   tsp. freshly ground black pepper

1½   Tbs. extra-virgin olive oil

FOR THE SALAD

½   lb. mixed baby salad greens (about 8 lightly packed cups)

1   small fennel bulb, trimmed, halved lengthwise, cored, and very thinly sliced crosswise

    Kosher salt and freshly ground black pepper

If you have fleur de sel, use it to season the finished salad. The salt flakes are an appealing contrast to the sweet and citrusy dressing.

START THE DRESSING

In a small bowl, combine the vinegar with the orange juice and zest, ¼ tsp. salt, and a few grinds of pepper. Stir in the dried cherries and set aside.

COOK THE SALMON

Season the salmon fillets on both sides with the salt and pepper. Heat the oil in a 12-inch skillet over medium-high heat. Cook the salmon, flipping once, until barely cooked through and a rich golden-brown crust develops on both sides, 4 to 5 minutes per side. Set aside on a plate.

FINISH THE DRESSING

Using a fork or slotted spoon, remove the cherries from the orange juice and set aside. In a thin stream, whisk the ½ cup olive oil into the orange juice mixture until blended. Season to taste with salt and pepper.

ASSEMBLE THE SALAD

Combine the greens and fennel in a large bowl. Add about half of the vinaigrette to the salad, toss, and season to taste with salt and pepper. Portion the salad onto 4 large plates or shallow bowls. Set a piece of salmon on each salad and sprinkle the cherries around the fish. Drizzle some of the remaining vinaigrette over each fillet and serve.
—*Maryellen Driscoll*

PER SERVING: 620 CALORIES | 41G PROTEIN | 14G CARB | 38G TOTAL FAT | 4.5G SAT FAT | 25G MONO FAT | 6G POLY FAT | 105MG CHOL | 650MG SODIUM | 4G FIBER

More about Fennel

Look for large, plump, rounded fennel bulbs. Some bulbs, depending on the variety and how they're grown, are flat and elongated. These tend to be tougher and not as sweet, so don't buy them if you don't have to. The bulb part should be largely white or pale green, with as few blemishes as possible. Fresh bulbs should look moist. If the outer layer of the bulb appears dry, tough, or discolored, the fennel has been out of the ground for a while and will not be at its freshest. The leafy dill-like fronds are another indication of freshness: They should be perky and upright, not limp.

Try to use fennel within 2 to 3 days of buying. It gradually loses moisture after harvest and becomes spongy and dry. Store it loosely wrapped in the refrigerator's crisper drawer.

oven-toasted ham, brie &
apple sandwiches
(recipe on p. 76)

sandwiches, burgers & more

brazilian chicken salad sandwiches

SERVES 4

¼ **cup mayonnaise**

2 **Tbs. fresh lime juice**

Kosher salt and freshly ground black pepper

4 **cups shredded roasted chicken meat (homemade or from a store-bought rotisserie chicken)**

¼ **cup golden raisins**

1 **large celery rib, finely chopped**

3 **Tbs. finely chopped yellow onion**

2 **Tbs. extra-virgin olive oil**

½ **cup grated carrots**

½ **cup grated beets**

½ **cup chopped fresh cilantro**

8 **Boston lettuce leaves**

8 **slices whole-wheat bread, toasted if you like**

This easy take on a sandwich sold by vendors along Rio de Janeiro's beaches is packed with grated vegetables, sweet raisins, fresh lime juice, and cilantro. It's like no chicken salad sandwich you've had before.

1. In a medium bowl, whisk the mayonnaise, 1 Tbs. of the lime juice, ½ tsp. salt, and ¼ tsp. pepper. Add the chicken, raisins, celery, and onion. Season to taste with salt and pepper.

2. In another medium bowl, combine the oil with the remaining 1 Tbs. lime juice, ½ tsp. salt, and ¼ tsp. pepper. Mix in the carrots, beets, and cilantro.

3. Put a lettuce leaf on 4 of the bread slices, then top with the chicken salad, carrot mixture, another lettuce leaf, and another slice of bread.
—*Ian Knauer*

PER SERVING: 690 CALORIES | 47G PROTEIN | 38G CARB | 39G TOTAL FAT | 8G SAT FAT | 16G MONO FAT | 11G POLY FAT | 130MG CHOL | 670MG SODIUM | 6G FIBER

arugula, prosciutto & tomato panini

SERVES 4

- **1** loosely packed cup baby arugula
- **3** Tbs. extra-virgin olive oil
- **1** tsp. red-wine vinegar
-     Kosher salt and freshly ground black pepper
- **8** ¾-inch-thick slices rustic white bread (like ciabatta)
- **1** large clove garlic, halved
- **2** tomatoes, cored and cut into eight ½-inch-thick slices
- **8** thin slices prosciutto (about 4 oz.)
- **½** lb. Danish Fontina, grated (about 2 cups)

Dressing the arugula in oil and vinegar before assembling the sandwich enhances the peppery flavor of the greens and adds tang, much like an aïoli spread or tapenade would. Instead of Italian Fontina, try the Danish version of this cheese for a milder flavor and softer texture.

1. In a medium bowl, toss the arugula with 1 Tbs. oil, the vinegar, ⅛ tsp. salt, and ¼ tsp. black pepper. Let sit for 5 minutes to wilt slightly. Set 4 slices of bread on a cutting board. Gently rub both sides of each piece of bread with the garlic. Top each slice of bread with 2 tomato slices and sprinkle evenly with ½ tsp. salt. Layer the prosciutto, Fontina, and arugula mixture over the tomatoes. Rub both sides of the remaining 4 slices of bread with the garlic and set these slices, garlic-rubbed side down, on top of the arugula. Discard the garlic. Brush the outsides of the bread slices with the remaining 2 Tbs. oil.

2. Heat a panini press according to the manufacturer's instructions. (Alternatively, heat a nonstick grill pan over medium heat.) Put 2 of the sandwiches on the press, pull the top down, and cook until browned, 5 to 7 minutes. (If using a grill pan, put a heavy pan on top of the sandwiches and cook for roughly the same amount of time, turning the sandwiches over once.) Cook the remaining sandwiches in the same manner. Cut in half and serve. —*Tony Rosenfeld*

oven-toasted ham, brie & apple sandwiches

SERVES 4

- **1** large baguette (about 1 lb.), cut into 4 pieces
- **7** oz. Brie, most of the rind trimmed off and thinly sliced
- **2** Tbs. unsalted butter
- **1½** medium Granny Smith apples, peeled (optional), cored, and cut into ¼-inch-thick wedges (about 1½ cups)
- **¾** lb. ham steak, thinly sliced on the diagonal
- **2** Tbs. whole-grain Dijon mustard
- **1** Tbs. honey
- **1** tsp. chopped fresh thyme

Remove the rind from the Brie while the cheese is still cold, and choose a thinly sliced ham steak rather than deli ham for a meaty flavor and texture. Look for a ham steak that's labeled "ham in natural juices."

1. Position a rack in the center of the oven and heat the oven to 425°F. Split the baguette pieces lengthwise, open them up like a book, and top one side with the Brie. Set on a baking sheet lined with parchment paper or aluminum foil, and bake until the cheese melts and the bread lightly browns, about 5 minutes.

2. Meanwhile, melt the butter in a large (12-inch), heavy-duty skillet over medium-high heat. Add the apples and cook, tossing every minute or so, until they start to soften and brown in places, 3 to 4 minutes. Add the ham and cook, gently tossing, until it warms. Remove from the heat and gently toss with the mustard, honey, and thyme until the ham and apples are evenly coated. Using tongs, distribute the ham mixture into the warm pieces of baguette, secure with 2 toothpicks, cut in half, and serve. *—Tony Rosenfeld*

Granny Smith apples, like other varieties, keep well. Refrigerate them and keep them away from strong-smelling foods, as apples easily absorb odors.

bison burgers with thousand island barbecue dressing

SERVES 4

- ¼ **cup mayonnaise**
- 1 **Tbs. chili sauce, such as Heinz®**
- 4 **tsp. smoky barbecue sauce**
- 1 **tsp. sweet pickle relish**
- ¼ **tsp. Worcestershire sauce**
- 1½ **lb. ground bison**

  Kosher salt and freshly ground black pepper

  Vegetable oil, for the grill
- 4 **rolls or hamburger buns, split**
- 4 **iceberg lettuce leaves**
- 1 **large vine-ripened tomato, preferably heirloom, sliced**

Bison (buffalo) meat is a great substitute for beef—just take care not to overcook it, as it can dry out quickly.

1. Prepare a medium-high gas or charcoal grill fire.

2. In a small bowl, mix the mayonnaise, chili sauce, 2 tsp. of the barbecue sauce, sweet pickle relish, and Worcestershire sauce. Set aside.

3. In a medium bowl, use your hands to gently mix the bison with the remaining 2 tsp. barbecue sauce, 1¼ tsp. salt, and ¾ tsp. pepper. Shape into four ½- to ¾-inch-thick patties.

4. Lightly oil the grill grate and place the patties on the grate. Cover and grill for 4 to 5 minutes. Flip the burgers, cover, and cook to desired doneness, about 5 minutes for medium (130° to 135°F on an instant-read thermometer).

5. While the burgers cook, toast the rolls on the grill. Spread some of the dressing on each half of the roll and arrange a lettuce leaf and a slice or two of tomato on the top halves. When the burgers are done, put them on the bottom halves. Assemble the sandwiches, cut in half if you like, and serve. *—Bruce Aidells*

PER SERVING: 570 CALORIES | 30G PROTEIN | 36G CARB | 34G TOTAL FAT | 11G SAT FAT | 11G MONO FAT | 8G POLY FAT | 95MG CHOL | 940MG SODIUM | 2G FIBER

grilled portabella and goat cheese sandwiches with green olive pesto

SERVES 4

- 1 cup tightly packed fresh basil leaves
- ½ cup pitted green olives, such as manzanilla, coarsely chopped
- 1 Tbs. walnuts or pine nuts
- 1 small clove garlic, coarsely chopped
- ½ cup plus 2 tsp. extra-virgin olive oil

  Kosher salt and freshly ground black pepper

- 8 small to medium fresh portabella mushrooms, stemmed, gills removed, and wiped clean
- 4 soft round rolls, such as Portuguese or kaiser, split
- 4 oz. fresh goat cheese, crumbled

The earthy flavor of the portabellas goes well with the mild, tangy goat cheese and salty olive pesto.

1. Heat a panini or sandwich press according to the manufacturer's instructions. (Alternatively, heat a nonstick grill pan over medium-high heat.)

2. While the press is heating, put the basil, olives, nuts, and garlic in a food processor and process until finely chopped. With the motor running, add 6 Tbs. of the olive oil in a slow, steady stream through the feed tube and continue to process until thick and smooth. Season to taste with salt and pepper.

3. Brush the mushrooms with 2 Tbs. of olive oil and sprinkle with salt and pepper. Put them on the press, pull the top down, and cook until softened and browned, 3 to 5 minutes (or cook in the grill pan, flipping once). Transfer to a plate and let cool slightly.

4. Spread the pesto on the bottom halves of the rolls. Put 2 mushrooms on each and then some cheese. Top the sandwiches with the other halves of the rolls. Brush both sides of the sandwiches with the remaining 2 tsp. oil.

5. Put the sandwiches, pesto side up, on the press, pull the top down, and cook until browned and crisp and the cheese is melted, 5 to 7 minutes. (If using a grill pan, put a heavy pan on top of the sandwiches and cook, turning the sandwiches once.) Carefully remove from the press and serve. *—Lauren Chattman*

PER SERVING: 590 CALORIES | 15G PROTEIN | 40G CARB | 42G TOTAL FAT | 9G SAT FAT | 26G MONO FAT | 6G POLY FAT | 15MG CHOL | 1010MG SODIUM | 4G FIBER

avocado BLTs

SERVES 4

- **2 large Hass avocados (about 1 lb.)**
- **1 Tbs. fresh lemon juice; more as needed**
- **Kosher salt**
- **1 large tomato (about ¾ lb.), cut into 8 slices**
- **2 Tbs. olive oil**
- **8 thick slices bacon (about 10 oz.)**
- **1 large Vidalia onion, cut into ½-inch-thick rounds (about 8 rounds)**
- **8 ½-inch-thick slices bread (rustic white, whole wheat, or sourdough), toasted**
- **8 Boston lettuce leaves**

> To pit an avocado, use a chef's knife to split the avocado in half lengthwise. The pit will be stuck in one of the halves. Carefully and gently tap the pit with the knife blade so that the blade notches into the pit. Rotate the avocado half so the pit twists free.

These sandwiches are wonderful as is, though you can layer on some sliced turkey or sharp Cheddar if you like. Pick up the best ingredients— a juicy heirloom tomato, fresh lettuce, and good-quality bacon—to ensure the best flavor in this classic sandwich.

1. In a small bowl, mash one of the avocados with the lemon juice and ¼ tsp. salt. Taste and season the avocado with more lemon juice and salt if needed. Slice the second avocado into thin slices. Fan the tomato slices on a large plate, drizzle with 1 Tbs. oil, and sprinkle with ½ tsp. salt.

2. In a large (12-inch), heavy-duty skillet (like cast-iron), cook the bacon with the remaining 1 Tbs. oil over medium heat, flipping occasionally, until it browns and renders much of its fat, about 5 minutes. Transfer the bacon to a plate lined with paper towels. Add the onion rounds to the skillet, sprinkle lightly with salt, and cook until they start to brown, about 2 minutes. Flip and cook until the other sides brown but are still firm, about 2 more minutes. Remove from the heat.

3. For each sandwich, spread the mashed avocado on one bread slice. Top with 2 slices of tomato, 2 onion rounds, bacon, lettuce, and avocado slices. Add the remaining slice of bread and serve.
—Tony Rosenfeld

smoky black bean & cheddar burritos with baby spinach

- **4** burrito-size (9- to 10-inch) flour tortillas
- **15** grape tomatoes, quartered lengthwise (from 1 pint)
- **2** Tbs. fresh lime juice; more as needed
- **¼** cup chopped fresh cilantro

  Kosher salt
- **2** Tbs. extra-virgin olive oil
- **¼** cup raw pepitas (optional)
- **1** tsp. seeded and minced chipotle plus 1 tsp. adobo sauce (from a can of chipotles en adobo)
- **¾** tsp. ground cumin
- **1** 19-oz. can black beans, drained and rinsed
- **½** cup grated sharp Cheddar
- **1½** oz. baby spinach (about 1½ cups)
- **¼** to ½ cup sour cream (optional)

Sandwich wraps make an easy lunch or dinner and are ideal for picnics or casual get-togethers. Chipotle chiles in adobo lend a smoky overtone to this meatless wrap, while pepitas give it crunch.

1. Heat the oven to 250°F. Wrap the tortillas in aluminum foil and warm in the oven.

2. Meanwhile, in a small bowl toss the tomatoes with 1 Tbs. of the lime juice, about 1½ Tbs. of the cilantro, and a generous pinch of salt. Set aside.

3. If using the pepitas, heat 1 Tbs. of the olive oil and the pepitas in a 12-inch skillet over medium heat. Cook, stirring frequently, until they are puffed and some are golden brown, 1 to 2 minutes. Using a slotted spoon, transfer the pepitas to a plate lined with a paper towel. Sprinkle with a generous pinch of salt and toss.

4. Return the pan to medium heat. Add the remaining 1 Tbs. olive oil. (Or if not using pepitas, heat the 2 Tbs. oil over medium heat.) Add the chipotle, adobo sauce, and cumin. Stir to blend into the oil, and then add the beans and 2 Tbs. water to the pan, stirring to blend. Simmer until warmed through, about 2 minutes. Reduce the heat to low. Mash about half of the beans with a fork. Stir in the Cheddar and the remaining 2½ Tbs. cilantro and 1 Tbs. lime juice. Season to taste with salt. If the beans seem too thick, add 1 to 2 Tbs. water to thin to a soft, spreadable consistency.

5. Working with one tortilla at a time, spread about a quarter of the beans along the bottom third of a tortilla. Top with a quarter of the spinach, and sprinkle with about a quarter of the tomatoes and pepitas (if using). If you like, add a little lime juice and sour cream on top. Fold the bottom edge over the filling, fold in the sides, and roll up the burrito. —*Maryellen Driscoll*

PER SERVING: 510 CALORIES | 19G PROTEIN | 63G CARB | 21G TOTAL FAT | 6G SAT FAT | 10G MONO FAT | 4G POLY FAT | 15MG CHOL | 1020MG SODIUM | 9G FIBER

grilled lamb burgers with marinated red onions, dill & sliced feta

Vegetable oil for the grill

1¼ lb. ground lamb

2 tsp. sweet paprika

2 tsp. dried oregano

1 small clove garlic, minced and mashed to a paste

Kosher salt

6 oz. feta, cut into ¼-inch-thick slices (about 8)

2 Tbs. extra-virgin olive oil

2 Tbs. chopped fresh dill

½ small red onion, thinly sliced

3 Tbs. red-wine vinegar

1 tsp. granulated sugar

4 whole-wheat pitas, warmed

4 thin slices tomato

8 thin slices English cucumber

When you tire of the basic burger, this Mediterranean-inspired version is just the ticket. The quick-pickled red onions add dimension and are a great addition to cucumber, tomato, and pasta salads. To keep with the Greek theme, serve the burgers in warm pita bread, though whole-wheat hamburger buns would work, too.

1. Prepare a medium charcoal or gas grill fire. Clean and oil the grill grates. Gently mix the lamb with the paprika, oregano, garlic, and 1 tsp. salt. Form into four ½-inch-thick patties.

2. On a large plate, lay out the slices of feta and sprinkle with the olive oil and 1 Tbs. of the dill. In a small bowl, toss the onion with the vinegar, sugar, ½ tsp. salt, and the remaining 1 Tbs. dill, and let sit for 10 to 15 minutes at room temperature.

3. Grill the burgers on one side until they have good grill marks, about 5 minutes. Flip and cook on the other side until it has good grill marks, too, and the burgers are just light pink inside (make a nick with a paring knife), about 5 minutes for medium doneness.

4. Serve the burgers in the warmed pita with the feta, tomato, cucumber, and a heaping teaspoon of pickled onions. *—Tony Rosenfeld*

Feta is best stored in the salty brine it is sometimes packed in. Once opened, it will keep in the refrigerator for at least a week. If the cheese is not in brine, mix 1 cup water with ¼ cup kosher salt to make a quick brine, and refrigerate in an airtight container.

moroccan grilled chicken sandwiches with onion marmalade

MAKES 12 SMALL SANDWICHES

Vegetable oil, as needed

Moroccan Spice Rub (recipe on the facing page)

4 **medium boneless, skinless chicken breast halves (7 to 8 oz. each), lightly pounded to an even thickness**

12 **2½-inch-square pieces focaccia, sliced in half horizontally and lightly toasted**

1 **to 2 cups baby arugula, washed and dried**

Onion Marmalade (recipe below)

Kosher salt and freshly ground black pepper

These full-flavored sandwiches pack well, so take them on your next picnic or as lunch. Covering the focaccia with a layer of arugula not only adds fresh flavor but also keeps the bread from getting soggy.

1. Heat a gas grill to medium high or prepare a medium-hot charcoal fire. Oil the grill grate. Spread the spice rub on a plate. Lightly rub each chicken breast with oil and press each breast into the spice rub to thoroughly coat one side of the meat.

2. When the grill is hot, arrange the chicken, spice-rub side down, at a 45-degree angle to the bars of the cooking grate. Grill until the chicken has grill marks, about 2 minutes. Rotate the breasts 90 degrees and continue grilling for 2 minutes. Flip the chicken and cook the second side the same way for another 4 to 6 minutes, until the chicken has crosshatched grill marks and the meat is cooked through. Transfer the breasts to a platter, let cool until barely warm, cover loosely, and refrigerate until you're ready to assemble the sandwiches.

3. To assemble the sandwiches, slice each breast thinly crosswise, holding the knife at a 45-degree angle. Cover the bottom pieces of focaccia with a layer of arugula. Top each with about 1 Tbs. of the onion marmalade, some of the sliced chicken, a sprinkle of salt and pepper, more onion marmalade, and another layer of arugula. Cover with the top pieces of toasted focaccia. Serve immediately.
—*Stu Stein*

PER SERVING: 234 CALORIES | 18G PROTEIN | 32G CARB | 4G TOTAL FAT | 1G SAT FAT | 1G MONO FAT | 1G POLY FAT | 37MG CHOL | 586MG SODIUM | 2G FIBER

onion marmalade

MAKES ABOUT 2½ CUPS

3 **medium yellow onions (about 1½ lb.), sliced into thin half-moons**

1 **cup sherry vinegar or white-wine vinegar**

½ **cup dry white wine**

¼ **cup granulated sugar**

1 **Tbs. finely chopped fresh thyme**

Kosher salt and freshly ground white pepper

In a 4-quart nonreactive saucepan, combine the onion, vinegar, wine, ½ cup water, sugar, and thyme. Bring to a boil over high heat; reduce the heat to medium low and simmer slowly, stirring occasionally, until the onion is very soft and the liquid has cooked down to a syrupy consistency, 45 minutes to 1¼ hours. The onion should be fairly moist but not swimming in syrup. Season with salt and pepper to taste and adjust the sugar and acid level to get a sweet-and-sour flavor. Let cool, transfer to an airtight container, and refrigerate for up to 2 weeks.

moroccan spice rub

MAKES ABOUT ¼ CUP

- 2 **Tbs. sweet paprika (preferably Hungarian)**
- 1 **tsp. granulated sugar**
- 1 **tsp. kosher salt**
- ½ **tsp. freshly ground black pepper**
- ½ **tsp. ground ginger**
- ½ **tsp. ground cardamom**
- ½ **tsp. ground cumin**
- ¼ **tsp. ground cloves**
- ¼ **tsp. ground cinnamon**
- ¼ **tsp. ground allspice**
- ¼ **tsp. cayenne**

If there's a commercially prepared North African–inspired spice rub that you like, feel free to use it instead of this version.

In a small bowl, stir together all the ingredients. Stored in an airtight container, the spice rub will keep at room temperature for up to 6 months.

salmon burgers with dill tartar sauce

SERVES 4

- 1½ lb. salmon fillet, skinned, cut into 1-inch cubes, and chilled
- 1 small shallot, finely diced (about 2 Tbs.)
- 1 Tbs. capers, rinsed and chopped
- 1 tsp. Dijon mustard

  Kosher salt and freshly ground black pepper
- ½ cup mayonnaise
- ⅓ cup dill pickle relish
- 2 Tbs. chopped fresh dill
- 2 Tbs. fresh lemon juice; more as needed
- 2 Tbs. olive oil
- 1 cup lightly packed baby spinach (about 1 oz.)
- 1 small red onion, cut into thin rings
- 1 large tomato, cut into 8 thin slices
- 4 hamburger buns, split and toasted

To make these burgers, "grind" the salmon fillet by pulsing it in a food processor. Make sure the fish is chilled so it chops easily. Because the burgers are somewhat loosely packed, it's easier to sear them on the stovetop than on the grill (where they are more inclined to fall apart).

1. Put half of the salmon in a food processor and pulse until it's coarsely chopped. Transfer to a medium bowl. Chop the remaining salmon in the same manner and add to the bowl. Fold in the shallot, capers, mustard, and ¾ tsp. each salt and pepper. Form into four ¾-inch-thick patties, set on a large oiled plate, cover, and refrigerate until ready to cook (up to 4 hours).

2. Meanwhile, make the tartar sauce. In a small bowl, mix the mayonnaise with the relish, dill, lemon juice, and ¼ tsp. each salt and pepper. Taste and add more lemon juice, salt, and pepper if needed. The sauce will keep for up to 1 day in the refrigerator.

3. Heat the oil in a large (12-inch), nonstick skillet over medium-high heat until it's shimmering. Add the salmon burgers (straight from the refrigerator; the cold temperature will help them hold together), reduce the heat to medium, and cook without touching until they brown at the edges, 2 to 3 minutes. Flip and cook the other sides until they, too, are browned and the burgers are just a little pink in the center (check by slicing into a thicker part of one of the burgers with a paring knife), 3 to 4 more minutes.

4. Put the spinach, onion, and 2 tomato slices on each of the buns; top with the burgers and a dollop of the tartar sauce; add the top of the bun and serve. —*Tony Rosenfeld*

shrimp salad rolls with tarragon and chives

SERVES 6

Kosher salt

2 **lb. large shrimp (31 to 40 per lb.), preferably easy-peel**

¾ **cup finely chopped celery with leaves**

½ **cup mayonnaise**

¼ **cup thinly sliced fresh chives**

1 **Tbs. finely chopped fresh tarragon**

1 **Tbs. fresh lemon juice; more to taste**

Freshly ground black pepper

6 **hot dog rolls, preferably New England–style split-top rolls**

Full of bright flavors, the shrimp salad is delicious off the roll, too. If you're really in a hurry, you can use precooked shrimp. As an alternative, substitute 1½ lb. (4 cups) cooked lobster meat for the cooked shrimp.

1. Bring a large pot of well-salted water to a boil over high heat. Add the shrimp and cook, stirring, until bright pink and cooked through, about 2 minutes—the water needn't return to a boil. Drain in a colander and run under cold water to stop the cooking. Shell the shrimp, devein if necessary, and cut into ½- to ¾-inch pieces.

2. In a large bowl, stir together the celery, mayonnaise, chives, tarragon, lemon juice, ¼ tsp. salt, and ¼ tsp. pepper. Stir in the shrimp and season to taste with more lemon juice, salt, and pepper.

3. Position a rack 6 inches from the broiler element and heat the broiler on high. Toast both outside surfaces of the rolls under the broiler, about 1 minute per side. Spoon the shrimp salad into the rolls, using about ⅔ cup per roll, and serve. —*Lori Longbotham*

PER SERVING: 390 CALORIES | 29G PROTEIN | 25G CARB | 18G TOTAL FAT | 3.5G SAT FAT | 1G MONO FAT | 1G POLY FAT | 230MG CHOL | 800MG SODIUM | 1G FIBER

mexican black bean burgers

SERVES 4

- **3** Tbs. olive oil
- **½** cup thinly sliced scallions (white and green parts)
- **⅓** cup finely chopped poblano chile (1 small)
- **2** large cloves garlic, finely chopped
- **1** 15-oz. can black beans, rinsed and drained
- **½** cup coarsely chopped fresh cilantro
- **½** cup toasted whole-grain breadcrumbs (about 1 slice of bread)
- **1** large egg, lightly beaten
- **½** tsp. pure chile powder, such as ancho or New Mexico
- **½** tsp. ground cumin
- Kosher salt
- Tomatillo and Avocado Salsa (recipe below)

It's better to sauté these burgers than to grill them, because they have a fragile texture and lack the protein that meat and fish have to hold everything together.

1. Heat 1 Tbs. of the oil in a 10-inch skillet over medium heat. Add the scallions, poblano chile, and garlic and cook until they're beginning to soften, 1 to 2 minutes. Transfer to a food processor. Add the beans and pulse 2 or 3 times to coarsely chop. Be careful not to overprocess.

2. Transfer the mixture to a large bowl and gently mix in the cilantro, breadcrumbs, egg, chile powder, cumin, and ¾ tsp. salt. Shape the mixture into 4 equal ¾-inch-thick patties. Refrigerate, covered, for at least 30 minutes and up to 4 hours.

3. Heat the remaining 2 Tbs. oil in a large skillet over medium heat. Cook the burgers until nicely browned on both sides, flipping carefully, about 5 minutes total. Serve with the Tomatillo and Avocado Salsa.
—*John Ash*

PER SERVING: 300 CALORIES | 9G PROTEIN | 26G CARB | 19G TOTAL FAT | 3G SAT FAT | 13G MONO FAT | 2.5G POLY FAT | 55MG CHOL | 490MG SODIUM | 9G FIBER

tomatillo and avocado salsa

MAKES ABOUT 1 CUP

- **1** medium tomatillo, husked, washed, and coarsely chopped
- **1** Tbs. thinly sliced scallion
- **½** tsp. chopped garlic
- **½** tsp. seeded and minced serrano chile; more as needed
- **1** large ripe avocado, pitted, peeled, and coarsely chopped
- Kosher salt and freshly ground black pepper

This salsa can be refrigerated in an airtight container for up to 2 days. It's also tasty on pork tacos or with quesadillas.

Put the tomatillo, scallion, garlic, and serrano chile in a food processor and process until finely chopped, about 15 seconds. Add the avocado and pulse until just combined. The salsa should be chunky. Season to taste with salt, pepper, and more serrano.

falafel pitas with tomato-cucumber salad

SERVES 4

- 1 15-oz. can chickpeas, rinsed and drained
- 7 Tbs. extra-virgin olive oil
- 1 tsp. ground cumin
- ½ tsp. ground coriander
- Kosher salt and freshly ground black pepper
- 1 medium yellow onion, diced
- ½ cup plain fine dry breadcrumbs; more as needed
- 1½ cups cherry tomatoes, quartered
- 1 medium pickling cucumber or ⅓ English cucumber, halved and sliced ¼ inch thick
- 1 Tbs. fresh lemon juice
- 4 pitas, warmed

Falafel are usually deep-fried, but pan-searing these chickpea fritters is healthier (and not as messy). Serve them in pita bread, topped with thick yogurt or tahini sauce, if you like.

1. Heat the oven to 425°F. In a food processor, pulse the chickpeas, 2 Tbs. of the oil, the cumin, coriander, 1 tsp. salt, and ½ tsp. black pepper into a chunky paste. Add the onion and breadcrumbs and pulse until the mixture tightens up. You should be able to easily form it into a patty—add more breadcrumbs as needed. Gently form the chickpea mixture into twelve ½-inch-thick patties.

2. Heat 2 Tbs. of the oil in a 10-inch nonstick skillet over medium heat until shimmering hot. Add 6 of the patties and cook until nicely browned, about 2 minutes. Flip and cook the other sides until browned, 1 to 2 minutes more. Transfer the patties to a baking sheet. Repeat with 2 Tbs. more oil and the remaining 6 patties. Bake the patties until heated through, about 5 minutes.

3. Meanwhile, toss the tomatoes and cucumber with the lemon juice, the remaining 1 Tbs. oil, and salt to taste.

4. Split the pitas and stuff them with the falafel and tomato-cucumber salad. —*Tony Rosenfeld*

PER SERVING: 640 CALORIES | 18G PROTEIN | 80G CARB | 28G TOTAL FAT | 4G SAT FAT | 18G MONO FAT | 4.5G POLY FAT | 0MG CHOL | 920MG SODIUM | 12G FIBER

farmer's market quesadillas

MAKES 4 QUESADILLAS

5 Tbs. vegetable oil

1 cup small-diced fresh mild chiles, such as Anaheim or poblano (from about 2 large chiles)

1½ cups small-diced summer squash (from about 2 small zucchini, yellow squash, or yellow crookneck)

Kosher salt and freshly ground black pepper

1 cup fresh corn kernels (from 2 medium ears)

⅛ tsp. chipotle chile powder

1 cup diced tomato (from 2 small tomatoes)

¼ cup chopped fresh cilantro

1 Tbs. fresh lime juice

4 9-inch flour tortillas

2 cups grated sharp Cheddar (½ lb.)

Sour cream, for serving (optional)

Chipotles are dried smoked jalapeños, and in any form they add an intriguing depth to dishes. Look for a ground chipotle, but a crushed chipotle would be a fine substitute; just add a bit more than you would of the ground.

1. Heat the oven to 200°F. Fit a rack over a baking sheet and put in the oven.

2. Heat 1 Tbs. of the oil in a 12-inch skillet over medium-high heat until hot. Add the chiles and cook, stirring, until soft, 3 to 4 minutes. Add the squash, season with salt and pepper, and cook, stirring, until the squash softens and starts to brown, 3 to 4 minutes. Stir in the corn and chipotle powder and cook for another 2 minutes. Spoon into a bowl, let cool for a few minutes, and then fold in the tomato, cilantro, and lime juice. Season to taste with salt and pepper. Set aside ¾ cup of the mixture.

3. Lay several layers of paper towel on a work surface. Wipe out the skillet, put it over medium-high heat, and add 1 Tbs. of the oil. When it's hot, put one tortilla in the pan. Quickly distribute ½ cup of the cheese evenly over the tortilla and about a quarter of the remaining vegetable mixture over half the tortilla. When the underside of the tortilla is browned, use tongs to fold the cheese-only side over the vegetable side. Lay the quesadilla on the paper towels, blot for a few seconds, and then move it to the rack in the oven to keep warm while you repeat with the remaining oil and tortillas. Cut the quesadillas into wedges and serve immediately with the reserved vegetable mixture and sour cream (if desired). —*Martha Holmberg*

PER SERVING: 660 CALORIES | 22G PROTEIN | 51G CARB | 42G TOTAL FAT | 15G SAT FAT | 16G MONO FAT | 9G POLY FAT | 60MG CHOL | 1090MG SODIUM | 5G FIBER

thai curry turkey burgers

SERVES 4

- 1¼ **lb. ground turkey (not ground turkey breast)**
- 2 **Tbs. red or green Thai curry paste**
- **Kosher salt and freshly ground black pepper**
- **Vegetable oil, for the grill**
- 1 **medium lime**
- ⅔ **cup mayonnaise**
- ¾ **cup thinly sliced seedless cucumber**
- ¼ **cup fresh cilantro leaves**
- 1 **small shallot, thinly sliced**
- 1 **Tbs. seasoned rice vinegar**
- 4 **sesame seed hamburger buns**
- **Sliced tomato, for serving**

Aromatic Thai curry paste mixed into the meat gives these turkey burgers a flavorful kick; look for it in the Asian section of most supermarkets.

1. Prepare a medium gas or charcoal grill fire.

2. In a medium bowl, gently mix the turkey, curry paste, and ¼ tsp. each salt and pepper with your hands just until blended. Form the mixture into four ½-inch-thick patties.

3. Oil the grill grate. Grill the burgers, flipping once, until an instant-read thermometer inserted into the centers of the burgers registers 165°F, 12 to 15 minutes total.

4. While the burgers cook, finely grate 1 tsp. zest from the lime, then squeeze the lime to yield 1 Tbs. juice. In a small bowl, combine the zest and juice, mayonnaise, and ¼ tsp. salt. In another small bowl, toss the cucumber with the cilantro, shallot, and vinegar.

5. Place the buns cut side down on the grill and toast until browned and heated through, 1 to 2 minutes.

6. Spread the tops and bottoms of the buns with the mayonnaise. Serve the burgers in the buns, topped with a slice of tomato and the cucumber mixture. *—Lori Longbotham*

PER SERVING: 610 CALORIES | 32G PROTEIN | 19G CARB | 41G TOTAL FAT | 12G SAT FAT | 22G MONO FAT | 3.5G POLY FAT | 115MG CHOL | 750MG SODIUM | 2G FIBER

broiled salmon
with ginger–shiitake glaze
(recipe on p. 100)

main dishes

zucchini tart with lemon thyme and goat cheese

SERVES 8

1¼ cups unbleached all-purpose flour

5 oz. cold unsalted butter

Kosher salt

½ tsp. white vinegar

1½ lb. zucchini, trimmed and sliced into ⅛-inch-thick rounds

2 Tbs. extra-virgin olive oil

Freshly ground black pepper

½ lb. plain goat cheese, softened

1 tsp. chopped fresh lemon thyme

If you can't find lemon thyme, use 1 tsp. chopped thyme and ¼ tsp. finely grated lemon zest instead.

When preparing the dough for this gorgeous tart, don't omit the white vinegar: It makes the crust flaky and tender.

1. In a food processor, pulse the flour, butter, and ¾ tsp. salt until the butter is the size of small peas. Add the vinegar and 3 to 4 Tbs. cold water, pulsing until the dough just comes together. Shape the dough into a 1-inch-thick disk; wrap in plastic and chill for 30 minutes. Roll the dough on a well-floured surface into an 11-inch round that's ¼ inch thick. Put the dough on a baking sheet, cover with plastic, and chill until ready to use, at least 30 minutes.

2. In a colander, toss the zucchini with 2 tsp. salt and drain for 30 minutes. Gently squeeze the slices with your hands to release excess water and transfer to a medium bowl.

3. Position a rack in the center of the oven and heat the oven to 400°F. Toss the zucchini with 1 Tbs. of the olive oil and pepper to taste. In a small bowl, mix the goat cheese with the lemon thyme and salt and pepper to taste. Spread the cheese over the dough, leaving a ½-inch border. Arrange the squash rounds in tightly overlapping concentric circles all the way to the edge of the dough. (The rounds will shrink as they cook.) Drizzle with the remaining 1 Tbs. olive oil and bake until the zucchini is golden brown, 40 to 50 minutes. —*Maria Helm Sinskey*

PER SERVING: 320 CALORIES | 8G PROTEIN | 18G CARB | 24G TOTAL FAT | 14G SAT FAT | 8G MONO FAT | 1G POLY FAT | 50MG CHOL | 500MG SODIUM | 1G FIBER

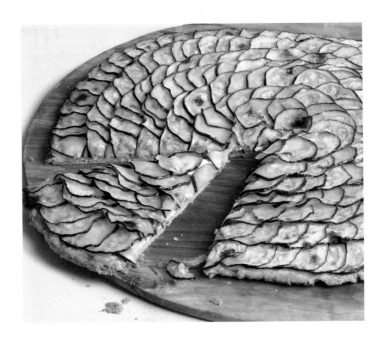

honey-lime-sake shrimp

SERVES 4

- ½ cup mild honey (such as clover)
- ½ cup sake
- 3 medium limes, finely grated to yield 2 tsp. zest, squeezed to yield ⅓ cup juice
- 1 Tbs. minced garlic
- 1 Tbs. minced fresh ginger
- 2 tsp. hot sauce (such as Cholula®)
- Kosher salt
- 24 colossal shrimp (13 to 15 per lb.; about 1 lb.), shelled (tails left intact, if you like) and deveined
- 1 Tbs. coarsely chopped fresh cilantro

These simple-to-make glazed shrimp have a surprisingly complex flavor. Sake, a Japanese rice wine, lends a savory-sweet note that's enhanced by the honey, while fresh limes and hot pepper sauce add zing. Serve over rice for a main dish or with toasted bread as an appetizer.

1. In a 12-inch skillet, combine the honey, sake, lime juice and zest, garlic, ginger, hot sauce, and 1 tsp. salt and stir until thoroughly mixed. Bring to a simmer over medium heat, then add the shrimp, toss to coat, and cook until just pink and opaque throughout, about 1 minute per side.

2. Transfer the shrimp to a serving bowl with a slotted spoon or tongs. Bring the sauce to a boil over medium-high heat and cook, adding any juice that has accumulated from the shrimp, until reduced to a syrupy consistency, about 10 minutes. Pour the sauce over the shrimp, sprinkle with the cilantro, and toss to coat. Serve immediately.
—Ronne Day

PER SERVING: 190 CALORIES | 19G PROTEIN | 20G CARB | 1.5G TOTAL FAT | 0G SAT FAT | 0G MONO FAT | 0.5G POLY FAT | 145MG CHOL | 310MG SODIUM | 0G FIBER

spicy chipotle shrimp, avocado & corn fajitas

SERVES 4

- **1** lb. shrimp (26 to 30 per lb.), peeled and deveined
- **¼** cup olive oil
- **1** tsp. chili powder
- **1** tsp. kosher salt
- **½** tsp. freshly ground black pepper
- **1** large Hass avocado (about ½ lb.), cut into ½-inch dice
- **1** chipotle, minced, plus 1 Tbs. adobo sauce (from a can of chipotles en adobo)
- **1** lime, ½ juiced (about 1 Tbs.) and ½ cut into wedges
- **1** large yellow onion, thinly sliced (about 3 cups)
- **1** large clove garlic, minced
- **1** cup frozen corn, thawed, or kernels from 2 ears corn
- **8** corn tortillas, warmed
- **¼** cup coarsely chopped fresh cilantro

To heat the corn tortillas but keep them from ripping or cracking, warm them in a nonstick skillet over medium-low heat for 10 to 15 seconds on each side, and then put them between layers of damp paper towels until they are ready to be served. Arrange the fajitas and fixings on a buffet table, bar style, for casual entertaining, or serve the components on various platters at the table.

1. Toss the shrimp with 1 Tbs. oil, the chili powder, ¼ tsp. salt, and the pepper. In a medium bowl, mash the avocado with the chipotle and adobo sauce, lime juice, and ¼ tsp. salt.

2. Heat 1½ Tbs. oil in a large (12-inch) skillet over medium-high heat until shimmering. Add the shrimp and cook, stirring, until they turn pink and become just firm to the touch, about 2 minutes. Transfer to a large plate.

3. Reduce the heat to medium, and add the remaining 1½ Tbs. oil to the pan. Add the onion, sprinkle with the remaining ½ tsp. salt, and cook, stirring, until the onion softens and starts to brown, about 6 minutes. Add the garlic and cook, stirring, for 30 seconds. Add the corn and shrimp, and cook, stirring, until they heat through, about 2 minutes.

4. Spread some avocado on a warm tortilla and top with some of the shrimp mixture, a squeeze of lime juice, and a sprinkling of cilantro.
—*Tony Rosenfeld*

asparagus, ham & mushroom strata

SERVES 8

2 Tbs. unsalted butter; more for the pan

1 lb. asparagus, ends snapped off, cut into 1½-inch pieces

1 tsp. kosher salt

1 tsp. freshly ground black pepper

3½ oz. oyster mushrooms (or shiitake or white mushrooms), stemmed and thinly sliced

6 scallions, trimmed and thinly sliced, white and green parts separated (½ cup green, 2 Tbs. white)

9 large eggs, beaten

2¾ cups milk (preferably whole)

1 large loaf (about 1 lb.) rustic white bread (like ciabatta), cut into 1-inch cubes

½ lb. thinly sliced deli ham, cut into 1-inch strips

3 cups grated extra-sharp Cheddar (about ½ lb.)

A strata is like an Italian quiche, but instead of an involved pastry crust, leftover bread forms the egg custard base. As with a bread pudding, assemble this dish ahead of time and bake it just before serving. It's up to you whether or not to trim the bread crust. When entertaining, trim it for a neat and pretty dish, or leave it intact for a heartier texture.

1. Melt the butter in a large (12-inch) skillet over medium-high heat. Add the asparagus, sprinkle with ½ tsp. each salt and pepper, and cook, stirring occasionally, until the spears start to brown and soften, about 3 minutes. Add the mushrooms and scallion whites and cook, stirring occasionally, until the mushrooms soften and cook through, about 2 minutes. Remove from the heat and let cool for a couple of minutes.

2. Butter a 9x13-inch baking dish. Whisk the eggs with the milk and ½ tsp. each salt and pepper. Spread half the bread in a single layer on the bottom of the baking dish. Top with half the egg mixture and then cover with half the ham, cheese, and asparagus mixture, and sprinkle with half the scallion greens. Repeat with the remaining custard, ham, cheese, asparagus mixture, and scallions. Cover with plastic wrap, pressing down so the bread is completely submerged in the egg mixture, and refrigerate for at least 4 hours and up to 2 days before baking.

3. Position a rack in the center of the oven and heat the oven to 350°F. Let the strata sit at room temperature while the oven heats. Bake until the custard sets and the top browns, about 30 minutes. Loosely cover with foil and bake for another 20 minutes. Let cool for 10 minutes, cut into square pieces, and serve. —*Tony Rosenfeld*

broiled salmon with ginger-shiitake glaze

SERVES 4

- **3 Tbs. canola oil; more for the baking sheet**
- **2 lb. salmon fillets, skin on**
- **¼ tsp. ground coriander**
- **¾ tsp. kosher salt**
- **½ tsp. freshly ground black pepper**
- **½ small red bell pepper, finely diced (about ¼ cup)**
- **3 scallions, trimmed and thinly sliced (white and green parts separated)**
- **2 Tbs. finely chopped fresh ginger**
- **3½ oz. shiitake mushrooms, stemmed and cut into ¼-inch dice (about 1 cup)**
- **¼ cup honey**
- **3 Tbs. rice vinegar**
- **1 Tbs. reduced-sodium soy sauce**
- **1 tsp. Asian chili sauce (like Sriracha)**
- **1 tsp. cornstarch**

Though most glazes are applied with a brush, this slightly chunky mixture of sautéed mushrooms and red peppers is spooned over the fish. The honey helps the crust brown, and a splash of vinegar and a spoonful of chili sauce perk up the fish while the vegetables add texture and color.

1. Position an oven rack about 8 inches away from the broiler element and heat the broiler to high.

2. Oil a large, rimmed baking sheet. Set the salmon skin side down on the baking sheet, sprinkle with 1 Tbs. oil, the coriander, ½ tsp. salt, and the pepper, and let sit at room temperature while you prepare the sauce.

3. In a large (12-inch) skillet over medium-high heat, cook the red pepper, scallion whites, and ginger in the remaining 2 Tbs. oil, stirring occasionally, until the red pepper and scallions start to soften and brown, about 3 minutes. Add the mushrooms, raise the heat to medium high, sprinkle with the remaining ¼ tsp. salt, and cook, stirring, until they soften and start to brown, about 3 minutes. Add the honey, vinegar, soy sauce, chili sauce, and ¼ cup water, and bring to a simmer. Whisk the cornstarch with 1 tsp. water and stir into the glaze. Return to a simmer and cook until the glaze thickens, about 1 minute. Remove from the heat.

4. Broil the salmon until it starts to brown and becomes almost firm to the touch, about 8 minutes. Momentarily transfer to the stovetop and spoon the glaze over the salmon. Return to the oven and broil for about 1 more minute so the glaze browns and the salmon almost completely cooks through (check by using a paring knife to flake a thicker part of the fillet). Sprinkle with the scallion greens, transfer to a large platter, and serve. *—Tony Rosenfeld*

skinning salmon

Though butchering fish can be complicated work, skinning salmon is quite simple. Make a little slice at one corner of the fillet a couple inches wide, separating the skin from the flesh of the salmon. Then with one hand holding the knife at a 30-degree angle and the other holding the corner of skin, firmly pull on the skin while slicing the knife back and forth (the skin hand will do most of the work) so the skin pulls free.

Skinning grilled salmon is just as easy. Grill the salmon fillet, but before removing the salmon from the grill, slip a spatula between the skin and the flesh, leaving the skin behind. By the time the grill is cool, the skin will have become ash and can be brushed off the grate.

chicken breasts with tarragon and vermouth

SERVES 2 OR 3

- **1** lb. boneless, skinless chicken breast halves (about 3)

  Kosher salt and freshly ground black pepper

- **2** Tbs. extra-virgin olive oil; more as needed

- **2** Tbs. minced shallot

- **½** cup dry vermouth or dry white wine

- **3** Tbs. cold unsalted butter, cut into 6 to 8 pieces

- **2** tsp. chopped fresh tarragon

Chicken and tarragon are a classic French combination. Serve with potatoes and steamed haricots verts.

1. Trim the chicken, removing the tenders, and slice on an angle into ¾-inch-thick pieces; season generously with salt and pepper. In a 10-inch straight-sided sauté pan, heat the oil over medium-high heat until it shimmers. Add half of the chicken and cook, flipping once, until lightly browned and just barely cooked through, 1 to 2 minutes per side. Transfer to a plate; repeat with the remaining chicken. Cover with foil to keep warm.

2. Return the pan to medium heat and, if it looks dry, add 1 Tbs. oil. Add the shallot and sauté, stirring with a wooden spoon, until softened, about 1 minute. Pour in the vermouth or wine and scrape the pan with the spoon to loosen any browned bits. Simmer until the vermouth is reduced slightly, about 2 minutes. Reduce the heat to low and add the cold butter 2 or 3 pieces at a time, stirring after each addition until completely melted. Stir in the tarragon, taste the sauce, and add salt and pepper as needed. Add the chicken and any accumulated juices to the sauce and turn to coat with the sauce. Serve immediately.

—Jennifer Armentrout

PER SERVING: 410 CALORIES | 31G PROTEIN | 6G CARB | 24G TOTAL FAT | 9G SAT FAT | 12G MONO FAT | 2G POLY FAT | 115MG CHOL | 560MG SODIUM | 0G FIBER

grilled sausage with summer squash, fresh herbs & olives

SERVES 4

- 1½ **lb. mixed summer squash, cut into 1-inch chunks**
- 2 **Tbs. extra-virgin olive oil**
- **Kosher salt and freshly ground black pepper**
- 1 **lb. Italian sausage links (chicken or pork)**
- ⅓ **cup mixed fresh herbs, such as cilantro, parsley, mint, and basil, chopped**
- ⅓ **cup pitted Kalamata olives, halved**
- 1 **Tbs. capers, rinsed**
- **Squeeze of fresh lemon juice**

If you like, add other summer vegetables, like peppers, eggplant, or sweet onions. Serve with grilled bread.

1. Prepare a medium-hot grill fire. Toss the squash with the olive oil in a medium bowl; season to taste with salt and pepper.

2. Grill the squash and the sausage, turning frequently, until the squash is just tender and the sausage is cooked through, 8 to 12 minutes. Cut the sausage into 1-inch chunks. Toss the squash and sausage with the herbs, olives, and capers. Season with lemon juice, salt, and pepper. —*Allison Ehri Kreitler*

PER SERVING: 320 CALORIES | 13G PROTEIN | 10G CARB | 26G TOTAL FAT | 7G SAT FAT | 14G MONO FAT | 3G POLY FAT | 35MG CHOL | 1260MG SODIUM | 2G FIBER

how to pit an olive

It's easiest to use a chef's knife or a small skillet or saucepan to pit olives. The action is the same for both tools: Apply pressure with the bottom of the pan or the side of the knife until the olive splits, exposing the pit enough that it can be plucked away by hand. For soft black olives, use a knife. For firm green olives, use a skillet because more pressure is needed and the knife might slip.

pork chops with cranberry-maple pan sauce

SERVES 4

4 1-inch-thick bone-in pork chops (about 2½ lb.)

2 tsp. chopped fresh thyme

   Kosher salt and freshly ground black pepper

1½ Tbs. olive oil

1 cup fresh or frozen cranberries

½ cup lower-salt chicken broth

½ cup pure maple syrup

2 tsp. cider vinegar

2 tsp. Dijon mustard

Fresh cranberries color the sauce a vibrant red, and their tart edge is a perfect counterpoint to the sweet maple syrup.

1. Pat the pork dry and season with 1 tsp. of the thyme, 1¼ tsp. salt, and ¾ tsp. pepper.

2. Heat the oil in a heavy-duty 12-inch skillet over medium heat until shimmering hot. Add the pork chops and cook without moving until the pork is browned around the edges and easily releases when you lift a corner, 3 to 4 minutes. Flip the pork chops and continue to cook until firm to the touch and an instant-read thermometer inserted horizontally into a chop close to but not touching the bone registers 140°F, about 9 minutes.

3. Transfer the chops to a plate and cover loosely with foil to keep warm. Add the cranberries, chicken broth, maple syrup, cider vinegar, mustard, and the remaining 1 tsp. thyme to the skillet and raise the heat to medium high. Cook, whisking to incorporate the mustard and any browned bits from the bottom of the pan, until the cranberries soften and the liquid has reduced to a saucy consistency, about 7 minutes.

4. Return the pork chops and any accumulated juice to the skillet, turning to coat both sides. Serve the pork chops with the sauce.
—Tony Rosenfeld

PER SERVING: 410 CALORIES | 34G PROTEIN | 31G CARB | 16G TOTAL FAT | 4.5G SAT FAT | 8G MONO FAT | 2G POLY FAT | 85MG CHOL | 500MG SODIUM | 1G FIBER

More about Thyme

Thyme is an herb that balances other flavors in a dish, perfuming foods with its warm, aromatic flavor. A few finely chopped leaves added at the last minute bring the other flavors into sharper focus, and it's equally at home in a caramel sauce served over roasted fruits as it is in baked macaroni and cheese.

For the broadest culinary use, French thyme (also called summer thyme) and English thyme are the two to look for at your local market, but there are many other variants.

Rinse fresh thyme well before using. Pat it dry and then pick the leaves from the stem if you'll be chopping the thyme (the stems are tough). Some thyme varieties can be tedious to pick, but English thyme is quite easy: Pinch the top of a sprig between thumb and forefinger, then zip your other thumb and forefinger down the stem, pulling off the leaves as you go.

tandoori chicken legs

SERVES 6

FOR THE CHICKEN

2 Tbs. fresh lemon juice

   Kosher or sea salt

6 whole chicken legs
   (2 to 3 lb.)

FOR THE MARINADE

1 Tbs. finely grated fresh
   ginger

1 large clove garlic, minced

   Kosher or sea salt

⅓ cup plain whole-milk yogurt

3 Tbs. vegetable oil

1½ tsp. fresh lemon juice

1 tsp. sweet paprika

¾ tsp. hot dry mustard

½ tsp. ground cumin

½ tsp. ground coriander

¼ tsp. ground nutmeg

¼ tsp. ground cardamom

¼ tsp. ground turmeric

¼ tsp. cayenne

¼ tsp. freshly ground black
   pepper

FOR FINISHING

   Vegetable oil for the grill

4 Tbs. unsalted butter, melted

½ cup fresh cilantro leaves

1 small red onion, thinly sliced

1 medium lime, cut into
   wedges

These legs get a triple blast of flavor: first from a soak in lemon juice and salt, then from a pungent marinade of spices and yogurt, and finally from a bit of butter brushed on at the end of cooking. Remove the skin from the chicken legs before grilling to help the marinade penetrate the meat more easily.

PREPARE THE CHICKEN

1. Combine the lemon juice and 1 tsp. salt in a large zip-top plastic bag and massage the bag until the salt crystals dissolve.

2. Pull the skin off the chicken legs. Using a sharp knife, make 2 or 3 deep slashes in each leg, almost to the bone. Toss the chicken legs in the lemon juice, seal the bag, and refrigerate for 15 minutes.

MARINATE THE CHICKEN

Mash the ginger, garlic, and 1 tsp. salt to a paste with the side of a large knife and transfer the paste to a small mixing bowl. Whisk in the remaining marinade ingredients. Add the marinade to the chicken legs and massage the bag to thoroughly coat the legs. Seal the bag and refrigerate the chicken for at least 4 hours but preferably 12 to 24 hours.

GRILL THE CHICKEN

1. Prepare a gas or charcoal grill fire for indirect grilling over medium-high heat (400°F).

2. If using a charcoal grill, bank the coals to one side. Put a 9x13-inch foil drip pan on the grate next to the coals and fill it halfway with water. Replace the grill grate.

3. If using a gas grill, put a 9x13-inch foil drip pan on the inactive burners and fill it halfway with water. Replace the grill grate.

4. Clean the grate with a wire brush and, using tongs, wipe the grate with a paper towel or cloth dipped in oil.

5. Arrange the legs over the drip pan and away from the heat. Grill, flipping once, until an instant-read thermometer inserted into the thickest part of the meat reads 170°F, 25 to 30 minutes.

6. Transfer the chicken to a platter and brush each leg with the melted butter. Garnish with the cilantro leaves, onion slices, and lime wedges and serve. —*Steven Raichlen*

PER SERVING: 390 CALORIES | 30G PROTEIN | 3G CARB | 28G TOTAL FAT | 10G SAT FAT | 10G MONO FAT | 6G POLY FAT | 125MG CHOL | 400MG SODIUM | 1G FIBER

southeast asian chicken wings

- 3½ lb. large whole chicken wings (12 to 16)
- 12 to 16 twelve-inch bamboo skewers, soaked in water for 30 minutes
- ½ cup unsweetened coconut milk
- 2 stalks fresh lemongrass, tender white core from the bottom third only, coarsely chopped (about 3 Tbs.)
- 2 medium cloves garlic, coarsely chopped
- 2 scallions, white parts coarsely chopped, green parts thinly sliced (3 to 4 Tbs.)
- 2 Thai bird chiles or 1 jalapeño, thinly sliced (including seeds)
- ¼ cup packed fresh cilantro
- 3 Tbs. fish sauce
- 1 Tbs. coarsely chopped fresh ginger
- 1 Tbs. fresh lime juice
- 1 Tbs. granulated sugar
- Vegetable oil for the grill
- ½ cup Thai sweet chili sauce (such as Mae Ploy®)

Buffalo does not have a monopoly on wings. In Thailand, you'll find them glazed with a sweet chili sauce; in Vietnam, they're seasoned with lemongrass and fish sauce. Here, several ingredients, including coconut milk, fish sauce, lemongrass, and sweet chili sauce, re-create a bit of that Asian flavor. The look may be unusual, but using a skewer to stretch out your chicken wings increases the amount of exposed skin that can crisp up during cooking as well as absorb the marinade and smoky flavors from the grill. What's more, wings on a stick are fun to eat.

1. Pat the chicken wings dry with paper towels. Thread each wing on a bamboo skewer, starting at the meaty end and ending at the wing tip so that the wing is stretched out as much as possible without ripping the skin. Arrange the wings in a large, shallow dish.

2. In a blender, purée the coconut milk, lemongrass, garlic, scallion whites, chiles, cilantro, fish sauce, ginger, lime juice, and sugar until smooth. Pour the marinade over the wings, turning to coat evenly. Cover with plastic wrap and refrigerate for 2 to 4 hours.

3. Prepare a gas or charcoal grill fire for direct grilling over medium heat (350°F). When ready to cook, clean the grate with a wire brush and, using tongs, wipe the grate with a paper towel or cloth dipped in oil.

4. Shake off any excess marinade from the wings and wrap the ends of each skewer with a small piece of aluminum foil to protect them from burning. Grill the wings (covered if using a gas grill), flipping halfway through cooking, until golden brown on the outside and an instant-read thermometer inserted in a thick part of a wing reads 165°F, 16 to 24 minutes total.

5. Brush the wings on both sides with the sweet chili sauce and grill until the glaze sizzles, 1 to 2 minutes per side. Transfer the wings to a platter, sprinkle with the scallion greens, and serve. —*Steven Raichlen*

PER SERVING: 520 CALORIES | 41G PROTEIN | 16G CARB | 31G TOTAL FAT | 9G SAT FAT | 12G MONO FAT | 6G POLY FAT | 130MG CHOL | 570MG SODIUM | 0G FIBER

grilled moroccan spice-crusted lamb with spicy chili sauce

SERVES 4

FOR THE LAMB

- **4** tsp. kosher salt
- **1** Tbs. light brown sugar
- **1** Tbs. ground cumin
- **1** Tbs. dried oregano
- **½** tsp. ground cinnamon
- **½** tsp. hot pimentón (smoked paprika) or chipotle powder
- **5** lb. boneless leg of lamb, trimmed

FOR THE SAUCE

- **¼** cup olive oil
- **1** large yellow onion, cut into ¼-inch dice (about 2 cups)
- **2** large jalapeños (preferably red), cored, seeded, and finely diced (about ¼ cup)
- Kosher salt
- **2** large cloves garlic, finely chopped (about 1 Tbs.)
- **2** tsp. ground coriander
- **1** tsp. ground cumin
- **½** tsp. crushed red pepper flakes
- **2** Tbs. tomato paste
- **2** Tbs. white vinegar; more as needed
- Vegetable oil, for the grill
- **¼** cup chopped fresh cilantro

Serve this grilled lamb with Mediterranean sides like saffron couscous and grilled zucchini and green and yellow bell peppers. Stuff any leftover lamb in a fresh pita with salad greens, tomatoes, and the chili sauce. The sauce is potent, so a little goes a long way.

PREPARE THE LAMB

In a small bowl, mix the salt with the sugar and spices. Sprinkle all over the lamb, transfer to a large nonreactive dish, and cover; refrigerate for at least 4 hours and up to 2 days.

MAKE THE SAUCE

Heat the oil in a medium (10-inch) sauté pan over medium heat until it's shimmering. Add the onion, jalapeños, and 1 tsp. salt, and cook, stirring occasionally, until the onion softens and becomes translucent, about 8 minutes. Add the garlic, coriander, cumin, and red pepper flakes, and cook, stirring, until the garlic becomes fragrant, about 1 minute. Add the tomato paste, and cook, stirring, until the paste starts to darken, about 1 minute. Add ¾ cup water and the vinegar; bring to a boil, then simmer until the onion is completely tender, about 10 minutes. Transfer to a food processor and purée. Let cool to room temperature, season to taste with more salt, pepper, and vinegar if needed. Set aside or transfer to an airtight container and refrigerate for up to 3 days.

GRILL THE LAMB

For a gas grill, light the front burner to medium-high and the back burner(s) to medium-low. For a charcoal grill, light a medium-hot fire (400°F) with two-thirds of the coals banked to one side. Clean and oil the grill grates. Grill the lamb over the hotter part of the fire without moving it until it's nicely browned, 6 to 8 minutes. Turn, move to the cooler part of the fire, and cook until an instant-read thermometer inserted into a thicker part of the lamb registers 135°F for medium-rare, 8 to 10 more minutes.

TO SERVE

Transfer the lamb to a cutting board, tent with foil, and let rest for 10 minutes. Thinly slice across the grain, transfer to a large platter, and sprinkle with the cilantro. Serve with the sauce on the side.

—Tony Rosenfeld

lamb chops crusted with fennel and black pepper

SERVES 4

- 2 tsp. fennel seeds, lightly crushed
- 1¼ tsp. ground coriander
- 1 tsp. dried rosemary, chopped
- ¾ tsp. garlic powder
- 1 tsp. kosher salt
- ¾ tsp. freshly ground black pepper
- 8 lamb loin chops, about 1 inch thick (4 to 5 oz. each)
- 1½ Tbs. extra-virgin olive oil; more for the pan

Need dinner fast? These broiled lamb loin chops cook in just 10 minutes.

1. Position a rack 4 inches from the broiler element and heat the broiler to high.

2. In a small bowl, combine the fennel seeds, coriander, rosemary, garlic powder, salt, and pepper; mix well. Brush the lamb chops with the olive oil to coat. Press an equal amount of the spice mix on both sides of the chops and let them sit for 10 minutes.

3. Coat a broiler pan with oil or nonstick cooking spray. Set the lamb chops on the pan and broil until the first side is well browned, about 5 minutes. Flip the chops and continue to cook until the second side is well browned and the center is cooked to your liking (cut into a chop near the bone to check), about another 5 minutes for medium rare.
—*David Bonom*

PER SERVING: 560 CALORIES | 45G PROTEIN | 2G CARB | 41G TOTAL FAT | 16G SAT FAT | 20G MONO FAT | 4G POLY FAT | 170MG CHOL | 720MG SODIUM | 1G FIBER

pepper-crusted duck breasts with cherry-port sauce

1½ cups fruity red wine, such as Zinfandel, Shiraz, or Merlot

1 cup ruby port

1 1¼-inch piece fresh ginger, peeled

1 to 2 Tbs. granulated sugar

1 Tbs. balsamic vinegar

1 tsp. cornstarch

2 cups fresh sweet or sour cherries (about 11 oz.), pitted and halved

Kosher salt and freshly ground black pepper

6 small or 3 large skin-on duck breasts (about 3 lb. total)

2 Tbs. coarsely cracked black peppercorns

In this elegant and easy dish, a quick sauce of red wine, port, and cherries tops seared duck breasts. Serve with haricots verts blanched and sautéed in brown butter, then tossed with hazelnuts.

1. In a medium saucepan, combine the wine, port, ginger, and sugar (1 Tbs. for sweet cherries, 2 Tbs. for sour) and set over high heat. Bring to a boil, reduce the heat as needed, and simmer until reduced by half, 8 to 12 minutes.

2. In a small bowl, mix the balsamic vinegar and cornstarch. Whisking constantly, add the cornstarch mixture to the wine mixture and simmer until slightly thickened, about another 1 minute. Discard the ginger. Turn the heat to low, add the cherries, and simmer slowly until the cherries are warm, another 1 to 2 minutes. Season to taste with salt and pepper. Set aside.

3. Put the duck breasts on a work surface skin side up. Using a sharp knife, score the skin in a grid pattern, cutting just halfway through the thickness of the skin. Season the duck generously with salt. Scatter the cracked pepper on a small rimmed baking sheet and press the duck into the pepper, coating both sides evenly.

4. Heat a heavy 12-inch skillet over medium-high heat. Arrange the duck breasts, skin side down, in the skillet and cook until the skin is deep golden brown and the fat from the skin has rendered, 6 to 8 minutes. Carefully spoon off and discard all but about 1 Tbs. of the fat. Turn the duck and continue to cook until an instant-read thermometer inserted in the thickest part of a breast reads 135°F for medium rare, 4 to 8 minutes. Transfer to a cutting board, cover loosely with foil, and let rest for 10 minutes.

5. Meanwhile, warm the sauce over very low heat. Cut each duck breast on the diagonal into ½-inch-thick slices and serve with the sauce. *—Joanne Weir*

PER SERVING: 360 CALORIES | 25G PROTEIN | 20G CARB | 11G TOTAL FAT | 3G SAT FAT | 5G MONO FAT | 1.5G POLY FAT | 135MG CHOL | 370MG SODIUM | 2G FIBER

marinated steak with grilled scallions

4   1-inch-thick top loin (New York strip) steaks (8 to 10 oz. each), trimmed

1¾ tsp. kosher salt

2½ tsp. freshly ground black pepper

5   Tbs. canola oil

2   Tbs. reduced-sodium soy sauce

4   tsp. chopped fresh thyme

1   Tbs. Worcestershire sauce

1   Tbs. Dijon mustard

1   Tbs. red-wine vinegar

1   large clove garlic, minced

    Vegetable oil, for the grill

10 scallions, bulbs split in half lengthwise if large

The intense flavor of this homemade marinade adds a special touch to these fine steaks. The grilled scallions make a perfect accompaniment to the beef.

1. Sprinkle the steaks with 1¼ tsp. salt and 2 tsp. pepper.

2. In a medium bowl, mix 4 Tbs. oil with the soy sauce, 3 tsp. thyme, the Worcestershire, mustard, vinegar, and garlic. Put the steaks in a large bowl and coat them with the soy sauce mixture. Cover the bowl and marinate the steaks in the refrigerator, turning occasionally, for at least 4 hours and up to 1 day.

3. For a gas grill, light the front burner to medium-high and the back burner(s) to medium-low. For a charcoal grill, light a medium fire (300° to 350°F) with two-thirds of the coals banked to one side. Clean and oil the grill grates. While the grill heats, set the steaks out at room temperature. Toss the scallions with the remaining 1 Tbs. oil and ½ teaspoon each salt and pepper.

4. Set the steaks over the hotter part of the fire and the scallions over the cooler zone. Cook, covered, until the scallions brown, about 3 minutes, and the steaks have good grill marks and easily release from the grate, about 4 minutes. Flip both the scallions and steaks. Cook the steaks until they're just firm to the touch, pink when you slice into a thicker part, and register 135°F on an instant-read thermometer for medium rare, about 4 minutes. Grill the scallions until browned and softened, about 3 more minutes.

5. Transfer the steaks to dinner plates, top with the remaining 1 tsp. thyme, and serve with the scallions. —*Tony Rosenfeld*

pan-roasted chicken breasts with orange-brandy sauce

SERVES 6

FOR THE CHICKEN

- **2 cups fresh navel or Valencia orange juice**
- **2 Tbs. finely grated orange zest**
- **Kosher salt**
- **6 6- to 7-oz. boneless, skin-on chicken breast halves**
- **2 Tbs. extra-virgin olive oil**
- **Freshly ground black pepper**

FOR THE SAUCE

- **3 Tbs. unsalted butter**
- **1 medium shallot, minced**
- **2 Tbs. brandy**
- **1 cup fresh navel or Valencia orange juice**
- **½ cup lower-salt chicken broth**
- **1 navel or Valencia orange, cut into segments, segments cut into thirds**
- **1 Tbs. chopped fresh flat-leaf parsley**
- **Kosher salt and freshly ground black pepper**

A quick soak in an orange juice brine infuses the chicken with lots of flavor. You'll need a total of about 9 medium oranges for this recipe.

BRINE THE CHICKEN

Combine the orange juice, zest, 6 Tbs. salt, and 4 cups water in a large bowl or pot; stir to dissolve the salt. Add the chicken breasts and refrigerate for 2 to 3 hours.

COOK THE CHICKEN

1. Position a rack in the center of the oven and heat the oven to 400°F.

2. Remove the chicken from the brine and pat it dry with paper towels.

3. Heat the olive oil in a 12-inch ovenproof skillet over medium-high heat until shimmering hot. Add the chicken, skin side down, in a snug single layer and cook until the skin is golden brown, 3 to 5 minutes. Turn the chicken, season with the salt and a few grinds of pepper, and put the pan in the oven. Roast the chicken until an instant-read thermometer registers 165°F in the center of the thickest breast, about 15 minutes. Remove from the oven, transfer the chicken to a carving board, tent with foil, and let rest while you make the sauce.

MAKE THE SAUCE

1. Pour the juices from the skillet into a heatproof measuring cup. Let the fat rise to the surface and then spoon it off.

2. Melt 2 Tbs. of the butter in the skillet over medium-high heat. Add the shallot and cook, stirring, until soft, 1 to 2 minutes. Off the heat, add the brandy. Return the pan to the heat and cook, scraping the bottom of the pan, until the brandy has almost evaporated, about 30 seconds. Increase the heat to high and add the orange juice. Boil until it's thick, syrupy, and reduced to about ⅓ cup, about 5 minutes. Add the chicken broth, pan juices, and any juices from the carving board. Boil until reduced to about ¾ cup, about 3 minutes.

3. Swirl in the orange segments. Then, off the heat, swirl in the remaining 1 Tbs. butter and the parsley until the butter is melted. Season to taste with salt and a few grinds of pepper.

4. To serve, cut the chicken on the diagonal into thin slices and arrange on 6 serving plates. Drizzle with the sauce. —*Joanne Weir*

PER SERVING: 380 CALORIES | 38G PROTEIN | 9G CARB | 20G TOTAL FAT | 7G SAT FAT | 9G MONO FAT | 3G POLY FAT | 120MG CHOL | 550MG SODIUM | 1G FIBER

A Buyer's Guide to Oranges

The most common orange varieties are Valencia, navel, and blood oranges. With a few exceptions, most subvarieties of these oranges aren't labeled at the market. That's because the differences have little to do with flavor and more to do with when the fruit matures during the year—only a grower would know one from the other.

Valencia

Valencia oranges—originally from Spain—are thin-skinned and almost seedless. They're your best bet when you need lots of juice. Valencias are also a great choice for any recipe that calls for sweet oranges.

Navel

Originally from Brazil, navel oranges get their name from a second, smaller orange that develops at the base. (This undeveloped twin looks like a belly button.) Seedless, with thick skins, navels are the best eating oranges. Though a little less juicy than Valencias, they're virtually interchangeable when it comes to cooking. At the store, you might see some called Cara Cara; these have dark pink flesh and a sweet, mildly acidic flavor.

Blood oranges

Blood oranges have a sweeter flavor and less acidity than navels or Valencias, with overtones of raspberries or strawberries. Their skins may be blushed with red, and the flesh is blood red. If you want sweetness, blood oranges are the way to go, especially if paired with slightly bitter ingredients. At the market, you might find varieties like Moro or Tarocco. Moros have dark purple flesh and a deep reddish rind. Taroccos have a blushed rind.

red-cooked tofu

SERVES 4

- 4 medium scallions, thinly sliced (white and green parts separated)
- 2 medium carrots, cut into small dice
- 1 cup lower-salt chicken broth or (preferably homemade) vegetable broth
- 6 Tbs. reduced-sodium soy sauce; more as needed
- ¼ cup Shaoxing (Chinese rice wine) or dry sherry
- 1½ Tbs. minced fresh ginger
- 2 tsp. granulated sugar
- Freshly ground black pepper
- 2 14-oz. packages firm tofu, cut into 1-inch pieces
- 2 Tbs. seasoned rice vinegar
- 2 tsp. arrowroot or cornstarch

Red-cooking is a traditional Chinese braising technique that uses soy sauce, sugar, and rice wine to flavor the food and give it a dark red color. This easy, aromatic stew is delicious served over cooked rice or mustard greens.

1. In a large saucepan, combine the scallion whites, carrots, broth, soy sauce, Shaoxing, ginger, sugar, and ¼ tsp. pepper. Bring to a simmer over medium-high heat, stirring once or twice. Cover, reduce the heat to low, and simmer gently for 5 minutes. Add the tofu, cover, and continue to simmer gently until the tofu is heated through and has absorbed some of the other flavors, 10 minutes.

2. In a small bowl, whisk the rice vinegar and arrowroot until smooth and then stir the mixture into the stew, taking care not to break up the tofu. Stir gently until thickened, about 1 minute. Add more soy sauce to taste, sprinkle with the scallion greens, and serve.

—*Mark Scarbrough* and *Bruce Weinstein*

PER SERVING: 350 CALORIES | 34G PROTEIN | 20G CARB | 18G TOTAL FAT | 2.5G SAT FAT | 4G MONO FAT | 10G POLY FAT | 0MG CHOL | 960MG SODIUM | 6G FIBER

braised sausage with balsamic-glazed onions and grapes

SERVES 4

- **3** Tbs. olive oil
- **8** links sweet Italian sausage (about 2 lb.), pricked with a fork
- **1** large yellow onion, thinly sliced (about 2 cups)
- **½** tsp. kosher salt
- **½** cup lower-salt chicken broth
- **2** Tbs. balsamic vinegar
- **20** seedless red grapes, halved
- **2** Tbs. chopped fresh oregano

Sausage and grapes are a classic Italian pairing. The addition of balsamic vinegar and caramelized onions turns this into a quick, warming braise. Piercing the sausages with the tines of a fork will allow them to release some of their juices and infuse the broth. Serve with a crusty baguette and a green salad.

1. Heat 1 Tbs. oil in a large (12-inch) skillet over medium heat until it's shimmering. Add the sausages and cook, turning every couple minutes, until they're browned all over, about 8 minutes. Transfer to a large plate.

2. Add the remaining 2 Tbs. oil and the onion to the skillet, sprinkle with the salt, and cook, stirring occasionally, until the onion softens completely and starts to turn light brown, about 7 minutes. Add the chicken broth and balsamic vinegar, and scrape the bottom of the skillet with a wooden spoon to incorporate any browned bits. Reduce to a gentle simmer (medium-low or low depending on your stovetop). Add the sausages and grapes, cover the skillet with the lid ajar, and cook, stirring occasionally, until the sausages are cooked through (slice into one to check), about 25 minutes. Serve sprinkled with the oregano. —*Tony Rosenfeld*

sautéed pork chops with balsamic onions

SERVES 4

- **3** Tbs. olive oil; more if needed
- **1** large red onion (about 13 oz.), cut in half and thinly sliced crosswise
- **4** bone-in center-cut pork chops (1 to 1½ inches thick)

  Kosher salt and freshly ground black pepper
- **⅓** cup balsamic vinegar
- **1** Tbs. fresh thyme leaves

Check with your market's butcher to see if they carry 1½-inch-thick chops. The thicker the chops, the juicier they'll be.

1. In a very large sauté pan, heat 1 Tbs. of the oil over medium heat. Add the onion and cook, stirring frequently, until soft and caramelized, about 20 minutes (if the onion starts to burn, reduce the heat to medium low). Transfer the onion to a bowl and set aside.

2. Pat the pork chops dry with paper towels and rub both sides with 1 Tbs. salt and 2 heaping tsp. pepper. Return the pan to the burner, add the remaining 2 Tbs. olive oil, and increase the heat to medium high until the oil is hot but not smoking. (If you don't have a sauté pan large enough to fit the chops without crowding, use two smaller sauté pans; heat 1½ Tbs. olive oil in each, and cook 2 chops in each.) Cook the chops until well browned on one side, 3 to 5 minutes. Turn and cook the other side until the meat is done, 2 to 4 minutes. (If they start to burn, turn down the heat slightly.) To check for doneness, make a small cut near the bone and look inside—the pork should have a hint of pinkness. If it's still red, cook for another minute and check again. Transfer the chops to a plate, tent with foil, and let rest for 3 to 5 minutes before serving.

3. Meanwhile, put the pan back over medium heat and add the balsamic vinegar and caramelized onions (if you used two pans for the chops, use just one for the onions). Simmer, scraping the pan with a wooden spoon, until the vinegar is reduced enough to just coat the onions, 2 to 3 minutes. Stir in the thyme and season with salt and pepper to taste. Serve immediately with the pork chops.
—*Chris Schlesinger*

PER SERVING: 400 CALORIES | 31G PROTEIN | 7G CARB | 27G TOTAL FAT | 8G SAT FAT | 15G MONO FAT | 2G POLY FAT | 100MG CHOL | 1850MG SODIUM | 1G FIBER

grilled salmon with walnut-arugula pesto

SERVES 4

- ¼ cup walnut halves
- 2 cups loosely packed fresh arugula (2½ oz.)
- 1 cup loosely packed fresh basil (about ½ oz.)
- 3 Tbs. freshly grated Parmigiano-Reggiano
- 1 medium clove garlic, peeled
- 5 Tbs. extra-virgin olive oil; more for the grill pan

   Kosher salt

- 4 6- to 8-oz. skinless salmon fillets

   Freshly ground black pepper

Arugula gives this pesto a deliciously peppery finish, which complements the richness of the salmon.

1. In a small skillet over medium heat, toast the walnuts, stirring occasionally, until fragrant and a shade darker, about 5 minutes. Let cool slightly on a plate, about 3 minutes, and then transfer to a food processor. Add the arugula, basil, Parmigiano, and garlic and process until the mixture is very finely chopped, about 1 minute. With the motor running, slowly add 4 Tbs. of the oil until well combined. If you like, add 1 Tbs. water to thin the pesto. Transfer to a bowl and season to taste with salt.

2. Heat a lightly oiled grill pan over medium-high heat. Rub the salmon fillets all over with the remaining 1 Tbs. oil. Sprinkle all over with ½ tsp. salt and ¼ tsp. pepper. Put the fillets on the grill pan, skinned side up, and cook until well marked, about 5 minutes. Flip and continue to cook until opaque in the center, about 5 minutes more. Serve with the pesto. *—David Bonom*

PER SERVING: 490 CALORIES | 42G PROTEIN | 2G CARB | 28G TOTAL FAT | 3.5G SAT FAT | 15G MONO FAT | 7G POLY FAT | 110MG CHOL | 290MG SODIUM | 1G FIBER

steamed mussels with bell peppers, watercress & herbed toasts

½ cup dry sherry

½ cup fresh orange juice

2 Tbs. tomato paste

4 tsp. sherry vinegar

2 tsp. honey

5 Tbs. extra-virgin olive oil

1½ tsp. coarsely chopped fresh thyme

12 ½-inch-thick slices baguette (cut on an angle)

 Kosher salt

2 Tbs. unsalted butter

¾ large red bell pepper, cut into medium dice (about ¾ cup)

¾ large yellow bell pepper, cut into medium dice (about ¾ cup)

2 Tbs. minced fresh garlic

1 tsp. minced fresh serrano chile

4 lb. mussels, scrubbed and debearded

4 oz. fresh watercress, tough stems trimmed, washed well

A wide Dutch oven (not a tall soup pot) is best for steaming mussels; if they're stacked no more than 3 or 4 layers deep, the mussels will all steam—and open—at about the same rate.

1. In a small bowl, combine ½ cup water with the sherry, orange juice, tomato paste, vinegar, and honey.

2. In another small bowl, mix 3 Tbs. of the olive oil with the thyme. Position a rack 6 inches from the broiler and heat the broiler on high. Arrange the baguette slices on a baking sheet. Brush both sides with some of the thyme oil and sprinkle lightly with salt. Toast under the broiler, flipping once, until golden brown on one side and lightly toasted on the other, about 5 minutes total.

3. Meanwhile, in a medium (6-quart) Dutch oven, heat the remaining 2 Tbs. olive oil and 1 Tbs. of the butter over medium heat. Add the bell peppers, raise the heat to medium high, and cook, stirring occasionally, until browned in spots and somewhat softened, 6 to 8 minutes. Add the garlic and chile and cook briefly, stirring, until fragrant and well combined. Add the sherry mixture, stir, and bring to a simmer. Add the mussels, cover the pot, and cook until the mussels have opened, 3 to 4 minutes. Remove from the heat, toss in all but a few sprigs of the watercress, and stir gently to partially wilt it.

4. Using a slotted spoon, transfer the mussels and watercress to 4 wide, shallow serving bowls. Add the remaining 1 Tbs. butter to the broth and stir until melted. Ladle the broth over the mussels. Garnish with the remaining watercress sprigs and serve with the toasts on the side. *—Susie Middleton*

PER SERVING: 410 CALORIES | 19G PROTEIN | 21G CARB | 26G TOTAL FAT | 7G SAT FAT | 15G MONO FAT | 3G POLY FAT | 55MG CHOL | 760MG SODIUM | 2G FIBER

sear-roasted halibut with blood orange salsa

SERVES 4

FOR THE SALSA

¾ cup fresh navel or Valencia orange juice (from 2 medium oranges)

3 small blood oranges, cut into segments, segments cut in half

2 Tbs. minced red onion

1 Tbs. chopped fresh cilantro

1 Tbs. extra-virgin olive oil

1 Tbs. finely grated navel or Valencia orange zest (from 2 medium oranges)

Kosher salt and freshly ground black pepper

FOR THE HALIBUT

1 tsp. finely grated navel or Valencia orange zest (from 1 small orange)

1 tsp. chopped fresh thyme

1½ tsp. kosher salt

½ tsp. freshly ground black pepper

4 6-oz. skinless halibut fillets

3 Tbs. olive oil

Sear-roasting allows the halibut to form a gorgeous crust while keeping the inside moist. The mild-flavored fish is the perfect vehicle for the blood orange salsa that's bursting with sweet citrusy flavor.

Position a rack in the center of the oven and heat the oven to 425°F.

MAKE THE SALSA

1. In a small saucepan, boil the orange juice over medium heat until reduced to ¼ cup, 8 to 10 minutes. Let cool.

2. In a medium bowl, combine the reduced orange juice, blood orange segments, onion, cilantro, olive oil, and orange zest. Season to taste with salt and pepper.

COOK THE HALIBUT

1. In a small bowl, mix the orange zest, thyme, salt, and pepper. Rub the mixture all over the halibut fillets. Heat the oil in a 12-inch oven-proof skillet over medium-high heat. When the oil is shimmering hot, arrange the fillets in the pan. Sear for about 2 minutes without moving; then use a thin slotted metal spatula to lift a piece of fish and check the color. When the fillets are nicely browned, flip them and put the pan in the oven.

2. Roast until the halibut is just cooked through, 3 to 5 minutes. Remove the pan from the oven and transfer the halibut to serving plates. Spoon some of the salsa over each fillet. *—Joanne Weir*

PER SERVING: 380 CALORIES | 37G PROTEIN | 18G CARB | 18G TOTAL FAT | 2.5G SAT FAT | 11G MONO FAT | 2.5G POLY FAT | 55MG CHOL | 510MG SODIUM | 3G FIBER

how to slice and segment oranges

Cut off the top and bottom of the orange, slicing off enough to expose a circle of the orange's flesh. Stand the orange on one of the cut ends.

With a paring knife, slice off a strip of peel from top to bottom. Try to get all of the white pith, but leave as much of the flesh as possible. Continue all the way around.

To make segments (a.k.a. suprêmes), cut on either side of each membrane, freeing the orange segment in between. Work over a bowl to catch the segments and juice.

To make slices, cut the orange crosswise in the thickness you want.

sesame beef and snap peas

SERVES 4

- **1** lb. flank steak or skirt steak, cut into thin strips
- **1** Tbs. plus 1 tsp. reduced-sodium soy sauce
- **1** Tbs. plus 1 tsp. Asian sesame oil
- **½** tsp. kosher salt
- **1** Tbs. ketchup
- **2** tsp. rice vinegar
- **1** tsp. granulated sugar
- **1** tsp. Asian chili sauce (like Sriracha)
- **2** tsp. sesame seeds, toasted
- **3** Tbs. canola or peanut oil
- **3** Tbs. finely chopped fresh ginger
- **10** oz. sugar snap peas, ends trimmed
- **1** tsp. cornstarch

A drizzle of chili sauce gives the tangy sauce in this dish a touch of heat, while toasted sesame seeds and sesame oil offer a double shot of flavor. Served with steamed rice, this dish comes together in minutes for a quick weekday meal.

1. Toss the beef with 1 tsp. each of soy sauce and sesame oil and ¼ tsp. salt. In a small bowl, mix the remaining 1 Tbs. each of soy sauce and sesame oil with the ketchup, vinegar, sugar, chili sauce, and half of the sesame seeds.

2. Heat 1½ Tbs. oil in a large (12-inch) skillet or wok over medium-high heat until shimmering. Add the beef and cook, stirring occasionally, until it loses its raw color and browns in places, 2 to 3 minutes. Transfer to a large plate. Cook the ginger with the remaining 1½ Tbs. oil until it sizzles steadily and starts to brown lightly around the edges, about 1 minute. Add the snap peas, sprinkle with the remaining ¼ tsp. salt, and cook, stirring, until they turn bright green and start to brown in places, 1 to 2 minutes. Add ⅓ cup water and cook, stirring, until about half of the liquid cooks off and the peas start to soften, about 1 minute. Add the soy sauce mixture and beef, and cook, stirring, for a couple minutes until the mixture heats through and coats the peas and beef. Whisk the cornstarch with ¼ cup water; add to the beef, and cook, stirring, until the sauce thickens, about 1 minute. Sprinkle with the remaining 1 tsp. sesame seeds, and serve. *—Tony Rosenfeld*

seared scallops with cauliflower, brown butter & basil

SERVES 4

- 3 Tbs. extra-virgin olive oil
- 1 small head cauliflower (1 lb.), trimmed and cut into bite-size florets (about 4 cups)
- 1 lb. all-natural (dry-packed) sea scallops
- 2 Tbs. unsalted butter
- 1 large shallot, minced
- ½ cup dry vermouth
- ¼ tsp. kosher salt
- ¼ tsp. freshly ground black pepper
- 8 large fresh basil leaves, thinly sliced

In this easily assembled meal, vermouth-laced brown butter imbues cauliflower with deep flavor, while a basil garnish adds color and freshness.

1. Heat 1 Tbs. of the oil in a 12-inch nonstick skillet over medium-high heat until shimmering hot. Add the cauliflower and cook, stirring often, until lightly browned, about 4 minutes. Transfer to a bowl.

2. Add the remaining 2 Tbs. oil to the skillet. When shimmering hot, add the scallops in a single layer. Cook without moving until golden brown on one side, about 2 minutes. Flip the scallops and cook until they're barely cooked through, about another 2 minutes (if you cut into one, the center should still be slightly translucent). Transfer to another bowl.

3. Swirl the butter into the skillet, add the shallot, and cook, stirring often, until the shallot softens and the butter begins to brown, about 1 minute.

4. Add the vermouth and bring it to a boil, scraping up any browned bits on the bottom of the skillet with a wooden spoon. Return the cauliflower to the skillet and season with the salt and pepper. Cover the skillet and reduce the heat to medium. Cook, stirring once or twice, until the cauliflower florets are tender, about 6 minutes.

5. Return the scallops to the pan and toss to heat through, about 1 minute. Remove from the heat, sprinkle with the basil, and serve.
—*Bruce Weinstein* and *Mark Scarbrough*

PER SERVING: 300 CALORIES | 21G PROTEIN | 8G CARB | 17G TOTAL FAT | 5G SAT FAT | 9G MONO FAT | 1.5G POLY FAT | 270MG CHOL | 55MG SODIUM | 2G FIBER

quinoa salad with apples, walnuts, dried cranberries & gouda

SERVES 6

- 1½ cups quinoa, preferably red

  Sea salt

- 5 Tbs. extra-virgin olive oil; more as needed

- 1 large red onion, quartered lengthwise and thinly sliced crosswise

- 2 Tbs. balsamic vinegar

- 4 oz. arugula, trimmed and thinly sliced (about 3 cups)

- 4 oz. aged Gouda, finely diced (about 1 cup)

- 3 medium celery ribs, thinly sliced

- 1 large, crisp apple, such as Fuji or Pink Lady, cut into ½-inch dice

- 1 cup walnuts, coarsely chopped

- 1 cup finely diced fennel

- ¾ cup dried cranberries

- 3 Tbs. sherry vinegar

  Freshly ground black pepper

With its dried fruit, walnuts, and apples, this sweet-and-savory meat-free dish is reminiscent of a Waldorf salad.

1. In a bowl, rinse the quinoa with water, rubbing it between your fingers for about 10 seconds. Drain and transfer it to a 3-quart pot. Add 2½ cups water and ½ tsp. sea salt and bring to a boil over medium-high heat. Reduce the heat to medium low and simmer, covered, until the quinoa is tender but still delicately crunchy, about 15 minutes.

2. Drain the quinoa and return it to the pot. Cover and let the quinoa rest for 5 minutes; then fluff it with a fork. Let cool to room temperature.

3. While the quinoa cooks, heat 2 Tbs. of the olive oil in a 12-inch non-stick skillet over medium-high heat. Add the onion and a pinch of salt; cook, stirring frequently, until tender and brown around the edges, 6 to 8 minutes. Add the balsamic vinegar and toss with the onion until the vinegar cooks away, about 1 minute. Remove from the heat and let cool to room temperature.

4. In a large bowl, mix the quinoa, onion, arugula, cheese, celery, apple, walnuts, fennel, and cranberries.

5. In a small bowl, whisk the remaining 3 Tbs. olive oil with the sherry vinegar, ½ tsp. sea salt, and a few grinds of pepper. Add the dressing to the salad and gently mix it in. Let rest for a moment, then season to taste with salt and pepper. Add more olive oil if the salad seems dry.
—*Anna Thomas*

PER SERVING: 330 CALORIES | 9G PROTEIN | 34G CARB | 19G TOTAL FAT | 4G SAT FAT | 7G MONO FAT | 7G POLY FAT | 15MG CHOL | 350MG SODIUM | 4G FIBER

thai-style stir-fried chicken and basil

SERVES 2 OR 3

- 2 **Tbs. vegetable oil**
- 4 **medium shallots, thinly sliced**
- 2 **medium cloves garlic, thinly sliced**
- ¼ **tsp. crushed red pepper flakes**
- 1 **lb. chicken breast cutlets (about ¼ inch thick), cut crosswise into 1-inch-wide strips**
- 1 **Tbs. fish sauce**
- 1 **Tbs. fresh lime juice**
- 2 **tsp. packed light brown sugar**
- 1 **cup lightly packed fresh basil leaves**

If you like, use a mix of fresh cilantro and mint instead of basil. Serve over cooked jasmine rice.

1. Heat the oil in a well-seasoned wok or a heavy-duty 12-inch skillet over medium-high heat until shimmering hot. Add the shallot, garlic, and red pepper flakes; cook, stirring frequently, until the shallot starts to soften but not brown, 1 to 2 minutes. Add the chicken and cook, stirring, until it's no longer pink and the shallot is beginning to brown, 2 to 3 minutes.

2. Add the fish sauce, lime juice, sugar, and ¼ cup water. Cook, stirring frequently, until the chicken is just cooked through and the liquid reduces to a saucy consistency, 2 to 3 minutes. (If the sauce reduces before the chicken is cooked through, add water, 1 Tbs. at a time.) Remove from the heat, add the basil, and stir to wilt it.

—Lori Longbotham

PER SERVING: 280 CALORIES | 32G PROTEIN | 8G CARB | 13G TOTAL FAT | 2G SAT FAT | 5G MONO FAT | 5G POLY FAT | 85MG CHOL | 540MG SODIUM | 0G FIBER

> To cook stir-fries evenly, a 12-inch skillet is your best choice. The pan's shallow sides allow extra moisture to evaporate, which helps keep vegetables crisp and meat tender.

swordfish with black olive and mint tapenade

SERVES 4

- 1 cup pitted Kalamata olives, coarsely chopped
- 2 oil-packed sun-dried tomatoes, chopped
- 2 Tbs. extra-virgin olive oil
- 8 fresh basil leaves, torn into small pieces
- 2 Tbs. coarsely chopped fresh mint
- 1 medium clove garlic, minced and mashed to a paste

    Large pinch of crushed red pepper flakes

FOR THE SWORDFISH

- 4 1-inch-thick swordfish fillets (6 to 7 oz. each)
- 1 tsp. freshly ground black pepper
- ½ tsp. kosher salt
- 1 Tbs. olive oil

FOR SERVING

- 1 pint ripe grape or cherry tomatoes, halved
- 2 Tbs. chopped fresh mint
- 2 Tbs. extra-virgin olive oil
- ½ tsp. kosher salt

Make a double batch of this versatile black olive paste and use the extra as a dressing for pasta, sandwiches, or sautés, or as a garnish for grilled or roasted chicken. It's paired with fish here, so anchovies (an ingredient in traditional tapenade) are omitted, but feel free to add them if you like.

MAKE THE TAPENADE

Put the olives, sun-dried tomatoes, and oil in a food processor and pulse until the mixture forms a coarse paste. Pulse in the basil, mint, garlic, and red pepper flakes until combined and transfer to a medium bowl.

MAKE THE SWORDFISH

1. Heat a gas grill to medium high, or prepare a medium-hot charcoal fire. Clean and oil the grates to prevent sticking.

2. Sprinkle the fish with the pepper and salt and drizzle with the oil. Grill the fish until it has good grill marks, about 4 minutes. Using both tongs and a spatula, carefully turn the fish. Continue cooking until the other side has good grill marks and the fish is just cooked through, about 8 minutes.

TO SERVE

Toss the tomatoes with the mint, oil, and salt. Transfer the fish to a platter, spread generously with the tapenade, and top with a spoonful of the tomatoes (and their juices). Serve immediately.

—Tony Rosenfeld

stir-fried ginger pork with carrots and snow peas

SERVES 4

- 2 **carrots, peeled**
- **Kosher salt**
- 8 **long, diagonal slices peeled fresh ginger, ⅛ inch thick**
- 2 **lb. pork tenderloin**
- ⅓ **cup peanut oil**
- ½ **lb. snow peas, stems and strings removed**
- 2 **scallions (white and some green parts), chopped**
- 4 **cloves garlic, minced**
- 2 **Tbs. dry white wine**
- ¼ **cup soy sauce**

You can use the recipe as is or as a guide, substituting as you like—perhaps chicken instead of pork or mushrooms and red peppers for the vegetables. Feel free to add a julienne of shiitake mushrooms, tossing them in with the rest of the vegetables.

1. Cut the carrots into strips ⅛ inch in diameter and 2 inches long. Bring a small pan of salted water to a boil and add the carrot julienne. Boil until just barely tender, drain, and set aside. Cut the ginger slices into ⅛-inch strips. Cut the pork into thin slices and then into ¼-inch strips.

2. Heat the oil in a frying pan or wok over high heat. Add the pork and stir while cooking. After 1 minute, add the blanched carrots, the snow peas, and the ginger. Stir-fry for another couple of minutes. Add the scallions and garlic and then the wine and soy sauce; stir and serve.
—Jackie Shen

More about Snow Peas

Snow peas are eaten pod and all while the pods are still thin and tender. They cook quickly and take well to blanching, steaming, and of course, stir-frying.

Choose dark green, dense-looking peas with no signs of drying or cracking. To prep, trim the peas by breaking off the stem and pulling off the tough "string" that runs across the top of the pod.

pan-seared steak with italian-style salsa verde

SERVES 4

4   ¾-inch-thick top loin
    (New York strip) steaks
    (8 to 10 oz. each), trimmed

1   tsp. chopped fresh thyme

2   tsp. kosher salt; more as
    needed

1½ tsp. freshly ground black
    pepper; more as needed

1½ cups chopped fresh flat-
    leaf parsley

½   cup plus 2 Tbs. extra-virgin
    olive oil

½   cup chopped cornichons or
    small sour gherkins

2   Tbs. fresh lemon juice;
    more as needed

2   Tbs. capers, rinsed and
    drained

1   large clove garlic, minced
    and mashed to a paste

Italian salsa verde is a lively herb paste that adds zest to grilled and roasted meats. Heap any leftover steak on a hoagie roll for a delicious sandwich.

1. Put the steaks on a large plate and sprinkle both sides with the thyme, 1½ tsp. salt, and ½ tsp. black pepper.

2. In a food processor, combine the parsley, ½ cup of the extra-virgin olive oil, the cornichons, lemon juice, capers, garlic, ½ tsp. salt, and 1 tsp. black pepper; process until smooth. Taste and add more lemon juice, salt, or pepper if needed.

3. Heat the remaining 2 Tbs. olive oil in a large (12-inch) sauté pan over medium-high heat. Add the steaks and cook without touching until they brown, about 2 minutes. Turn and cook until the second side browns; for medium rare, the steaks should be light pink when you slice into a thicker part, and an instant-read thermometer should read 135°F, about 2 to 3 additional minutes. Let the steaks rest for 3 to 5 minutes before serving with the salsa verde. —*Tony Rosenfeld*

spinach, cheese & caramelized red onion frittata

SERVES 8

¼ cup olive oil

1 large red onion, thinly sliced (about 1 cup)

Kosher salt

1 jalapeño, cored, seeded, and finely diced (about 2 Tbs.)

10 oz. whole leaf spinach, trimmed, washed, and spun dry

10 large eggs, beaten

1¼ cups freshly grated Grana Padano

3 oil-packed sun-dried tomatoes, finely diced (about 2 Tbs.)

8 fresh basil leaves, torn into small pieces

Freshly ground black pepper

This Italian omelet is perfect for brunch or a quick weeknight dinner. It also reheats nicely in the microwave as a midday snack. To add heft, fold diced boiled potatoes into the spinach mixture before adding it to the eggs. Incorporating strips of roasted red peppers adds more color.

1. Position a rack in the center of the oven and heat the oven to 450°F.

2. Heat 2 Tbs. oil in a large (12-inch), ovenproof nonstick skillet over medium-high heat. Add the onion, sprinkle with ½ tsp. salt, and cook, stirring, until it starts to color and soften, about 2 minutes. Reduce the heat to medium, add the jalapeño, and continue cooking until the onion softens almost completely, about 5 minutes. Add the spinach, sprinkle with ½ tsp. salt, and increase the heat to high; cook, tossing, until the spinach just wilts, about 2 minutes. Remove from the heat and let cool for a couple of minutes.

3. In a large bowl, whisk the eggs with the Grana Padano, sun-dried tomatoes, basil, 1 tsp. pepper, and ¼ tsp. salt. Add the vegetables from the skillet to the egg mixture and stir to combine.

4. Wipe the skillet with a paper towel and heat the remaining 2 Tbs. oil in it over medium heat. Add the egg mixture and cook, running a spatula along the bottom of the pan to prevent sticking, until the eggs begin to set around the edges, about 3 minutes. Transfer the skillet to the oven and bake until the eggs puff, are firm to the touch, and are browned on top, about 12 minutes. Let cool for a couple of minutes, then slide onto a cutting board, cut into wedges, and serve.
—*Tony Rosenfeld*

turkey cutlets and black beans with tangerine-habanero mojo sauce

SERVES 4

- **5** to 6 Tbs. olive oil
- **3** medium cloves garlic, thinly sliced
- **½** tsp. plus ⅛ tsp. ground cumin
- **½** cup fresh tangerine juice (from 2 tangerines)
- **2** Tbs. fresh lime juice (from 1 lime)
- **½** tsp. seeded and minced habanero chile

  Kosher salt and freshly ground black pepper
- **1** small red onion, chopped
- **1** 15½-oz. can black beans, rinsed and drained
- **2** Tbs. chopped fresh cilantro
- **4** turkey breast cutlets (about 1¼ lb.)

Habaneros are becoming more readily available in grocery stores; however, if they're scarce, try a Scotch bonnet, jalapeño, or serrano chile instead.

1. In a 10-inch skillet, heat 2 Tbs. of the oil and the garlic over medium heat until the garlic is golden, about 3 minutes. Stir in ⅛ tsp. of the cumin. Add the tangerine juice, lime juice, and habanero. Bring to a simmer and cook for about 3 minutes. Season to taste with salt and pepper; set the mojo sauce aside. (The sauce can be served warm or at room temperature.)

2. Heat 2 Tbs. of the oil in a 12-inch nonstick skillet over medium-high heat. Add the onion and ¼ tsp. salt and cook, stirring occasionally, until softened, 3 to 5 minutes. Add the beans and the remaining ½ tsp. cumin and cook until the beans are heated through, 2 to 3 minutes. Stir in the cilantro and season to taste with salt and pepper. Transfer the beans to a bowl and cover with foil to keep warm.

3. Wash and dry the skillet. Season the turkey cutlets on both sides with salt and pepper. Heat 1 Tbs. of the oil in the skillet over medium-high heat until very hot. Add as many cutlets as will comfortably fit in a single layer and cook until browned on both sides and just cooked through, about 2 minutes per side. Transfer to a plate and tent with foil to keep warm. Repeat with the remaining cutlets, adding the remaining 1 Tbs. oil if needed.

4. Portion the cutlets and black beans among individual plates. Spoon the mojo sauce over and serve. *—Dawn Yanagihara-Mitchell*

PER SERVING: 410 CALORIES | 39G PROTEIN | 22G CARB | 18G TOTAL FAT | 2.5G SAT FAT | 13G MONO FAT | 2G POLY FAT | 95MG CHOL | 210MG SODIUM | 5G FIBER

eggplant ragoût with tomatoes, peppers & chickpeas

SERVES 4 TO 6

- **1½ lb. eggplant, preferably plump round fruits**
- **2 Tbs. olive oil; more for brushing the eggplant**
- **1 large red onion, cut into ½-inch dice**
- **1 large bell pepper, red or yellow, cored, seeded, and cut into 1-inch pieces**
- **2 plump cloves garlic, thinly sliced**
- **2 tsp. paprika**
- **1 tsp. ground cumin**
- **Generous pinch of cayenne**
- **2 Tbs. tomato paste**
- **5 plum tomatoes, peeled, quartered lengthwise, and seeded**
- **1 15-oz. can chickpeas, rinsed and drained**
- **Kosher salt and freshly ground black pepper**
- **¼ cup coarsely chopped fresh flat-leaf parsley**

Broiling the eggplant first helps it keep its shape in the stew.

1. Position a rack in the oven 3 to 4 inches from the broiler element and heat the broiler on high. Cut the eggplant crosswise into ¾-inch rounds and brush both sides with olive oil. Broil until light gold on each side, about 2 minutes per side. Let cool and cut into 1-inch pieces.

2. In a medium Dutch oven, heat 2 Tbs. olive oil over medium-high heat. Add the onion and bell pepper; sauté until the onion is lightly browned, 12 to 15 minutes. During the last few minutes of browning, add the garlic, paprika, cumin, and cayenne. Stir in the tomato paste and cook, stirring, for 1 minute. Stir in ¼ cup water and boil, using a wooden spoon to scrape up the juices from the bottom of the pan. Add the tomatoes, eggplant, chickpeas, 1 cup water, and 1 tsp. salt. Bring to a boil and then simmer, covered, until the vegetables are quite tender, about 25 minutes, stirring once or twice. Season with salt and pepper to taste, stir in the parsley, and serve. —*Deborah Madison*

PER SERVING: 220 CALORIES | 6G PROTEIN | 32G CARB | 8G TOTAL FAT | 1G SAT FAT | 5G MONO FAT | 1G POLY FAT | 0MG CHOL | 550MG SODIUM | 8G FIBER

corn and amaranth griddlecakes with spicy black beans

SERVES 4

This hearty meatless main course is chock full of flavor and texture. The griddlecakes are crisp, tender, and slightly peppery from the amaranth flour, and the beans deliver a kick. Serve with sliced avocado and pico de gallo.

FOR THE BLACK BEANS

- ½ lb. dried black beans
- 1 Tbs. crumbled dried epazote, or 2 to 3 fresh epazote leaves (optional)
- 3 medium cloves garlic, peeled

  Fine sea salt
- ½ cup chopped fresh cilantro
- ½ to 1 Tbs. finely chopped chipotle chile (from a can of chipotles en adobo)
- 1½ tsp. cumin seeds, toasted and ground

FOR THE GRIDDLECAKES

- 2¼ oz. (½ cup plus 2 Tbs.) amaranth flour
- 1 oz. (¼ cup) unbleached all-purpose flour
- 1 tsp. baking powder
- ¼ tsp. baking soda

  Fine sea salt
- 3 oz. (½ cup) medium-grind cornmeal
- ¼ cup pine nuts, coarsely chopped
- 3 Tbs. unsalted butter
- ½ cup buttermilk
- 1 large egg
- 1 4-oz. can diced fire-roasted green chiles, drained
- ½ cup fresh or thawed frozen corn kernels
- ½ cup thinly sliced scallions (white and green parts)
- ½ medium jalapeño, stemmed, seeded, and finely chopped

  Olive oil, for the pan

MAKE THE BLACK BEANS

1. Rinse the beans and combine them in a 4-quart pot with the epazote (if using), garlic, and about 6 cups water. Bring to a boil over high heat, stirring occasionally, then reduce the heat to low and simmer, covered, until the beans are just tender, about 1 hour. Add 1 tsp. salt and simmer gently for another 10 minutes. Remove the beans from the heat and let them cool in their liquid. (You can prepare the beans up to 1 day ahead; refrigerate them in their liquid.)

2. Drain the cooked beans, reserving the liquid. Return the beans to the pot and add the cilantro, chipotle, cumin, and about 1 cup of the reserved bean liquid. Simmer over medium heat, stirring occasionally, for about 10 minutes. The beans should be very moist; if necessary, add more of the bean liquid.

MAKE THE GRIDDLECAKES

1. In a large bowl, sift the amaranth flour, all-purpose flour, baking powder, baking soda, and ¾ tsp. salt. Whisk in the cornmeal and pine nuts.

2. Melt 2½ Tbs. of the butter. In a medium bowl, whisk the buttermilk, egg, and melted butter. Stir in the chiles.

3. Melt the remaining ½ Tbs. butter in a 10-inch nonstick pan over medium heat. Add the corn kernels, scallions, jalapeño, and a pinch of salt; cook, stirring, until the corn shows a few light brown spots, about 5 minutes. Stir the corn mixture into the wet ingredients. (You can prepare the griddlecakes to this point up to 4 hours ahead.)

4. When ready to cook the cakes, combine the wet and dry ingredients, being careful not to overmix. Heat about 2 tsp. olive oil in a large nonstick pan or on a griddle over medium-high heat. Drop ¼ cup of the batter at a time onto the hot pan and gently spread with the tip of a spoon to make 3-inch cakes. Cook the griddlecakes until tiny air bubbles begin to pop through the tops, 3 to 4 minutes; then flip them and cook until deep golden brown and crisp on the bottom, about another 3 minutes. Transfer to a plate and keep warm. Repeat until all of the batter is cooked.

5. Ladle the beans into shallow bowls and top with the griddlecakes.
—*Anna Thomas*

PER SERVING: 600 CALORIES | 22G PROTEIN | 75G CARB | 26G TOTAL FAT | 8G SAT FAT | 10G MONO FAT | 5G POLY FAT | 75MG CHOL | 1410MG SODIUM | 17G FIBER

sesame chicken with ginger and snow peas

SERVES 4

- **1** to 1¼ lb. boneless, skinless chicken breast halves (2 or 3), very thinly sliced on the diagonal
- **2** Tbs. soy sauce
- **1** Tbs. Asian sesame oil
- **1** Tbs. plus 1 tsp. rice vinegar
- **2** Tbs. ketchup
- **8** scallions
- **6** oz. snow peas, trimmed (about 1½ cups)
- **2** Tbs. minced fresh ginger
- **3** Tbs. canola oil
- **2** Tbs. lightly toasted sesame seeds

Before cutting the chicken, freeze it for 10 minutes so that it firms up, making it easier to slice thinly.

1. In a large bowl, toss the chicken with 1 Tbs. of the soy sauce, 1½ tsp. of the sesame oil, and 1 tsp. of the rice vinegar.

2. In a 1-cup liquid measuring cup or another bowl, combine ¼ cup water with the ketchup and the remaining 1 Tbs. soy sauce, 1 Tbs. vinegar, and 1½ tsp. sesame oil.

3. Trim the scallions and separate the dark green tops from the light-green and white bottoms. Slice the tops into 2-inch pieces and the bottoms into thin rounds. Combine both in a medium bowl with the snow peas and ginger.

4. Heat 1½ Tbs. of the oil in a 12-inch nonstick skillet or large stir-fry pan over medium-high heat until shimmering hot. Add the chicken and cook, stirring occasionally, until it loses most of its raw appearance, 1 to 2 minutes. Transfer to a large plate.

5. Add the remaining 1½ Tbs. oil and the scallions, snow peas, and ginger, and cook, stirring occasionally, until the ginger and scallions start to brown, about 2 minutes.

6. Return the chicken to the pan and add the ketchup mixture and half of the sesame seeds. Cook, stirring, until the chicken is cooked through and the snow peas are crisp-tender, 2 to 3 minutes. Transfer to a platter, sprinkle with the remaining sesame seeds, and serve. *—Tony Rosenfeld*

PER SERVING: 310 CALORIES | 26G PROTEIN | 10G CARB | 19G TOTAL FAT | 2.5G SAT FAT | 9G MONO FAT | 6G POLY FAT | 65MG CHOL | 800MG SODIUM | 2G FIBER

mexican tomato rice and beans

SERVES 6 TO 8

- **1 cup uncooked medium-grain white rice**

- **1 14½-oz. can diced tomatoes (preferably "petite-cut")**

- **2 Tbs. extra-virgin olive oil**

- **6 medium cloves garlic, finely chopped**

- **1 medium fresh jalapeño, cored and finely chopped (if you like spicy foods, leave in the ribs and seeds; if not, remove them)**

- **1 15-oz. can black beans, rinsed and drained**

- **2 tsp. ground cumin**

- **1 tsp. chili powder**

- **Kosher or fine sea salt**

- **¼ cup finely chopped fresh oregano leaves and tender stems**

- **¼ cup finely chopped fresh cilantro leaves and tender stems**

Hot Mexican spices and cool cilantro add zing to this hearty dish.

1. In a 1-quart saucepan, combine the rice with 2 cups cold water. Bring to a boil over medium-high heat, cover, reduce the heat to low, and cook for 20 minutes. Remove from the heat and let the pan stand, covered, for another 5 minutes.

2. While the rice steams, set a fine-mesh sieve in a bowl and drain the can of tomatoes. Pour the tomato juices into a 1-cup liquid measure. Add enough water to the tomato juices to equal 1 cup.

3. Heat a 10- to 12-inch skillet over medium-high heat. Pour in the oil and stir-fry the garlic and jalapeño until the garlic browns and the jalapeño smells pungent, about 1 minute. Add the black beans, cumin, chili powder, and 2 tsp. salt; stir two or three times to incorporate the mixture and cook the spices, about 30 seconds. Stir in the tomato juice and water mixture and bring to a boil. Adjust the heat to maintain a gentle boil and cook, stirring occasionally, until the beans absorb much of the liquid, 5 to 7 minutes. Add the tomatoes, oregano, cilantro, and cooked rice and cook, stirring occasionally, until the rice is warm, 1 to 2 minutes. Serve immediately. —*Raghavan Iyer*

PER SERVING: 200 CALORIES | 6G PROTEIN | 34G CARB | 4G TOTAL FAT | 0.5G SAT FAT | 3G MONO FAT | 0.5G POLY FAT | 0MG CHOL | 620MG SODIUM | 5G FIBER

wild mushroom and arugula risotto

SERVES 4

1½ cups (1 oz.) dried mushrooms, rehydrated and
chopped, plus ¾ cup
soaking liquid

5 cups lower-salt chicken
broth

4 Tbs. unsalted butter

1 medium yellow onion,
finely diced (about 1 cup)

Kosher salt

1½ cups carnaroli or arborio
rice

½ cup dry sherry

3 oz. baby arugula (4 cups,
loosely packed)

1 cup freshly grated
Parmigiano-Reggiano or
Grana Padano

⅓ cup sliced fresh chives

Freshly ground black pepper

Bulk dried mushrooms typically include more exotic types like oyster, shiitake, and morel. This satisfying risotto makes a meal on its own when accompanied by a green salad.

1. Heat the mushroom soaking liquid with the chicken broth in a 3-quart saucepan over medium heat. Meanwhile, in a large (4-quart) pot, melt 2 Tbs. butter over medium-high heat. Add the onion and sprinkle with ½ tsp. salt. Cook the onion, stirring, until it softens and turns a light brown, about 3 minutes. Add the rice and mushrooms and cook, stirring, for 1 minute. Add the sherry; raise the heat to high, and cook, stirring, until it almost completely reduces, about 1 minute.

2. Reduce the heat to medium; add ¾ cup of the broth to the rice, and cook, stirring often, until the rice absorbs the broth, 2 to 3 minutes. Add another ¾ cup of broth and cook until absorbed. Continue adding broth in this manner until the rice is creamy and tender, about 20 minutes total—you may or may not need all of the broth. Stir in the arugula, Parmigiano, all but a couple tablespoons of the chives, and the remaining 2 Tbs. butter and continue stirring until the arugula is just wilted, about 1 minute. Serve immediately in individual bowls, sprinkled with a few grinds of black pepper and the remaining chives. *—Tony Rosenfeld*

quinoa and avocado salad with dried fruit, toasted almonds & lemon-cumin vinaigrette

SERVES 4

- 3 Tbs. raisins (preferably a mix of dark and golden)
- 2 Tbs. dried apricots, thinly sliced
- 1 cup red or white quinoa, rinsed well

  Kosher salt
- 1 large lemon
- 3 Tbs. extra-virgin olive oil
- ¼ tsp. ground coriander
- ¼ tsp. ground cumin
- ¼ tsp. sweet paprika
- 2 medium firm-ripe avocados (6 to 7 oz. each), pitted, peeled, and cut into ½-inch chunks
- 2 medium scallions (white and light green parts only), thinly sliced
- 2 to 3 Tbs. coarsely chopped toasted almonds

  Freshly ground black pepper

Besides its attractive maroon color, red quinoa has a slightly deeper, nuttier flavor than white quinoa. Either, however, is excellent in this bright, lemony salad.

1. In a medium bowl, soak the raisins and apricots in hot water for 5 minutes. Drain and set aside.

2. In a 2-quart saucepan, bring 2 cups water, the quinoa, and ½ tsp. salt to a boil over high heat. Cover, reduce the heat to medium low, and simmer until the water is absorbed and the quinoa is translucent and tender, 10 to 15 minutes. (The outer germ rings of the grain will remain chewy and white. Some germ rings may separate from the grain and will look like white squiggles.) Immediately fluff the quinoa with a fork and turn it out onto a baking sheet to cool to room temperature.

3. Finely grate the zest from the lemon and then squeeze 1 Tbs. juice. In a small bowl, whisk the lemon zest and juice with the olive oil, coriander, cumin, paprika, and ¼ tsp. salt. In a large bowl, toss the vinaigrette with the quinoa, raisins, apricots, avocado, scallions, and almonds. Season to taste with salt and pepper and serve.

—Deborah Madison

PER SERVING: 460 CALORIES | 9G PROTEIN | 46G CARB | 29G TOTAL FAT | 4G SAT FAT | 19G MONO FAT | 4.5G POLY FAT | 0MG CHOL | 220MG SODIUM | 11G FIBER

sesame-ginger tofu and shiitake kebabs

MAKES 8 KEBABS; SERVES 4

- 8 bamboo skewers
- 1 14-oz. package water-packed extra-firm tofu, well drained
- ¼ cup reduced-sodium soy sauce
- 3 Tbs. rice wine (sake or Shaoxing)
- 3 Tbs. hoisin sauce
- 2 Tbs. peanut oil
- 2 Tbs. Asian sesame oil
- 2 Tbs. chopped fresh ginger
- 1 Tbs. honey
- 40 medium fresh shiitake mushrooms (about 1 lb.), stemmed
- 2 bunches scallions (white and light green parts only), cut into 1-inch lengths to yield 40 pieces
- 1 orange
- Nonstick cooking spray

Serve these kebabs with brown rice or somen noodles.

1. In a shallow pan, soak eight 12-inch bamboo skewers in water while you work. Sandwich the tofu between paper towels and put on a plate. Set a small heavy pot or cutting board on the tofu to press out excess moisture. Let sit for 20 to 30 minutes.

2. Cut the tofu into 40 cubes by first slicing the tofu block in half horizontally and then cutting each half into 20 cubes.

3. In a large bowl, whisk the soy sauce, rice wine, hoisin sauce, peanut oil, sesame oil, ginger, and honey. Add the tofu, mushrooms, and scallions. Marinate at room temperature for 30 to 45 minutes, stirring frequently but gently.

4. Trim the ends of the orange, cut it lengthwise into quarters, and then slice each quarter crosswise into 6 slices to yield 24 slices total.

5. Line a large, heavy-duty rimmed baking sheet with foil and coat the foil with cooking spray. Position a rack 8 inches from the broiler element and heat the broiler on high.

6. Thread 5 scallion pieces, 5 shiitake, 5 pieces of tofu, and 3 orange slices onto each skewer in an alternating pattern. Arrange the skewers on the baking sheet. Broil until nicely browned on one side, 5 to 6 minutes. Gently turn the kebabs over and cook until golden brown on the other side, another 5 to 6 minutes.

7. Meanwhile, pour the remaining marinade into a small (1-quart) saucepan. Bring to a boil over medium-high heat. Reduce the heat to maintain a gentle simmer and cook until slightly reduced and the flavors meld, about 2 minutes.

8. Arrange the kebabs on a serving platter or on individual plates. Drizzle with the sauce and serve. —*Susie Middleton*

PER SERVING: 230 CALORIES | 13G PROTEIN | 29G CARB | 10G TOTAL FAT | 1G SAT FAT | 6G MONO FAT | 2G POLY FAT | 0MG CHOL | 200MG SODIUM | 5G FIBER

thai-style steak with red curry sauce and spicy carrot salad

SERVES 4

1½ lb. sirloin steak

Kosher salt and freshly ground black pepper

2 Tbs. canola oil

3 Tbs. fresh lime juice

2 Tbs. fish sauce

2 tsp. light brown sugar

6 medium carrots, peeled and grated

¼ cup tightly packed fresh cilantro, coarsely chopped

1 or 2 fresh jalapeño or serrano chiles, stemmed, seeded, and finely chopped

⅔ cup canned unsweetened coconut milk

1 Tbs. Thai red curry paste

You can find Thai red curry paste in the Asian section of your super-market, or try an Asian market, which might have more brand options. Be sure to shake the coconut milk vigorously before you open the can.

1. Season the steak all over with 1½ tsp. salt and ¼ tsp. pepper. Heat 1 Tbs. of the oil in a large heavy-duty skillet over medium-high heat. Cook the steak, flipping once, until well browned outside and medium rare inside, 10 to 12 minutes total.

2. Meanwhile, put the remaining 1 Tbs. oil, 2 Tbs. of the lime juice, 1½ Tbs. of the fish sauce, and 1 tsp. of the sugar in a large bowl and whisk to combine and dissolve the sugar. Add the carrots, cilantro, and chiles and toss well to coat.

3. When the steak is done, transfer to a large plate, cover loosely with foil, and keep warm. Return the skillet to medium-low heat. Add ⅓ cup water and bring to a boil, scraping with a wooden spoon to release any browned bits. Add the coconut milk, curry paste, and the remaining 1 Tbs. lime juice, 1½ tsp. fish sauce, and 1 tsp. sugar; cook, whisking constantly, until thickened and fragrant, 4 to 5 minutes. Season with salt and pepper to taste.

4. Thinly slice the steak across the grain and transfer to plates. Spoon the sauce over the top and serve with the carrot salad on the side.
—Liz Pearson

PER SERVING: 400 CALORIES | 30G PROTEIN | 15G CARB | 25G TOTAL FAT | 11G SAT FAT | 9G MONO FAT | 2.5G POLY FAT | 75MG CHOL | 1300MG SODIUM | 3G FIBER

vegetable tacos with cilantro pesto

SERVES 8

FOR THE GRILLED VEGETABLES

- 2 small zucchini, cut length-wise into ¼-inch-thick slices

- 2 small yellow squash, cut lengthwise into ¼-inch-thick slices

- 2 medium chayote, peeled, seeded, and cut into ¼-inch-thick slices

- 3 Tbs. sunflower or vegetable oil

- 1 tsp. minced garlic

- 1 serrano chile, minced

  Kosher salt and freshly ground black pepper

FOR ASSEMBLING THE TACOS

- 8 6-inch corn tortillas, warmed

  Cilantro Pesto (recipe on the facing page)

- ¾ cup crumbled queso fresco or feta (optional)

  Coarsely chopped fresh cilantro (optional)

If you can't find the squash-like Mexican chayote, substitute an additional zucchini and yellow squash.

GRILL THE VEGETABLES

1. Prepare a medium-high gas or charcoal grill fire. In a large bowl, combine the zucchini, yellow squash, and chayote. Add the oil, garlic, serrano, 1 tsp. salt, and 1 tsp. pepper and toss gently to coat. Grill, covered, until the vegetables become tender and have grill marks on both sides, 2 to 3 minutes per side. The chayote will soften but won't become limp like the zucchini and squash.

2. Let the vegetables cool slightly and then slice crosswise into thin strips. Season to taste with more salt and pepper. The filling can be warm or at room temperature.

ASSEMBLE THE TACOS

Spoon some of the vegetable mixture on top of each tortilla and top with a drizzle of the pesto and some crumbled cheese and chopped cilantro (if using). —*Sue Torres*

PER SERVING: 290 CALORIES | 6G PROTEIN | 18G CARB | 23G TOTAL FAT | 3.5G SAT FAT | 5G MONO FAT | 14G POLY FAT | 5MG CHOL | 260MG SODIUM | 3G FIBER

cilantro pesto

1 cup packed coarsely chopped fresh cilantro

½ cup sunflower or vegetable oil

2 Tbs. toasted pine nuts

1 medium clove garlic

½ tsp. kosher salt

Combine all the ingredients in a blender and purée until smooth. Set aside, or refrigerate in an airtight container for up to 3 days.

swiss chard, sweet potato & feta tart in a teff crust

SERVES 8

FOR THE CRUST

5½ oz. (1 cup) teff flour

4½ oz. (1 cup) unbleached all-purpose flour

¾ tsp. table salt

6 oz. (¾ cup) cold unsalted butter, cut into ½-inch pieces

4 to 5 Tbs. ice water

FOR THE FILLING

1½ lb. sweet potatoes (2 medium)

3 Tbs. extra-virgin olive oil

2 medium red onions, halved and sliced lengthwise into ¼-inch-thick slices (4 cups)

Sea salt

2 Tbs. balsamic vinegar

3 medium cloves garlic, chopped

1 large bunch (15 oz.) Swiss chard, thick stems removed, leaves coarsely chopped (8 cups)

½ lb. feta, crumbled (1⅓ cups)

Crushed red pepper flakes

2 large eggs

Freshly ground black pepper

Adding teff flour to this tart's crust gives it the texture of shortbread and a rich, nutty flavor. The filling is vegetable heaven—chard, sweet potatoes, and red onions—topped off with a salty sprinkle of feta. Serve with a green salad to round out the meal.

MAKE THE CRUST

1. Combine both flours and the salt in a food processor; pulse to combine. Add the butter and pulse until it breaks down to the size of small peas. Sprinkle 4 Tbs. of the ice water over the mixture and pulse again until the pastry just holds together (if it's too dry to hold together, pulse in tiny amounts of the remaining water until it holds). Transfer the dough to a large sheet of plastic wrap and, using the plastic as an aid, shape it into a thick disk. Wrap the dough in the plastic and refrigerate for about 30 minutes.

2. Meanwhile, position a rack in the center of the oven and heat the oven to 375°F.

3. Unwrap and roll the dough on a lightly floured surface into a 14-inch round. (If the pastry cracks, just press it back together.) Wrap the pastry around the rolling pin and unroll it over an 11-inch fluted tart pan with a removable bottom. Without stretching the dough, very gently work it into the pan, pressing the pastry against the sides. Roll the pin over the pan to trim the excess dough. Use the scraps as needed to make the edge even and about ¼ inch thick (at the narrowest points). Press gently all around the edge so the dough comes up slightly above the rim of the pan.

4. Prick the bottom of the crust all over with a fork, line with parchment, and fill with dried beans or pie weights. Put the tart pan on a baking sheet and bake until the edge looks dry, about 10 minutes. Carefully remove the beans and parchment and bake until the bottom is just set and looks dry, 5 to 7 minutes more. Let cool on the baking sheet on a rack.

MAKE THE FILLING

1. Scrub the sweet potatoes, poke them once or twice with a fork, and put them on a small foil-lined baking sheet. Roast until tender when pierced, 50 to 60 minutes. Let cool, peel, and cut into ¾-inch dice.

2. While the sweet potatoes are roasting, heat 2 Tbs. of the olive oil in a 12-inch nonstick skillet over medium-high heat. Add the onions and a generous pinch of salt; cook, stirring, until the onions wilt and develop dark brown charred spots, about 10 minutes. Reduce the heat to medium low, cover the pan, and stir frequently until softened and caramelized, 8 to 9 minutes more. Add 1 Tbs. of balsamic vinegar and stir until it evaporates and glazes the onions.

3. Transfer the onions to a small bowl and wipe out the pan. Heat the remaining 1 Tbs. olive oil in the pan over medium-low heat. Add the garlic and cook until fragrant and just beginning to color, 1 to 2 minutes. Increase the heat to medium high, add the chopped chard and a pinch of salt, and toss over medium-high heat until the chard is completely wilted, about 4 minutes. Sprinkle the remaining 1 Tbs. balsamic vinegar over the chard and toss it until the vinegar cooks away, about 1 minute. Transfer to a large bowl.

4. Add the diced sweet potatoes, about three-quarters of the feta, and a pinch of crushed red pepper to the chard; toss gently. In a small bowl, whisk the eggs with a pinch of salt and pepper and add the eggs to the chard mixture.

BAKE THE TART
1. Spread the filling evenly in the tart shell and scatter the remaining feta on top. Bake the tart on the baking sheet until the cheese is nicely browned, 25 to 30 minutes.

2. Spoon the balsamic onions over the top of the tart, allowing bits of feta to peek through here and there. Let the tart cool slightly, about 10 minutes; then remove the rim of the pan. Slice and serve the tart warm or at room temperature. *—Anna Thomas*

PER SERVING: 490 CALORIES | 12G PROTEIN | 44G CARB | 31G TOTAL FAT | 16G SAT FAT | 10G MONO FAT | 1.5G POLY FAT | 125MG CHOL | 1270MG SODIUM | 6G FIBER

millet and cheddar polenta with roasted vegetables

SERVES 4

FOR THE ROASTED VEGETABLES

- **1** lb. cremini (baby bella) mushrooms, trimmed and halved if medium, quartered if large
- **1** lb. fresh pearl onions (any color), peeled, or frozen pearl onions, thawed
- **1** lb. Brussels sprouts, trimmed and halved
- **¼** cup extra-virgin olive oil
- **4** medium cloves garlic, minced
- **2** tsp. fresh thyme leaves

  Sea salt and freshly ground black pepper
- **1** Tbs. sherry vinegar

FOR THE MILLET POLENTA

- **1** cup millet
- **5** to 6 cups vegetable broth, preferably homemade
- **3** Tbs. unsalted butter
- **4** oz. extra-sharp white Cheddar, grated (1½ cups)

  Sea salt (optional)

  Extra-virgin olive oil or melted butter, for serving (optional)

Millet makes a rich, soft polenta, and sharp Cheddar highlights the mild, slightly sweet flavor of the grain. Roasted winter vegetables complete this warming vegetarian supper.

ROAST THE VEGETABLES

1. Position a rack in the top third of the oven and heat the oven to 450°F.

2. In a large bowl, toss the mushrooms, onions, and Brussels sprouts with 2 Tbs. of the oil, the garlic, thyme, 1½ tsp. salt, and a few grinds of pepper. Spread on a large rimmed baking sheet. Roast for 20 minutes, stir the vegetables, and continue roasting until tender and browned, about 35 minutes total. Transfer to a serving bowl and toss with the remaining 2 Tbs. oil and the vinegar.

MAKE THE MILLET POLENTA

1. Meanwhile, rinse and drain the millet. Put it in a heavy 4-quart saucepan and stir over medium-high heat until it smells toasty and turns deeply golden, 7 to 8 minutes.

2. Add 5 cups of the vegetable broth and the butter and bring to a boil over medium-high heat. Reduce the heat to a simmer and cover. Allow the millet to simmer gently, stirring after the first 20 minutes and then every 7 to 8 minutes thereafter to prevent sticking, until it becomes a thick, creamy porridge with a chewy texture, about 35 minutes total. If it seems too thick, stir in a little more broth. Stir in the cheese and season to taste with salt, if needed.

3. Serve the polenta in wide, shallow bowls with the roasted vegetables on top. Drizzle a little olive oil or melted butter over each serving, if you like. *—Anna Thomas*

PER SERVING: 640 CALORIES | 20G PROTEIN | 68G CARB | 34G TOTAL FAT | 14G SAT FAT | 13G MONO FAT | 3G POLY FAT | 55MG CHOL | 1280MG SODIUM | 13G FIBER

spicy penne tossed with chicken,
broccoli & chopped olives
(recipe on p. 162)

pasta & noodles

penne with ricotta, arugula & basil

SERVES 4 TO 6

Kosher salt and freshly ground black pepper

- **1** lb. dried penne
- **8** oz. whole-milk ricotta (about 1 cup)
- **1** oz. freshly grated Parmigiano-Reggiano (about 1 cup); more for serving
- **2** Tbs. extra-virgin olive oil
- **2** tsp. lightly packed finely grated lemon zest
- **5** oz. baby arugula (about 6 loosely packed cups), coarsely chopped
- **1½** oz. fresh basil (about 2 loosely packed cups), coarsely chopped

Parmigiano-Reggiano, ricotta, and lemon zest form the base of a creamy, no-cook pasta sauce that comes together in minutes.

1. Bring a large pot of well-salted water to a boil over high heat. Cook the pasta in the water until al dente, about 11 minutes. Reserve about ⅓ cup of the cooking water and drain the pasta.

2. Meanwhile, in a large bowl, mix the ricotta, Parmigiano, 1 Tbs. of the oil, the zest, ½ tsp. salt, and ¾ tsp. pepper.

3. Heat the remaining 1 Tbs. oil in a 12-inch nonstick skillet over medium heat. Add the arugula and basil and ½ tsp. salt and cook, tossing with tongs, until just wilted, about 2 minutes. Transfer the arugula mixture to the bowl with the ricotta and mix well.

4. Add the hot pasta to the ricotta mixture and toss to coat. Add the reserved cooking liquid as needed to moisten the pasta. Season to taste with salt and pepper. Serve, passing more Parmigiano at the table. —*Lori Longbotham*

PER SERVING: 430 CALORIES | 18G PROTEIN | 59G CARB | 13G TOTAL FAT | 5G SAT FAT | 5G MONO FAT | 1.5G POLY FAT | 25MG CHOL | 500MG SODIUM | 4G FIBER

baked orzo with shrimp, lemon & feta

SERVES 6 TO 8

- 5 Tbs olive oil; more for the dish
- 1 lb. shrimp (26 to 30 per lb.), peeled and deveined

  Kosher salt and freshly ground black pepper
- 1 large clove garlic, minced
- 5 oz. baby spinach
- 1 lb. orzo
- 6 oz. feta, crumbled (about 1½ cups)
- 2 tsp. chopped fresh thyme

  Finely grated zest of 1 lemon
- ¾ cup panko

All sorts of ingredients— sun-dried tomatoes, olives, peas, or corn—can be added to this baked pasta for extra flavor and color. Serve this side with a seared steak for a Mediterranean version of surf and turf.

1. Position a rack in the center of the oven and heat the oven to 425°F. Bring a large pot of well-salted water to a boil. Lightly coat a 2-quart baking dish with oil.

2. Heat 2 Tbs. oil in a 12-inch skillet over medium-high heat until shimmering. Add the shrimp, sprinkle with ½ tsp. each salt and pepper, and cook, stirring, until the shrimp start to lose their raw color (but don't cook through), about 2 minutes. Add the garlic and cook, stirring, for 30 seconds. Stir in the spinach and cook, tossing, until it starts to wilt, about 1 minute. Remove from the heat.

3. Add the pasta to the boiling water and cook according to the package instructions until al dente. Drain well and toss with the shrimp mixture, feta, 2 Tbs. oil, half the thyme, and lemon zest.
Transfer to the prepared baking dish. In a small bowl, toss the breadcrumbs with the remaining 1 Tbs. oil, the remaining 1 tsp. thyme, and ¼ tsp. salt. Sprinkle on top of the pasta.

4. Bake the pasta until the breadcrumbs brown and the pasta heats through, about 20 minutes (cover with foil if the top browns too quickly). Let cool for a couple of minutes and then serve. *—Tony Rosenfeld*

linguine with roasted asparagus and almond pesto

SERVES 4 TO 6

Kosher salt and freshly ground black pepper

¾ **lb. asparagus, trimmed**

2 **cups grape tomatoes**

¼ **cup extra-virgin olive oil**

½ **cup sliced almonds**

¼ **cup fresh basil leaves**

2 **Tbs. finely grated Parmigiano-Reggiano**

1 **lb. dried linguine**

This pesto recipe doubles easily; keep any extra in a sealed container in the refrigerator for up to a week. It's delicious on crostini for a quick bite or served with roast chicken or salmon.

1. Position racks in the upper and lower thirds of the oven and heat the oven to 425°F. Bring a large pot of well-salted water to a boil over high heat.

2. Arrange the asparagus in a single layer on half of a large rimmed baking sheet. Arrange the tomatoes on the other half of the sheet. Drizzle both with 1 Tbs. of the oil, season with ¼ tsp. salt, and toss to coat. Roast on the top rack until the tomatoes have collapsed and the asparagus is bright green, about 20 minutes.

3. While the vegetables roast, put the almonds on another rimmed baking sheet and toast on the bottom rack, stirring occasionally, until fragrant and lightly browned, 10 to 12 minutes.

4. Reserve a heaping 1 Tbs. of the almonds for garnish and put the remaining almonds in a food processor. Remove the tips from the asparagus and set aside. Roughly chop the remaining asparagus and add to the food processor, along with the basil, Parmigiano, ½ tsp. salt, and the remaining 3 Tbs. olive oil. Pulse until a coarse paste forms, about 10 seconds. Season to taste with salt and pepper and transfer to a large serving bowl.

5. Cook the linguine in the boiling water according to the package directions until al dente. Drain the pasta and reserve ½ cup of the pasta cooking water. Add the pasta to the pesto and toss to coat. If necessary, add some or all of the reserved cooking water to loosen the pesto to a saucy consistency. Garnish with the tomatoes, asparagus tips, and reserved almonds, and serve.
—*Allison Fishman*

PER SERVING: 430 CALORIES | 14G PROTEIN | 61G CARB | 15G TOTAL FAT | 2G SAT FAT | 9G MONO FAT | 2.5G POLY FAT | 0MG CHOL | 390MG SODIUM | 5G FIBER

sesame, snow pea & shiitake pasta salad

SERVES 8

Kosher salt and freshly ground black pepper

½ lb. dried rolled, tubular pasta (such as cavatelli or strozzapreti)

½ cup frozen baby green peas

40 fresh snow peas (4 to 5 oz.), trimmed

3 Tbs. vegetable oil

1 cup thinly sliced yellow onion

½ lb. fresh shiitake mushrooms, stemmed, caps sliced ¼ inch thick (about 3 cups)

1 tsp. minced garlic

1 tsp. minced fresh ginger

4 tsp. soy sauce

1 Tbs. rice vinegar

2 tsp. Asian sesame oil

¼ tsp. granulated sugar

½ cup thinly sliced scallions (white and green parts)

2 Tbs. toasted white sesame seeds

Two kinds of green peas, sesame, ginger, and soy give this earthy pasta salad bold flavor.

1. Bring a large pot of well-salted water to a boil over high heat. Add the pasta and cook until barely al dente, about 1 minute less than the package directions. Add the green peas and cook for about 30 seconds. Add the snow peas, stir, and immediately drain the vegetables and pasta in a colander set in the sink. Rinse with cool water to stop the cooking. Drain well, toss with 1 Tbs. of the vegetable oil, and set aside.

2. Heat 1 Tbs. of the vegetable oil in a 12-inch skillet over medium heat. Add the onion, shiitake, garlic, ginger, ½ tsp. salt, and a few grinds of pepper. Cook, stirring occasionally, until the onion is opaque and the mushrooms have released their juices, 3 to 4 minutes—don't let the vegetables brown. Remove the pan from the heat, transfer the vegetables and any juices to a small bowl, and let cool to room temperature.

3. In another small bowl, whisk the remaining 1 Tbs. vegetable oil with the soy sauce, vinegar, sesame oil, and sugar.

4. In a large bowl, combine the cooled pasta and vegetables, the scallions, and 1 Tbs. of the sesame seeds. Toss with the dressing and season to taste with salt and pepper. Serve at room temperature, garnished with the remaining sesame seeds. *—Ed Shoenfeld*

PER SERVING: 220 CALORIES | 6G PROTEIN | 30G CARB | 8G TOTAL FAT | 1G SAT FAT | 3G MONO FAT | 3.5G POLY FAT | 0MG CHOL | 390MG SODIUM | 3G FIBER

fettuccine with chicken, goat cheese & spinach

SERVES 4

1 cup dry white wine (like Sauvignon Blanc)

2 Tbs. minced shallots (from about 2 small)

5 oz. goat cheese, at room temperature, cut up or crumbled

Kosher salt and freshly ground black pepper

Pinch of crushed red pepper flakes

½ lb. dried fettuccine

2 boneless, skinless chicken breast halves (about 1 lb. total)

2 Tbs. olive oil

4 oz. fresh baby spinach (about 6 cups)

2 Tbs. chopped fresh basil

Here, the sharp flavor of goat cheese blends perfectly with the sweet richness of shallots.

1. In a medium saucepan, combine the white wine and shallots. Over high heat, reduce the liquid by half, about 5 minutes. Whisk in the goat cheese until the mixture is smooth, then season with ½ tsp. salt, ¼ tsp. pepper, and the red pepper flakes. Set aside.

2. Bring a large pot of salted water to a boil over high heat. Add the pasta and cook until just done, 9 to 11 minutes. Reserve ½ cup of the pasta water, drain the pasta, and set aside.

3. Meanwhile, pound the chicken breasts with a meat mallet or the bottom of a heavy skillet to flatten them to about ¾ inch and season them with salt and pepper. Heat 1 Tbs. of the olive oil in a sauté pan over medium-high heat. Add the chicken and sauté until browned and just cooked through, about 5 minutes on each side. Remove the chicken from the pan. Add the remaining 1 Tbs. olive oil and the spinach and sauté until it's wilted, about 2 minutes. Let the chicken cool for 2 minutes and then cut it diagonally into strips.

4. In a large bowl, combine the pasta with the goat cheese sauce; add the spinach and the chicken with its juices. If the pasta is dry, stir in some of the reserved pasta water until the sauce reaches the consistency you want. Season with salt and pepper and serve in warm bowls, topped with the basil. —*Jennifer Bushman*

PER SERVING: 550 CALORIES | 40G PROTEIN | 46G CARB | 21G TOTAL FAT | 9G SAT FAT | 9G MONO FAT | 2G POLY FAT | 90MG CHOL | 590MG SODIUM | 3G FIBER

Buying and Storing Spinach

Fresh, unpackaged spinach, whether loose or bunched, is usually fresher than the prepacked type, and the flavor can be superior. It's also easier to see what you're getting, as sealed plastic bags can hide slimy spinach. Use the large leaves for cooking; save the smaller ones for salads. A pound of fresh leaves will cook down to about a cup. For a side dish of cooked spinach, figure ½ lb. raw spinach per serving.

Fresh spinach keeps well for 2 to 3 days sealed in a plastic bag in the fridge.

spicy penne tossed with chicken, broccoli & chopped olives

SERVES 4 TO 6

Kosher salt

½ **cup olive oil**

4 **cloves garlic, smashed**

2 **tsp. chopped fresh rosemary**

½ **tsp. crushed red pepper flakes**

½ **lb. (about 1 large) boneless, skinless chicken breast, cut into thin strips**

⅔ **cup pitted Kalamata olives, coarsely chopped**

1 **lb. dried penne**

½ **lb. broccoli florets, cut into 1½-inch pieces (about 3 cups)**

2 **Tbs. fresh lemon juice**

1 **cup freshly grated pecorino romano**

Kalamata olives enhance any dish with their salty, rich flavor. Here, they add a twist to a basic chicken and broccoli pasta. For a vegetarian option, omit the chicken and add red and green peppers, chickpeas, or any other legume or vegetable of your choice when the pasta and pasta water are added to the skillet.

1. Bring a large pot of well-salted water to a boil over high heat. Meanwhile, heat the oil and garlic in a 12-inch skillet over medium heat, stirring gently so the cloves don't break up, until they become light brown in places and very fragrant, 2 to 3 minutes. Add the rosemary and red pepper flakes and cook until they start to sizzle, about 15 seconds. Add the chicken, sprinkle with ¼ tsp. salt, and cook, stirring often, until the chicken loses its raw color, about 2 minutes. Remove from the heat and stir in the olives.

2. Add the penne to the boiling water and cook, stirring occasionally, until just barely al dente, 1 to 2 minutes less than the package instructions. Add the broccoli and cook until it turns bright green and the pasta is tender, about 1 minute. Reserve ½ cup of the pasta water, and then drain the pasta and broccoli. Discard the garlic from the olive mixture. Add the pasta and the pasta water to the skillet and cook uncovered over medium-high heat, stirring, until the pasta absorbs most of the liquid, about 2 minutes. Stir in the lemon juice and half of the pecorino. Serve sprinkled with the remaining pecorino.

—Tony Rosenfeld

angel hair pasta with sautéed cherry tomatoes, lemon & tuna

SERVES 3 OR 4

Kosher salt

2 **Tbs. extra-virgin olive oil**

4 **cups cherry or grape tomatoes (about 1½ lb.; a mix of colors, if possible)**

1 **large clove garlic, minced**

1 **6-oz. can light tuna in oil, drained and separated into chunks**

2 **Tbs. minced jarred pepperoncini (about 4 medium peppers, stemmed and seeded)**

1 **Tbs. lightly chopped capers**

1 **tsp. fresh lemon juice**

1 **tsp. cold unsalted butter**

½ **tsp. packed finely grated lemon zest**

½ **lb. dried angel hair pasta**

3 **Tbs. coarsely chopped fresh flat-leaf parsley**

This dish is built around summer's luscious offerings yet designed for speed. The sauce only looks like you slaved over it, and its strong flavors are perfectly in balance.

1. Bring a large pot of generously salted water to a boil over high heat. Meanwhile, in an 11- to 12-inch skillet, heat the oil over medium-high heat until very hot. Add the tomatoes (be careful because the oil and juice can spatter) and cook until they begin to collapse and their juices run and start to thicken, 6 to 10 minutes. (If you have big, stubborn tomatoes, you may need to crush them a bit with a spatula or pierce them with a knife.) Add the garlic and cook for 30 seconds.

2. Remove the pan from the heat and stir in the tuna, pepperoncini, capers, lemon juice, butter, and lemon zest. Season the sauce to taste with salt and keep it warm while you cook the pasta.

3. Cook the pasta in the boiling water according to package directions. Drain well, arrange in individual pasta bowls, and top with the sauce and the parsley. —*Martha Holmberg*

PER SERVING: 400 CALORIES | 22G PROTEIN | 49G CARB | 13G TOTAL FAT | 2.5G SAT FAT | 7G MONO FAT | 2.5G POLY FAT | 10MG CHOL | 880MG SODIUM | 5G FIBER

penne with crisp prosciutto, zucchini & corn

SERVES 4

Kosher salt

5 Tbs. olive oil

8 thin slices prosciutto (about 4 oz.), cut into strips

1 medium yellow onion, thinly sliced (1 cup)

2 small zucchini (about ¾ lb.), trimmed, quartered lengthwise, and cut into 1½-inch pieces

2 ears corn, shucked and kernels sliced off (about 1 cup), or 1 cup frozen corn kernels, thawed

½ cup freshly grated pecorino romano

3 Tbs. chopped fresh mint

1 lb. dried penne

2 tsp. sherry vinegar or apple cider vinegar

Freshly ground black pepper

Sautéing the prosciutto in a skillet crisps and intensifies its texture and flavor so it becomes like a refined version of bacon. Instead of overpowering the dish, the prosciutto complements the sweetness of the corn, brightness of the mint, and delicate flavor of the zucchini.

1. Bring a large pot of well-salted water to a boil. Meanwhile, put 2 Tbs. oil and the prosciutto in a large (12-inch) skillet, place over medium heat, and cook, stirring occasionally, until the prosciutto browns in places and becomes crisp, about 5 minutes. Transfer the prosciutto to a large plate lined with paper towels.

2. Add 1 Tbs. oil and the onion to the skillet, sprinkle with ½ tsp. salt, and cook, stirring occasionally, until the onion softens completely and turns light brown, about 6 minutes; add 1 or 2 Tbs. water to the skillet if the onion starts to stick or burn. Add the zucchini and corn, sprinkle with ¼ tsp. salt, and cook, tossing occasionally, until the zucchini becomes tender, 4 to 5 minutes. Remove from the heat and stir in half the pecorino romano and all the mint.

3. Add the penne to the pot of boiling water and cook according to the package directions. Reserve ½ cup of the pasta water and then drain the pasta. Add the pasta, the remaining 2 Tbs. oil, the vinegar, and 1 tsp. black pepper to the skillet with the zucchini and corn mixture. Set the skillet over medium heat and cook, stirring, for 1 minute so the pasta mixes with the vegetables. Add the reserved pasta water and stir. Serve sprinkled with the crisp prosciutto and the remaining pecorino romano. *—Tony Rosenfeld*

spring vegetable ragoût with fresh pasta

SERVES 4

Kosher salt and freshly ground black pepper

¾ **lb. fresh pasta sheets**

1 **small clove garlic, minced**

3 **cups mixed spring vegetables (such as medium-thick asparagus, baby carrots, baby turnips, spring onions, and sugar snap peas), trimmed and cut into pieces measuring 1 to 3 inches long by ½ to ¾ inch wide**

½ **cup shelled peas or peeled fava beans (see note below)**

⅓ **cup loosely packed pea shoots or watercress sprigs; more for garnish**

¼ **cup loosely packed chopped mixed fresh herbs, such as basil, chervil, mint, parsley, and tarragon; more for garnish**

4 **Tbs. cold unsalted butter, cut into ½-inch pieces**

1½ **tsp. freshly grated lemon zest**

Freshly grated Parmigiano-Reggiano, for garnish (optional)

Here's a dish that lets spring vegetables shine. Purchased fresh pasta sheets get cut into noodles for a rustic look.

1. Bring a large pot of well-salted water to a boil. With a pizza cutter or chef's knife, cut the pasta sheets into rustic strips about ½ inch wide.

2. In a 10- to 11-inch straight-sided sauté pan, bring 2½ cups water, the garlic, 1 tsp. salt, and ¼ tsp. pepper to a simmer over high heat. Add the mixed vegetables and simmer briskly, adjusting the heat as necessary, until just crisp-tender, 3 to 4 minutes. With a slotted spoon, transfer to a large plate. If using peas, simmer them until barely tender, about 2 minutes, and transfer to the plate with the slotted spoon. (If using favas, skip this step.) Raise the heat to high and boil the liquid until reduced to 1 cup, 3 to 4 minutes.

3. Meanwhile, cook the pasta in the boiling water until barely al dente, 2 to 4 minutes. Drain.

4. Add the cooked pasta, vegetables, favas (if using), pea shoots or watercress, herbs, butter, and lemon zest to the broth. Toss over medium-high heat until the butter is melted, about 1 minute.

5. Season to taste with salt and pepper. Serve garnished with pea shoots or watercress, fresh herbs, and Parmigiano (if using).
—Allison Ehri Kreitler

PER SERVING: 390 CALORIES | 12G PROTEIN | 55G CARB | 14G TOTAL FAT | 8G SAT FAT | 3G MONO FAT | 1.5G POLY FAT | 95MG CHOL | 460MG SODIUM | 6G FIBER

> **To peel fava beans, shuck them and cook them in boiling salted water until tender, 1 to 2 minutes, then rinse them with cold water and peel off the skin.**

udon with tofu and stir-fried vegetables

SERVES 4

Kosher salt

¾ lb. dried udon noodles

3 cups homemade or lower-salt chicken broth

1 Tbs. plus 2 tsp. oyster sauce

1 Tbs. plus 2 tsp. rice vinegar

4 tsp. Asian sesame oil

¼ cup minced fresh ginger

2 Tbs. canola oil

¾ lb. bok choy, cut crosswise into ¾-inch pieces (4 cups)

3½ oz. fresh shiitake mushrooms, stemmed, caps thinly sliced (1½ cups)

½ lb. extra-firm tofu, cut into ½-inch cubes

2 medium carrots, cut into matchsticks

3 medium scallions, trimmed and thinly sliced, for garnish

These wheat-based Japanese noodles are available both dried (used in this recipe) and fresh. Dried udon are flatter than their fresh counterparts and closer in texture to linguine.

1. Bring a medium pot of well-salted water to a boil. Add the noodles and cook, stirring, until tender, about 8 minutes. Transfer to a colander and run under cold water to cool slightly. Drain well.

2. In a medium bowl, mix the chicken broth, oyster sauce, vinegar, and 2 tsp. of the sesame oil.

3. Heat the ginger and canola oil in a large skillet over medium-high heat until the ginger sizzles steadily for about 30 seconds. Add the bok choy and shiitake, sprinkle with the remaining 2 tsp. sesame oil and ¾ tsp. salt, and cook, tossing after 1 minute, until the bok choy turns dark green and begins to soften, 3 to 5 minutes. Add the chicken broth mixture, tofu, and carrots and bring to a boil. Reduce to a simmer, cover, and cook until the carrots are soft and the tofu is heated through, 5 to 7 minutes.

4. Portion the noodles among 4 bowls. Spoon the vegetables, tofu, and broth over the noodles. Sprinkle with the scallions and serve.

–Tony Rosenfeld

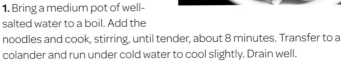

PER SERVING: 540 CALORIES | 24G PROTEIN | 71G CARB | 19G TOTAL FAT | 2G SAT FAT |

9G MONO FAT | 4.5G POLY FAT | 0MG CHOL | 820MG SODIUM | 8G FIBER

spaghetti frittata with arugula and fresh herbs

SERVES 4 TO 6

Kosher salt and freshly ground black pepper

3 oz. uncooked dried spaghetti (or 1⅓ cups cooked)

2 Tbs. extra-virgin olive oil

1 Tbs. unsalted butter

1 large or 2 small shallots, trimmed, peeled, and thinly sliced crosswise

2 oz. arugula (about 2 cups lightly packed), stemmed if necessary

8 large eggs (preferably at room temperature)

⅔ cup heavy cream

1 cup freshly grated Parmigiano-Reggiano (use the large holes on a box grater)

2 Tbs. finely chopped fresh mint

2 Tbs. chopped fresh flat-leaf parsley

2 Tbs. sliced fresh chives

If you have leftover cooked pasta in the fridge, this is a great way to use it up.

1. Position a rack in the center of the oven and heat the oven to 375°F. Bring a large pot of well-salted water to a boil over high heat.

2. Cook the spaghetti in the boiling water according to package directions. Drain well and let cool. Transfer to a medium bowl.

3. In an ovenproof, 10-inch nonstick skillet, heat 1 Tbs. of the olive oil and 1½ tsp. of the butter over medium heat. Add the shallot and a pinch of salt and cook, stirring occasionally, until the shallot is softened and lightly golden, about 8 minutes. Add the arugula and toss with tongs until wilted, about 1 minute. With a heatproof spatula, scrape the arugula mixture and any fat left in the pan into the bowl with the pasta. Toss lightly to combine.

4. In a large bowl, whisk the eggs, cream, ½ tsp. salt, and several grinds of pepper. Add the pasta mixture, Parmigiano, mint, parsley, and chives. Mix gently but thoroughly.

5. Heat the remaining 1 Tbs. oil and 1½ tsp. butter in the skillet over medium-high heat. When the butter has melted and is bubbling, add the egg mixture. Use the heatproof spatula to gently distribute the ingredients evenly. Reduce the heat to medium low and cook until the eggs have set just along the outside edge of the pan, 4 to 5 minutes. Transfer the skillet to the oven and bake until the frittata is puffed, golden, and set, 22 to 24 minutes.

6. Let the frittata cool in the pan for 15 to 20 minutes. Run the spatula gently around the edge and underneath the frittata, and slide it onto a cutting board. Let sit for 5 to 10 minutes. Cut into wedges and serve.
—*Susie Middleton*

PER SERVING: 320 CALORIES | 13G PROTEIN | 13G CARB | 25G TOTAL FAT | 1G SAT FAT | 9G MONO FAT | 2G POLY FAT | 325MG CHOL | 230MG SODIUM | 1G FIBER

mint and pine nut pesto with gemelli and asparagus

SERVES 4 TO 6

FOR THE PESTO

- **6** **scallions (dark and light green parts only), trimmed and thinly sliced (about ½ cup)**
- **½** **cup freshly grated Parmigiano-Reggiano**
- **½** **cup pine nuts, toasted**
- **⅓** **cup firmly packed fresh mint leaves, chopped**
- **5** **Tbs. extra-virgin olive oil; more as needed**
-   **Kosher salt and freshly ground black pepper**

FOR THE PASTA

- **1** **lb. dried gemelli**
- **¾** **lb. asparagus, ends snapped off, cut into 1½-inch pieces**
- **2** **tsp. fresh lemon juice; more as needed**
- **¼** **cup freshly grated Parmigiano-Reggiano**

You could also spread the pesto on top of chicken breasts or a firm-fleshed fish like cod or salmon and roast.

MAKE THE PESTO

Put the scallions, Parmigiano, pine nuts, and mint in a food processor and process until finely chopped. With the processor on, pour the oil down the feed tube in a steady stream, so the mixture thins into a slightly loose paste. Add more oil if needed. Add ½ tsp. salt and ¾ tsp. pepper and pulse once more. The pesto will keep in an airtight container in the refrigerator for up to 4 days.

MAKE THE PASTA

Bring a large (6-quart) pot of well-salted water to a boil over high heat. Add the pasta and cook, stirring occasionally, until nearly tender, about 2 minutes less than the package timing. Add the asparagus and cook with the pasta until both are tender, about 2 minutes more. Drain well and toss with the pesto and lemon juice. Add more lemon juice, salt, and pepper to taste. Serve sprinkled with black pepper and the Parmigiano. —*Tony Rosenfeld*

> To keep pine nuts from going rancid, store them in a zip-top bag in the freezer, where they'll keep for up to 6 months.

roasted fingerling potato crisps
with shallots and rosemary
(recipe on p. 180)

sides

sautéed sugar snap peas with mushrooms and bacon

- **3 slices thickly sliced bacon, cut into strips**
- **3 cloves garlic, smashed**
- **2 Tbs. olive oil**
- **¾ lb. sugar snap peas, ends trimmed**
- **Kosher salt**
- **10 oz. small white mushrooms, halved (or large white mushrooms, quartered)**
- **⅓ cup dry sherry**
- **1 tsp. sherry vinegar**
- **1½ Tbs. coarsely chopped fresh tarragon**

With the addition of bacon and mushrooms, this dish is quite substantial and filling. It is a perfect side for a Sunday dinner of roast lamb or roast beef.

1. In a large (12-inch) skillet over medium heat, cook the bacon and garlic with 1 Tbs. oil until the bacon lightly browns and renders most of its fat, about 6 minutes. Transfer the bacon to a plate lined with paper towels; let it drain and cool, and then crumble it. Discard the garlic from the skillet.

2. Raise the heat to medium high; add the snap peas, sprinkle with ¾ tsp. salt, and cook, stirring, until they turn bright green and start to brown in places, about 2 minutes. Transfer the peas to a plate.

3. Add the remaining 1 Tbs. oil and the mushrooms to the pan, sprinkle with ½ tsp. salt, and cook, stirring, until the mushrooms brown and start to soften, about 5 minutes. Add the sherry and cook, stirring, until the liquid almost completely reduces, about 2 minutes. Return the snap peas to the skillet, drizzle in the sherry vinegar, and cook, tossing, for 1 minute. Transfer to a serving dish, toss with the tarragon, and sprinkle with the bacon just before serving. *—Tony Rosenfeld*

grilled summer squash
with pesto and balsamic syrup

SERVES 4

1½ lb. assorted summer squash, trimmed and sliced diagonally into ½-inch-thick ovals

  Kosher salt

1 cup packed fresh basil leaves

2 Tbs. grated Parmigiano-Reggiano

¼ cup plus 2 Tbs. extra-virgin olive oil; more for drizzling

½ cup balsamic vinegar

  Freshly ground black pepper

2 Tbs. pine nuts, toasted

Summer squash takes on a deliciously smoky, caramelized flavor when grilled. Try to slice the squash into ovals, which are easier than rounds to manage on the grill grate.

1. Prepare a high gas or charcoal grill fire. In a colander, toss the squash with 2 tsp. salt and drain for 30 minutes; transfer to a large bowl.

2. Meanwhile, put the basil, Parmigiano, ¼ cup of the olive oil, and ½ tsp. salt in a food processor and purée until smooth.

3. In a small saucepan over medium-low heat, boil the balsamic vinegar until syrupy and reduced to about 2 Tbs., 8 to 10 minutes.

4. Toss the squash with the remaining 2 Tbs. olive oil and a few grinds of black pepper. Grill, flipping once, until golden and tender, 8 to 12 minutes. Arrange on a platter, dot with the pesto, and drizzle with olive oil and the balsamic syrup to taste. Sprinkle with pine nuts and serve. *—Maria Helm Sinskey*

PER SERVING: 270 CALORIES | 4G PROTEIN | 11G CARB | 24G TOTAL FAT | 3.5G SAT FAT | 16G MONO FAT | 4G POLY FAT | 0MG CHOL | 750MG SODIUM | 2G FIBER

quick-braised baby artichokes with garlic, mint & parsley

SERVES 4

16 baby artichokes, trimmed and halved, or 12 large artichokes, trimmed to the heart and quartered, submerged in acidulated water as they're cut

¼ cup extra-virgin olive oil

Kosher salt and freshly ground black pepper

4 medium cloves garlic, minced (1½ Tbs.)

1 Tbs. fresh lemon juice

½ cup chopped fresh flat-leaf parsley

½ cup chopped fresh mint

This classic Roman dish includes two of the artichoke's best friends: fresh herbs and lemon juice. Its simplicity requires the freshest artichokes you can find.

1. Drain the artichokes and blot dry with a dishtowel.

2. In a 12-inch skillet, heat 2 Tbs. of olive oil over medium-high heat until shimmering hot. Add half of the artichokes, cut side down, sprinkle with salt and pepper, and cook until golden brown, 3 to 4 minutes. As each one browns, flip it and brown the outside, about another 2 minutes. Transfer to a bowl and repeat with the remaining 2 Tbs. oil and the second batch of artichokes. Reduce the heat to medium and add the reserved cooked artichokes to the ones in the skillet, along with the garlic. Cook, stirring, until fragrant, about 1 minute. Add ½ cup water and the lemon juice; bring to a boil. Reduce the heat to low, cover, and simmer until just tender, about 20 minutes. Uncover the pan, stir in the parsley and mint, raise the heat to medium, and simmer until any remaining liquid is mostly evaporated, 1 to 2 minutes. Season to taste with salt and pepper and serve.
—*Sara Jenkins*

PER SERVING: 210 CALORIES | 6G PROTEIN | 20G CARB | 14G TOTAL FAT | 2G SAT FAT | 10G MONO FAT | 1.5G POLY FAT | 0MG CHOL | 300MG SODIUM | 10G FIBER

how to prep artichokes

Here are three ways to clean and trim artichokes. Try the method for baby artichokes when you make this recipe.

baby artichoke

Snap off the dark green outer leaves of the artichoke until only the pale, tender inner leaves remain.

Cut off the top ¼ inch of the artichoke.

Trim the stem end and any dark parts around the bottom. Rub a lemon half over all the cut ends.

whole artichoke

Cut off the bottom of the stem, leaving about ½ inch.

Pull off any small fibrous dark leaves around the base. Cut off the top ½ inch of the artichoke.

Using scissors, trim off the sharp, pointed tips of the remaining leaves.

artichoke heart

Snap off the dark green outer leaves. Cut off the top third of the artichoke and all but 1 inch of the stem.

Using a paring knife, peel away the stem's tough outer layer and remove the base of the leaves all around.

Cut the artichoke in half lengthwise. With a spoon or melon baller, scoop out and discard the hairy choke and thorny inner leaves.

carrots and parsnips with shallot-herb butter

- **5** large carrots (about 1 lb.), peeled
- **4** large parsnips (about 1 lb.), peeled
- **3** Tbs. extra-virgin olive oil
- **1½** tsp. kosher salt
- **½** tsp. freshly ground black pepper
- **4** Tbs. unsalted butter, softened at room temperature
- **2** Tbs. minced shallot
- **2** Tbs. finely chopped fresh chives
- **1½** tsp. finely chopped fresh rosemary
- **1½** tsp. chopped fresh thyme
- **1** clove garlic, minced

A flavorful toss-in transforms roasted carrots and parsnips into a vibrant side dish. Cutting the vegetables into similar-size pieces helps to ensure they cook at about the same rate.

1. Position a rack in the center of the oven and heat the oven to 450°F.

2. Cut the carrots and parsnips into ¼ x 2-inch matchsticks. Put them in a large bowl and toss with the oil. Sprinkle with salt and pepper and toss again. Transfer the vegetables to a 10x15-inch Pyrex® dish or other heavy pan and roast, stirring every 15 minutes, until the vegetables are nicely browned, 40 to 45 minutes.

3. Meanwhile, combine the butter, shallot, chives, rosemary, thyme, and garlic in a small bowl and stir well. Add the butter to the roasted vegetables and toss to coat. Serve immediately.
—*Julie Grimes Bottcher*

PER SERVING: 470 CALORIES | 4G PROTEIN | 50G CARB | 30G TOTAL FAT | 12G SAT FAT | 15G MONO FAT | 2G POLY FAT | 40MG CHOL | 1050MG SODIUM | 12G FIBER

More about Parsnips

While there are several varieties of parsnips, most markets don't usually indicate which they're selling, mainly because the differences in flavor, texture, and appearance are minimal. Your best bet is to choose what looks freshest. Parsnips should be firm and of uniform color; blemishes can be a sign of decay. Opt for medium parsnips, as very large ones can be woody and bitter.

When you get home, wrap unwashed parsnips in paper towels or newspaper and store them in a loosely closed plastic bag in the crisper drawer of the refrigerator for up to 2 weeks.

roasted fingerling potato crisps with shallots and rosemary

SERVES 4

- **1 lb. fingerling potatoes, thinly sliced lengthwise (about ⅛ inch thick)**
- **3 Tbs. olive oil**
- **2 large shallots, sliced ¼ inch thick and broken into individual rings**
- **2 tsp. chopped fresh rosemary**
- **1½ tsp. kosher salt**
- **½ tsp. freshly ground black pepper**

Try to cut the fingerlings no larger than ⅛ inch thick, so that the potatoes will crisp in the oven. (Using a mandolin will allow you to cut them even thinner.) These crisps make a great accompaniment to grilled steak or roasted fish.

1. Position a rack in the center of the oven and heat the oven to 425°F. Line a large, rimmed baking sheet with parchment paper or aluminum foil.

2. In a large bowl, toss the potato slices with the oil, shallot, rosemary, salt, and pepper, and then spread the chips flat on the baking sheet. Bake the potatoes, turning after 10 minutes, until they brown and start to crisp, 25 to 30 minutes; the shallot should be tender and browned. Serve immediately. —*Tony Rosenfeld*

What Are Fingerling Potatoes?

Like heirloom tomatoes, fingerling potatoes are an old variety that has been resuscitated by the advent of farmer's markets and organic growers. They get their name from their small, finger-length size and come in a range of colors, from white, yellow, and orange to red and purple. The Russian banana, the most common fingerling variety, has yellow flesh and a buttery texture similar to that of Yukon Gold. Fingerlings are delicious sliced and roasted, pan-fried, or mashed with butter and fresh herbs.

grilled hearts of palm, radicchio & asparagus

SERVES 4

- 5 hearts of palm, rinsed and patted dry
- ½ head radicchio, halved lengthwise (about 4 oz.)
- ½ bunch asparagus, ends trimmed (about ½ lb.)
- ¼ cup extra-virgin olive oil
- ½ tsp. kosher salt

  Freshly ground black pepper
- 1 Tbs. fresh lemon juice
- ½ tsp. finely grated lemon zest

  Pinch of granulated sugar
- 3 very thin slices prosciutto di Parma, torn into strips (about 1¾ oz.)
- 1 oz. shaved Parmigiano-Reggiano (scant ½ cup)

This makes a great accompaniment to grilled chicken or pork. Use a vegetable peeler to shave the Parmigiano.

1. Heat a gas grill on high or prepare a hot charcoal grill fire.

2. In a large bowl, toss the hearts of palm, radicchio, and asparagus with 2 Tbs. of the olive oil, ¼ tsp. salt, and several grinds of pepper. Grill, flipping as needed, until nicely marked all over and tender, 4 to 5 minutes total. Set aside until cool enough to handle.

3. Meanwhile, in a small bowl, whisk the remaining 2 Tbs. olive oil with the lemon juice, zest, sugar, the remaining ¼ tsp. salt, and a pinch of pepper.

4. Core the radicchio. Cut the radicchio, asparagus, and hearts of palm into pieces about 3 inches long by ½ inch wide. Return to the large bowl and toss with the prosciutto, Parmigiano, and 2 Tbs. of the vinaigrette. Serve drizzled with the remaining vinaigrette, if desired.
—*Allison Ehri Kreitler*

PER SERVING: 190 CALORIES | 7G PROTEIN | 7G CARB | 16G TOTAL FAT | 3G SAT FAT | 10G MONO FAT | 1.5G POLY FAT | 10MG CHOL | 800MG SODIUM | 3G FIBER

minty quinoa tabbouleh

1½ cups quinoa

    Kosher salt

1½ cups seeded and finely
    diced tomato (from about
    1 large tomato)

1 cup finely chopped fresh
    flat-leaf parsley (from
    about 2 bunches)

1 cup peeled, seeded,
    finely diced cucumber
    (from about ¾ of a large
    cucumber)

½ cup thinly sliced scallion
    greens

½ cup extra-virgin olive oil;
    more as needed

6 Tbs. fresh lemon juice;
    more as needed

¼ tsp. ground cumin

⅛ tsp. ground cinnamon

½ cup finely chopped fresh
    mint

Tabbouleh, a lemony Middle Eastern parsley and grain salad, is traditionally made with bulgur wheat. This version, fragrant from a touch of cumin and cinnamon, uses quinoa instead.

1. Rinse the quinoa well in a bowl of cool water and drain. Bring the quinoa, ½ tsp. salt, and 3 cups water to a boil in a medium saucepan over high heat. Cover, reduce the heat to medium low, and simmer until the water is absorbed and the quinoa is translucent and tender, 10 to 15 minutes. (The outer germ rings of the grain will remain chewy and white. Some germ rings may separate from the grains and will look like white squiggles.) Immediately fluff the quinoa with a fork and spread on a baking sheet to cool.

2. When cool, fluff the quinoa again and transfer to a large bowl. Add the tomato, parsley, cucumber, scallions, oil, lemon juice, cumin, cinnamon, and 1 tsp. salt. Toss well. Cover and refrigerate to let the flavors mingle, at least 2 hours or overnight.

3. Before serving, let sit at room temperature for 20 to 30 minutes. Stir in the mint. Taste and add more oil and lemon juice (you'll probably need at least 1 Tbs. of each), and more salt as needed.
—*Jennifer Armentrout*

PER SERVING: 130 CALORIES | 3G PROTEIN | 13G CARB | 8G TOTAL FAT | 1G SAT FAT | 6G MONO FAT | 1G POLY FAT | 0MG CHOL | 110MG SODIUM | 2G FIBER

sautéed spinach with golden raisins, pine nuts & fresh breadcrumbs

SERVES 4

¼ cup golden raisins

¼ cup pine nuts, toasted

¼ cup olive oil

½ cup fresh, coarse breadcrumbs

1 large clove garlic, minced

Kosher salt

1 bunch spinach (about 1 lb.), trimmed

This spinach side mixes the sweetness of raisins with savory garlic breadcrumbs. Making fresh breadcrumbs is simple. Use stale bread or toast fresh bread in a 300°F oven for a few minutes until crisp, and then pulse in a food processor until the bread is the size of peas.

In a large (12-inch) skillet over medium heat, heat the raisins and pine nuts in 2 Tbs. oil for about 1 minute. With a slotted spoon, transfer the raisins and pine nuts to a plate. Add the breadcrumbs and garlic to the pan, and sprinkle with ¼ tsp. salt. Cook over medium-low heat until slightly brown, 5 to 7 minutes. Transfer to a plate. Put the remaining 2 Tbs. oil in the pan with the spinach, and cook until the spinach just wilts. Transfer to a serving platter, toss with the raisins and pine nuts, top with breadcrumbs, and serve. —*Tony Rosenfeld*

italian green beans with tomatoes and balsamic vinegar

Kosher salt and freshly ground black pepper

¾ **lb. haricots verts, trimmed**

2 **Tbs. olive oil**

2 **medium cloves garlic, smashed and peeled**

2 **large plum tomatoes, coarsely chopped and puréed in a food processor**

1 **Tbs. balsamic vinegar**

Shavings of Parmigiano-Reggiano, for garnish (optional)

This is a speedy version of slow-cooked Italian green beans, elegant in its simplicity. Sauté the haricots verts quickly to preserve their delicate texture, then toss them with a sauce of plum tomatoes and balsamic vinegar.

1. Bring a pot of well-salted water to a boil. Add the beans and cook until bright green and just tender, 3 to 4 minutes. Drain and immediately plunge in a large bowl of ice water. Let cool for 3 to 4 minutes. Drain and set aside.

2. Heat the oil in a large (12-inch) skillet over medium heat. Add the garlic and cook for about 1 minute. Add the tomatoes and vinegar, sprinkle with ½ tsp. each salt and pepper, and cook, stirring until the mixture reduces by half, about 2 minutes. Add the beans to the pan and cook until warmed through and coated with the tomato mixture, about 1 minute. Taste the beans and season with salt and pepper if needed; garnish with shavings of Parmigiano, if desired. Serve immediately. —*Tony Rosenfeld*

roasted asparagus with buttery breadcrumbs

SERVES 4

2 oz. day-old bread, crust removed, or four ½-inch-thick baguette slices

1½ Tbs. unsalted butter

¼ tsp. chopped fresh thyme leaves

Kosher salt

1½ lb. asparagus, trimmed

1 Tbs. extra-virgin olive oil

1½ tsp. fresh lemon juice

> Roasting, which works best with thin asparagus, amps up the taste, because none of the flavor is lost to boiling water.

For the crumbs, choose a baguette or country-style loaf. The two-step method for breadcrumbs—they're baked, then sautéed—results in a more consistent texture.

1. Position a rack in the center of the oven and heat the oven to 250°F. Put the bread in a food processor and pulse until coarse crumbs form. Spread the crumbs on a rimmed baking sheet; bake until they're dry and lightly crisped, about 20 minutes. Let cool and then grind again in the processor to get a scant ¼ cup fine crumbs.

2. Melt the butter in a skillet over moderately low heat. Add the bread-crumbs and thyme. Cook slowly, stirring often, until the crumbs are a uniform deep golden brown, about 18 minutes. Season with ⅛ tsp. salt and set aside to let cool. The crumbs will crisp as they cool.

3. Raise the oven temperature to 450°F. Put the asparagus on a baking sheet in a single layer and drizzle with the olive oil. Using your hands, toss the spears to coat evenly with the oil. Season with ½ tsp. salt. Roast until the spears are tender and lightly blistered, 12 to 14 minutes for medium spears. Transfer them to a platter or individual plates, sprinkle with the lemon juice, and top with the breadcrumbs. Serve immediately. —*Janet Fletcher*

PER SERVING: 150 CALORIES | 5G PROTEIN | 15G CARB | 8G TOTAL FAT | 3G SAT FAT | 4G MONO FAT | 1G POLY FAT | 10MG CHOL | 370MG SODIUM | 4G FIBER

risotto with peas, mint & lemon

SERVES 4

5 to 6 cups vegetable broth

4 Tbs. unsalted butter

1 medium onion, cut into ¼-inch dice

Kosher salt

2 cups arborio rice (or other risotto rice)

½ cup dry white wine (like Pinot Grigio)

2 cups frozen peas

⅓ cup chopped fresh mint

2 Tbs. fresh lemon juice

1 Tbs. finely grated lemon zest

¼ cup freshly grated Parmigiano-Reggiano; more for serving

> The key to risotto is adding hot broth incrementally. This slowly draws starch from the rice and gives you the creamiest texture.

Chop mint with your sharpest knife to avoid bruising, which causes it to turn black.

1. Heat the broth in a saucepan over medium-high heat until very hot and then reduce the heat to keep the broth hot. In another wide, heavy saucepan, melt 2 Tbs. of the butter over medium heat. Add the onion and a generous pinch of salt and sauté, stirring occasionally with a wooden spoon, until the onion softens and starts to turn lightly golden, 3 to 5 minutes. Add the rice and stir until the grains are well coated with butter and the edges become translucent, 1 to 2 minutes. Pour in the wine and stir until it's absorbed, about 1 minute. Add another generous pinch of salt and ladle enough of the hot broth into the pan to barely cover the rice, about 1 cup. Bring to a boil and then adjust the heat to maintain a lively simmer. Cook, stirring occasionally, until the broth has been mostly absorbed, 2 to 3 minutes.

2. Continue adding broth in ½-cup increments, stirring and simmering until it has been absorbed each time, at intervals of 2 to 3 minutes.

3. After about 16 to 18 minutes, the rice should be creamy but still fairly firm. At this point, add the peas and another ½ cup broth. Continue to simmer and stir until the peas are just cooked and the rice is just tender to the tooth, another 3 to 4 minutes. Stir in another splash of broth if the risotto is too thick. Remove the pot from the heat and stir in the mint, lemon juice, lemon zest, the remaining 2 Tbs. butter, and the Parmigiano. Season with salt to taste. Serve the risotto immediately with a sprinkling of Parmigiano. *—Tasha DeSerio*

PER SERVING: 270 CALORIES | 9G PROTEIN | 31G CARB | 10G TOTAL FAT | 6G SAT FAT | 3G MONO FAT | 1G POLY FAT | 25MG CHOL | 520MG SODIUM | 3G FIBER

sautéed escarole with raisins, pine nuts & capers

SERVES 4

Kosher salt

2 lb. escarole (about 2 heads), trimmed, rinsed, and cut into roughly 2-inch pieces

2 Tbs. extra-virgin olive oil

3 large cloves garlic, smashed and peeled

2 Tbs. pine nuts

2 Tbs. raisins

1 Tbs. capers, rinsed

Pinch of crushed red pepper flakes

1 tsp. fresh lemon juice

You can blanch the escarole up to 1 hour ahead. Wait until just before serving to add the lemon juice, though, as the acid in the juice will dull the escarole's color if it sits too long.

1. Bring a large pot of well-salted water to a boil over high heat. Add the escarole and cook until the stem pieces start to soften, about 2 minutes (the water needn't return to a boil). Drain, run under cold water to cool, and drain again.

2. In a 12-inch skillet, heat the olive oil and garlic over medium heat, stirring occasionally, until the garlic browns lightly, 2 to 3 minutes. Remove the garlic with tongs and discard. Add the pine nuts, raisins, capers, and red pepper flakes and cook, stirring, until the pine nuts are golden and the raisins puff, about 1 minute. Add the escarole, increase the heat to medium high, and cook, tossing often, until heated through and tender, 3 to 4 minutes. Sprinkle with the lemon juice and season to taste with salt. —*Jennifer Armentrout*

PER SERVING: 140 CALORIES | 3G PROTEIN | 11G CARB | 10G TOTAL FAT | 1G SAT FAT | 6G MONO FAT | 2.5G POLY FAT | 0MG CHOL | 530MG SODIUM | 6G FIBER

More about Escarole

Escarole goes by a few aliases, including Batavian endive, common chicory, and broad chicory. Whatever you call it, escarole is a bitter leafy green that's closely related to frisée, radicchio, curly endive, and Belgian endive. It grows into an open, somewhat flat head of broad, crumpled-looking, light to dark green leaves with wide, fleshy stems.

Escarole's bitterness is relatively mild, and you can eat it raw or cooked. Raw escarole has a crisp texture and a slightly sweet flavor that tempers the bitterness, making it a perfect choice for spring salads. It's especially delicious paired with apples, pears, cheeses (blue or goat), olives, and nuts. Once cooked, escarole develops a tender, melting texture, and its bitterness becomes a little more pronounced. It's great in soups or sautéed with other strong flavors, like capers and garlic, as a side dish. Escarole and white beans is a classic pairing.

Buying and storing

Choose escarole with fresh-looking leaves. Avoid any with tough-looking outer leaves and browning around the tops. Store escarole in a plastic bag in your refrigerator's crisper bin for up to 3 days.

Cooking

To use escarole in a soup, simply chop it up, stems and all, and add it to the soup in the last 15 or 20 minutes of cooking—enough time to become very tender. If you're planning to sauté escarole, blanch it in boiling water for a couple of minutes first, which will give it a succulent texture and a bright green color.

potato and butternut squash gratin with corn and bacon

SERVES 6

- **1** Tbs. plus ½ tsp. unsalted butter
- **4** slices bacon
- **1½** cups fresh breadcrumbs
- **½** cup plus 2 Tbs. finely grated Parmigiano-Reggiano
- **1** Tbs. extra-virgin olive oil
- **1½** tsp. chopped fresh thyme leaves

  Kosher salt and freshly ground black pepper
- **1** large or 2 medium leeks (white and light green parts only), halved and sliced ¼ inch thick
- **2** tsp. minced fresh garlic
- **1¾** to 2 cups fresh corn kernels (from 3 to 4 large ears)
- **⅔** cup heavy cream
- **¾** cup lower-salt chicken broth
- **½** tsp. finely grated lemon zest
- **¾** lb. peeled, seeded butternut squash, cut into ½-inch dice (about 2½ cups)
- **½** lb. Yukon Gold potatoes, cut into ⅓-inch dice (about 1½ cups)

You can make this a day ahead, if you like; the flavors will develop even more overnight. Reheat at 375°F, covered, for 20 minutes.

1. Position a rack in the center of the oven and heat the oven to 400°F. Rub a 2-quart shallow gratin dish with ½ tsp. of the butter.

2. In a 12-inch nonstick skillet over medium heat, cook the bacon until crisp, about 8 minutes. Transfer the bacon to paper towels. Reserve 2 Tbs. of the fat in the skillet; discard the remainder. When the bacon is cool, crumble or mince it.

3. In a small bowl, combine 1 Tbs. of the crumbled bacon with the breadcrumbs, 2 Tbs. of the Parmigiano, the olive oil, ½ tsp. of the thyme, and a large pinch of salt. Mix well.

4. Add the remaining 1 Tbs. butter to the skillet with the bacon fat and melt over medium heat. Add the leeks and a pinch of salt, and cook, stirring, until softened and just starting to turn golden, 6 to 7 minutes. Add the garlic and stir well. Add the corn, ¼ tsp. salt, and a few grinds of pepper. Cook, stirring, until the corn has lost its raw look and is slightly shrunken, 2 to 3 minutes. Let cool slightly.

5. Combine the cream and chicken broth in a 2-cup liquid measure. Add the lemon zest, ½ tsp. salt, and a few grinds of pepper. Stir to mix well.

6. In a large bowl, combine the remaining bacon, the corn-leek mixture, diced squash, potatoes, and the remaining 1 tsp. thyme. Toss lightly to combine. Spread the mixture evenly in the gratin dish. Sprinkle the remaining ½ cup Parmigiano on top. Stir the cream mixture one more time and pour it over everything as evenly as possible. (Be sure to scrape out any seasonings left in the cup.) Press down on the vegetables with a spatula so that the liquid surrounds them and everything is evenly distributed. Sprinkle the breadcrumb mixture evenly over all.

7. Cover with foil and bake for 20 minutes. Remove the foil and continue to bake until the crumb topping is deeply golden and the squash and potatoes are tender when pierced with a fork, about 25 minutes. The liquid should have bubbled below the surface of the vegetables, leaving browned bits around the edge of the pan. Let cool for 20 to 25 minutes before serving. —*Susie Middleton*

PER SERVING: 350 CALORIES | 8G PROTEIN | 32G CARB | 23G TOTAL FAT | 11G SAT FAT | 8G MONO FAT | 2G POLY FAT | 55MG CHOL | 390MG SODIUM | 4G FIBER

smashed fingerling potatoes with red-wine vinegar and chives

SERVES 6

- **2 lb. fingerling potatoes, cut into 1-inch pieces**

  Kosher salt and freshly ground black pepper

- **2 Tbs. red-wine vinegar**

- **⅓ cup extra-virgin olive oil**

- **½ cup thinly sliced fresh chives**

This dish—a cross between mashed potatoes and a warm potato salad—is proof that fingerling potatoes need little adornment. Good olive oil, red-wine vinegar, and thinly sliced chives do the trick. As with German potato salads, the potatoes are tossed with the vinegar while they're still hot so that they absorb the tangy flavor.

Put the potatoes in a medium pot, cover with cold water by a couple of inches, stir in 1 Tbs. salt, and bring to a boil. Reduce to a simmer, cover, and cook until the potatoes are completely tender when pierced with a fork, 10 to 15 minutes. Drain well and transfer to a large mixing bowl. Drizzle with the vinegar and add 1 tsp. pepper; gently smash (not quite mashing) and toss the potatoes with a large fork. Once the potatoes have absorbed all of the vinegar, drizzle the oil over the potatoes and gently smash and toss the potatoes again so that they absorb all of the oil. Fold in the chives, taste, and season with salt and pepper if needed. —*Tony Rosenfeld*

wheat berry salad with green beans and corn

SERVES 8 TO 10

2¼ cups wheat berries

    Kosher salt and freshly ground black pepper

½ cup plus 1 Tbs. extra-virgin olive oil; more as needed

⅓ cup sherry vinegar; more as needed

2 Tbs. roasted walnut oil

1 cup cut green beans (1-inch pieces), steamed until crisp-tender

1 cup fresh corn kernels, blanched or frozen corn kernels, thawed

1 cup diced roasted golden beets (roast until tender, peel, and cut into ½-inch dice)

1 cup crumbled blue cheese

¼ cup thinly sliced fresh chives

This hearty salad is perfect summer-picnic fare: chewy wheat berries, crisp-tender corn and green beans, sweet golden beets, and pungent blue cheese crumbles.

1. Fill a large bowl with cold water, add the wheat berries, and let soak for 10 to 18 hours. Drain. Bring 7 cups of water to a boil in a 4-quart pot over high heat. Add ¾ tsp. salt. Add the wheat berries, reduce the heat to a simmer, and cook, uncovered until tender, 1 to 1½ hours. Stir occasionally and add more boiling water as necessary to keep the wheat berries covered. Drain and rinse the wheat berries with cold water to stop the cooking.

2. Transfer the wheat berries to a foil-lined rimmed baking sheet, drizzle with 1 Tbs. of the olive oil, and toss lightly to coat. Spread the wheat berries on the baking sheet and cool completely at room temperature or in the refrigerator.

3. Put the vinegar in a small bowl and gradually whisk in the remaining ½ cup of olive oil. Whisk in the walnut oil. Taste and season with salt, pepper, and additional vinegar or olive oil as needed.

4. Put the cooked and cooled wheat berries in a large serving bowl and toss to break up any clumps. Add the green beans, corn, beets, blue cheese, chives, and ½ cup vinaigrette and toss. Taste and season as needed with more vinaigrette, salt, and pepper; serve. *–Joanne Weir*

PER SERVING: 340 CALORIES | 8G PROTEIN | 37G CARB | 20G TOTAL FAT | 4.5G SAT FAT | 11G MONO FAT | 4G POLY FAT | 10MG CHOL | 490MG SODIUM | 5G FIBER

Make Ahead

The salad can be refrigerated for up to 1 day. If making ahead, let sit at room temperature so it's not refrigerator-cold and season with more vinaigrette, salt, and pepper before serving.

stir-fried green beans with ginger and black bean sauce

SERVES 4

- **1** Tbs. low-sodium soy sauce
- **2** Tbs. Chinese black bean sauce (like Lee Kum Kee®)
- **1** Tbs. rice vinegar
- **2** tsp. Asian sesame oil
- **1** tsp. granulated sugar
- **3** Tbs. canola oil
- **1** lb. haricots verts, trimmed
- **¼** tsp. kosher salt
- **2** Tbs. minced fresh ginger
- **1** medium clove garlic, minced

Though delicate haricots verts are traditionally saved for fancy French preparations, they're also perfect for a quick stir-fry. Jarred black bean sauce serves as a light base for the sauce, while minced ginger and garlic impart a heady punch.

1. In a small bowl, mix the soy sauce, black bean sauce, vinegar, sesame oil, and sugar; set aside.

2. Heat the canola oil in a large (12-inch) straight-sided sauté pan over medium-high heat until shimmering. Add the beans, sprinkle with salt, and cook, tossing occasionally, until most of the beans are browned, shrunken, and tender, 8 to 10 minutes. Reduce the heat to low and add the ginger and garlic; cook for about 45 seconds.

3. Add the soy sauce mixture to the pan, cook for another 30 seconds, until the beans are coated and the sauce is warmed through, and serve.
—*Tony Rosenfeld*

More about Ginger

Though referred to as a root, ginger is a rhizome of a tropical plant. Fresh ginger's tangy freshness, light spiciness, and mellow sweetness complement a range of dishes.

Choosing

Ginger's aroma, texture, and flavor vary depending upon the timing of its harvest. Early-harvest or young ginger (harvested after 6 months) is tender and sweet, while older, more mature ginger (harvested between 10 and 12 months) is more fibrous and spicy. Mature ginger is usually all that's available in American supermarkets, but young ginger can often be found in Asian markets. It's easily identified by its thin, papery skin, which can be left on, and pink-tinged tips. Look for ginger with skin (the thinner the better) that's smooth, unblemished, and almost translucent. When you break off the piece you want, the interior should be firm, crisp, and not overly fibrous (making it easier to slice). It should have a fresh, spicy fragrance.

Prepping

Fresh ginger should almost always be peeled. Try using the edge of a metal spoon to scrape off the skin. It takes a bit more effort than using a paring knife or a peeler, but it's less wasteful—and it lets you maneuver around the knobs and gnarls.

Ginger can be sliced into matchsticks, chopped, grated, puréed, and minced. Ginger's flavor fades as it cooks, so add ginger at the end of cooking for the most gingery oomph.

Storing

Refrigerate peeled fresh ginger in a zip-top bag in the vegetable crisper drawer and it will keep for weeks. Dried and crystallized ginger may be kept at room temperature.

raspberry and
blackberry mousse
(recipe on p. 214)

desserts

gingered lemon bars

MAKES SIXTEEN 2-INCH BARS

5 oz. (1 cup plus 2 Tbs.) unbleached all-purpose flour; more as needed

6¼ oz. (1¾ cups plus 1 tsp.) confectioners' sugar

1 Tbs. lightly packed finely grated lemon zest

½ tsp. plus a tiny pinch of ground ginger

Table salt

4 oz. (½ cup) chilled unsalted butter, cut into small pieces; more for the pan

½ tsp. baking powder

3 large eggs, at room temperature

6 Tbs. fresh lemon juice

If you're not a ginger lover, feel free to leave it out of this recipe— you'll still get a luscious, tart, tangy, and sweet lemon bar. To cut the neatest squares, use a flat metal spatula or a bench scraper and cut straight down.

1. Position a rack in the center of the oven and heat the oven to 350°F. Butter an 8-inch-square baking pan.

2. In a medium bowl, whisk 1 cup (4½ oz.) of the flour with ¼ cup of the confectioners' sugar, the lemon zest, ½ tsp. of the ginger, and a pinch of salt. Cut in the butter with a pastry blender or 2 table knives until the mixture resembles small peas. Knead the dough in the bowl just until it begins to come together. Transfer the dough to the baking pan and, with floured hands, press it evenly over the bottom. Bake until very light golden brown, about 20 minutes. Let cool on a rack while you make the filling.

3. In a small bowl, whisk 1½ cups of the confectioners' sugar, the remaining 2 Tbs. (½ oz.) flour, the baking powder, and a pinch of salt. In a medium bowl, beat the eggs with an electric mixer on high speed until tripled in volume, pale yellow, and very light and fluffy, 3 to 5 minutes (the eggs will hold soft peaks very briefly). Reduce the speed to low, add the sugar and flour mixture, and beat just until blended, scraping the bowl as needed. Add the lemon juice and beat just until blended. Pour the lemon mixture over the warm crust.

4. Bake until the filling is just set in the center, is golden brown on top, and doesn't jiggle when the pan is nudged, 18 to 20 minutes. Let cool completely in the pan on a rack.

5. Just before serving, stir the remaining 1 tsp. confectioners' sugar with the pinch of ginger in a small bowl. Transfer to a small sieve and sift over the lemon filling. Using a bench scraper or a metal spatula, cut into 2-inch squares, slicing straight down (rather than dragging). Store in an airtight container. *—Lori Longbotham*

PER SERVING: 140 CALORIES | 2G PROTEIN | 18G CARB | 7G TOTAL FAT | 4G SAT FAT | 2G MONO FAT | 0G POLY FAT | 55MG CHOL | 45MG SODIUM | 0G FIBER

chocolate-dipped strawberries

MAKES 12 STRAWBERRIES

- 3 oz. bittersweet chocolate, chopped into almond-size pieces
- 2 tsp. grapeseed or canola oil
- 12 medium strawberries (about 1 pint) preferably with stems, rinsed and dried

The secrets to perfection: Use the best strawberries and chocolate you can, and be sure your strawberries are bone-dry before you dip them into the melted chocolate or the chocolate will seize into a mass.

1. Melt the chocolate with the oil in a small, deep heatproof bowl set in a skillet holding about 1 inch of barely simmering water, whisking occasionally, until smooth. Remove the bowl from the heat.

2. Line a small rimmed baking sheet with waxed paper. Tilt the bowl to pool the chocolate on one side. Dip each strawberry into the chocolate to cover about two-thirds of the berry, or until the chocolate reaches the strawberry's shoulders. Turn the berry to coat it evenly, lift it out of the chocolate, and gently shake off any excess. Carefully lay it on the waxed paper. If the dipping chocolate begins to cool and thicken, return the bowl to the water bath to heat it briefly.

3. Let the strawberries stand at room temperature for 15 minutes and then refrigerate until the chocolate is set, 20 minutes. Carefully remove the berries from the waxed paper. Serve immediately or refrigerate for up to 8 hours before serving. —*Lori Longbotham*

PER SERVING: 105 CALORIES | 1G PROTEIN | 12G CARB | 6G TOTAL FAT | 3G SAT FAT | 2G MONO FAT | 1G POLY FAT | 0MG CHOL | 14MG SODIUM | 3G FIBER

Handling and Storing Strawberries

Strawberries are delicate, so handle them as little as possible to prevent bruising. When you bring them home, carefully sort out any that are mushy, moldy, or discolored. One bad berry can spoil the whole bowl. Spread the berries in a single layer on a baking sheet or shallow baking dish lined with paper towels. Stored in the refrigerator, they can keep for up to 3 days, but the sooner you eat them, the better. Don't wash them until you're ready to use them and then be very gentle and use as little water as possible. If your recipe calls for hulling the berries, don't do that until after you've washed and dried them.

upside-down apricot cake

SERVES 8 TO 10

FOR THE CARAMEL

½ cup granulated sugar

FOR THE CAKE

4 medium ripe apricots, pitted and cut into 4 wedges each

9 oz. (2 cups) unbleached all-purpose flour

1½ tsp. baking powder

¼ tsp. ground cinnamon

Table salt

4 oz. (½ cup) unsalted butter, at room temperature

1 cup granulated sugar

½ tsp. pure vanilla extract

2 large eggs

¾ cup milk

The light spice cake is the perfect base to soak up the juiciness of the fruit. It also provides a slightly savory contrast to the fruit's sweetness.

Position a rack in the center of the oven and heat the oven to 350°F. Lightly butter the sides of a 9-inch-square cake pan.

MAKE THE CARAMEL

In a small, heavy-based saucepan or skillet, combine the sugar and 3 Tbs. water. Set over medium heat, stirring frequently to help dissolve the sugar. Once the sugar boils, stop stirring. Increase the heat to high and cook until the liquid is deep amber. Immediately pour the caramel into the cake pan and swirl to cover the bottom evenly. Set aside to cool.

MAKE THE CAKE

1. Arrange the apricot wedges over the caramel and set the pan aside. In a medium bowl, whisk the flour, baking powder, cinnamon, and ¼ tsp. salt until blended. In another bowl, beat the butter, sugar, and vanilla with an electric mixer until well blended, about 3 minutes. Add the eggs one at a time and beat until just incorporated. Using a wide rubber spatula, fold the flour mixture and the milk alternately into the butter mixture, beginning and ending with the flour. Spoon large dollops of batter evenly into the cake pan, taking care not to disturb the fruit. Tap the pan gently on the counter to release air bubbles.

2. Bake until lightly browned and a pick comes out clean, 50 to 55 minutes. Working quickly (while the caramel is still hot), run a knife around the edge of the cake. Set a serving plate or a small cutting board on top of the pan and invert it (be careful—it's hot). Let the cake rest, upside down, for 5 minutes before removing the pan so the fruit and caramel will settle. Serve slightly warm or at room temperature.

—Abigail Johnson Dodge

PER SERVING: 320 CALORIES | 5G PROTEIN | 52G CARB | 11G TOTAL FAT | 6G SAT FAT | 3G MONO FAT | 1G POLY FAT | 70MG CHOL | 115MG SODIUM | 1G FIBER

More about Apricots

Ripeness cues can vary slightly between varieties, but you'll know a ripe, juicy apricot by its fruity fragrance and deep, uniform golden color, especially right around the stem, the portion that's the last to ripen. Hold the fruit in your hand and press it gently on its shoulders; the fruit should give slightly.

Ripen apricots in a paper bag at room temperature for up to 5 days. Like other stone fruit, once ripe, they can be stored in the refrigerator (which slows the ripening process) if you need to buy yourself some time.

balsamic-macerated strawberries with basil

SERVES 4

- 2 lb. strawberries, rinsed, hulled, and sliced ⅛ to ¼ inch thick (about 4 cups)
- 1 Tbs. granulated sugar
- 2 tsp. balsamic vinegar
- 8 to 10 medium fresh basil leaves

  Pound cake (optional)

  Sweetened whipped cream (optional)

For this recipe, there's no need for an expensive, artisanal balsamic vinegar—a grocery-store vinegar is perfectly well suited. The acid softens the fruit, draws out moisture, and brightens the berry flavor.

1. In a large bowl, gently toss the strawberries with the sugar and vinegar. Let sit at room temperature until the strawberries have released their juices but are not yet mushy, about 30 minutes. (Don't let the berries sit for more than 90 minutes or they'll start to collapse.)

2. Just before serving, stack the basil leaves on a cutting board and roll them vertically into a loose cigar shape. Using a sharp chef's knife, very thinly slice across the roll to make a fine chiffonade of basil.

3. Portion the strawberries and their juices among 4 small bowls and scatter with the basil to garnish, or spoon over pound cake and top with whipped cream. —*Sarah Breckenridge*

PER SERVING: 40 CALORIES | 1G PROTEIN | 10G CARB | 0G TOTAL FAT | 0G SAT FAT | 0G MONO FAT | 0G POLY FAT | 0MG CHOL | 0MG SODIUM | 2G FIBER

chocolate bark with ginger and pistachios

SERVES 4

6 oz. bittersweet dark chocolate (70% to 72% cacao), chopped (1 cup)

2 oz. white chocolate, chopped (⅓ cup; optional)

3 Tbs. chopped salted pistachios

3 Tbs. chopped dried apricots

2 Tbs. chopped crystallized ginger

With a cup of coffee or tea, this is a quick and sweet end to dinner.

1. In a small bowl, melt the dark chocolate in the microwave on high for 1 to 2 minutes. Stir until smooth.

2. Line a baking sheet with a silicone baking mat or waxed paper. Spread the melted dark chocolate into an approximately 5x8-inch rectangle.

3. If using the white chocolate, melt it in the same manner as the dark chocolate and drizzle it in a zigzag pattern across the dark chocolate.

4. Sprinkle with the chopped pistachios, apricots, and ginger and press gently to set them into the chocolate. Chill in the refrigerator for 10 minutes. Break into pieces and serve. Store any leftovers in the refrigerator. —*Mark Scarborough* and *Bruce Weinstein*

PER SERVING: 380 CALORIES | 6G PROTEIN | 45G CARB | 19G TOTAL FAT | 11G SAT FAT | 7G MONO FAT | 1G POLY FAT | 0MG CHOL | 80MG SODIUM | 6G FIBER

grilled cinnamon-sugar bananas with vanilla ice cream and bourbon

SERVES 6 TO 8

Vegetable oil for the grill

4   bananas, ripe but not overly soft

1   Tbs. granulated sugar

1   tsp. ground cinnamon

1   pint vanilla ice cream

½   to ¾ cup pecan pieces, toasted

2   Tbs. bourbon, such as Maker's Mark or Woodford Reserve®

This dessert is reminiscent of a grilled bananas Foster. The secret to grilling bananas is leaving them in their skin to hold them together and protect them from the flame. The bonus is that you know that your bananas are done when the skin starts to separate from the flesh.

1. Prepare a medium charcoal or gas grill fire. Brush the grill grate clean.

2. Slice the bananas, still in their skin, in half lengthwise and then crosswise so that each banana yields 4 pieces. In a small bowl, mix the sugar and cinnamon. Lightly sprinkle the cut sides of the bananas with some of the cinnamon sugar (you may not need it all). Let sit for 5 minutes so the sugar starts to dissolve.

3. Put the bananas, cut side down, on the grate and cover the grill. Grill until marks appear, 2 to 3 minutes. Using tongs, flip the bananas, cover the grill, and cook until the skin starts to pull away from the banana, about another 5 minutes. Remove from the grill and let cool for 2 to 3 minutes. Peel and serve the bananas on top of vanilla ice cream, sprinkled with the pecan pieces and drizzled with bourbon.

—Elizabeth Karmel

blackberry-apple turnovers

MAKES 12 TURNOVERS

FOR THE DOUGH

- **11¼ oz. (2½ cups) unbleached all-purpose flour; more for rolling**
- **2 Tbs. granulated sugar**
- **½ tsp. kosher salt**
- **6 oz. (¾ cup) cold unsalted butter, cut into 12 pieces**
- **6 oz. cold cream cheese, cut into 6 pieces**
- **½ cup heavy cream**

FOR THE FILLING

- **6 oz. (1¼ cups) blackberries, halved**
- **1 large Pink Lady apple, peeled, cored, and cut into ¼-inch dice**
- **½ cup light brown sugar**
- **1 Tbs. unbleached all-purpose flour**
- **½ tsp. ground allspice**
- **¼ tsp. kosher salt**

FOR ASSEMBLY

- **1 large egg yolk**
- **Granulated sugar**

With a dense crispness and a high sugar-to-acid ratio, Pink Lady apples are ideal for these pies. Even when tender, they hold their shape and retain some firmness, for a nice contrast to the juicy, collapsed berries.

MAKE THE DOUGH

1. Put the flour, sugar, and salt in a food processor. Add the butter and cream cheese and pulse until the mixture resembles coarse meal, 8 to 10 pulses. Add the cream and pulse, pausing to scrape the bowl once or twice, just until the dough starts to come together, 8 to 10 pulses more. Do not overprocess. Turn the dough out onto a clean work surface, gather it together, and pat it into a rectangle. Wrap it in plastic and refrigerate for at least 2 hours and up to 3 days.

2. When ready to bake, position racks in the bottom and top thirds of the oven and heat the oven to 400°F. Line 2 large rimmed baking sheets with parchment.

3. On a lightly floured surface with a lightly floured rolling pin, roll the dough into a 13x18-inch rectangle. Be sure to loosen the dough several times and reflour underneath so it doesn't stick. Trim the edges straight to form a 12x16-inch rectangle, then cut the dough into twelve 4-inch squares. Put 6 squares on each baking sheet.

MAKE THE FILLING

In a medium bowl, lightly toss the blackberries, apple, brown sugar, flour, allspice, and salt until combined.

ASSEMBLE AND BAKE THE TURNOVERS

1. In a small bowl, beat the egg yolk with 1 tsp. water. Brush the outer edges of each dough square with egg wash. Spoon 2 rounded Tbs. of the filling into the center of each square. Bring the points together into a triangular shape, pressing to seal the edges. Lightly brush the top of each turnover with egg wash and sprinkle with a scant ½ tsp. granulated sugar. With the tip of a paring knife, cut a steam vent in the center of the top crust of each turnover.

2. Bake until the turnovers are browned and the filling is bubbling, 25 to 30 minutes, swapping and rotating the baking sheets' positions about halfway through baking. (Don't worry if juice leaks out.)

3. Transfer the baking sheets to racks and allow to cool for 5 minutes. Then loosen the turnovers with an offset spatula and cool completely on the sheets. The turnovers are best the day they're made.
—*Karen Barker*

PER SERVING: 350 CALORIES | 4G PROTEIN | 38G CARB | 21G TOTAL FAT | 13G SAT FAT | 5G MONO FAT | 1G POLY FAT | 75MG CHOL | 125MG SODIUM | 2G FIBER

More about Blackberries

Blackberries are "aggregate" fruits, meaning that one berry is not one fruit, but rather a cluster of small fruits called drupes. When ripe, their skin is delicate, shiny, and black (if they are reddish, they are not ripe yet), and unlike raspberries, which are hollow in the center, blackberries have a tiny white core. At the market, look for berries without stems, because stems indicate that they were picked before ripening, and they do not get sweeter off the bush.

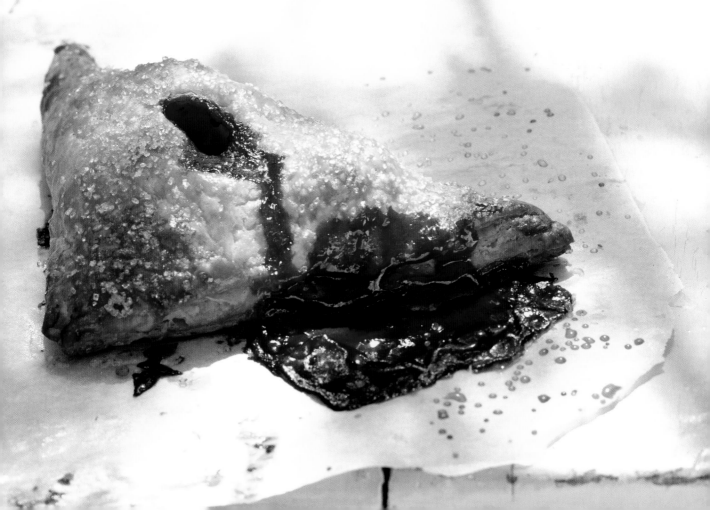

minty melon granita

SERVES 4 TO 6

1 **cup granulated sugar**

1 **small ripe melon (4 lb.)**

2 **Tbs. finely chopped fresh mint**

1 **Tbs. fresh lime juice**

If you don't have limes on hand, feel free to substitute fresh lemon juice.

1. Arrange a 9x13-inch baking dish or 9½-cup rectangular plastic container in the freezer, making sure it's level and secure.

2. Put the sugar and 1 cup water in a medium saucepan. Cook, stirring, over medium heat until the sugar is dissolved, about 3 minutes. Set aside to cool completely or refrigerate for up to 1 day. For faster cooling, set the bowl over a bowl filled with ice and stir occasionally until well chilled.

3. Halve the melon, scoop out the seeds, and cut the flesh into 1- to 2-inch chunks. Pile the melon into a food processor and process until smooth, about 1 minute. Add 2½ cups of the fruit purée to the sugar syrup, along with the mint and lime juice, and stir until blended. Pour the chilled mixture into the baking dish and freeze for about 2 hours. After that, every 30 minutes, stir, smash, and scrape the mixture with a table fork until the ice crystals are loose and frozen.
—*Abigail Johnson Dodge*

> **Store mint bunches with the cut stems in a glass of water and cover the leaves with a plastic bag. Refrigerate, changing the water every couple of days. The mint should stay fresh for at least a week.**

blackberry summer pudding

About ½ loaf firm, white bread, such as Pepperidge Farm® or challah

1 cup granulated sugar

6 cups blackberries

¼ cup Grand Marnier® or strained freshly squeezed orange juice

Whipped cream

Make this homey dessert the day before you want to serve it so the ingredients come together properly. You can also make this pudding with a mélange of summer berries and other soft fruits, such as red or black currants.

1. Line the bottom and sides of a 5- to 6-cup deep bowl or mold with plastic wrap, allowing enough excess wrap so it will cover the top of the container completely. Remove the crusts from the bread, trimming as many slices as needed to line the bottom and sides of the bowl completely. Cut and place the bread so there are no gaps between the pieces.

2. Place the sugar and ½ cup water in a heavy saucepan and cook over medium heat until the sugar is completely dissolved, about 3 minutes. Add 5 cups of the berries, reduce the heat, partially cover, and simmer for 5 minutes. Spoon the cooked berries into the lined bowl, reserving the excess juice. Measure out ¾ cup juice and stir in the Grand Marnier or orange juice.

3. Cover the berries with additional slices of crustless bread, cut to fit, and again make sure there are no gaps. Spoon the juice–Grand Marnier mixture over the bread. Cover with the overhanging plastic wrap. Weight the pudding with a 1-lb. weight, such as an unopened can placed on a small plate, and refrigerate overnight.

4. At serving time, remove the weight, fold back the plastic wrap, and invert the pudding onto a serving plate. Remove the plastic wrap from the sides of the pudding. Cut into wedges and serve, garnished with the remaining berries and whipped cream. —*Jane Adams Finn*

roasted red grapes
with mascarpone and rum

- **1 lb. seedless red grapes, left on the stems and cut into small clusters**
- **4 tsp. honey**
- **1 tsp. extra-virgin olive oil**
- **½ tsp. flaky sea salt**
- **½ cup mascarpone**
- **1½ Tbs. regular or spiced dark rum**
- **1 tsp. finely grated orange zest**

You can use any grape variety in this 15-minute dessert, although some types will collapse and get juicy more quickly than others. Adjust the baking time as needed.

1. Position a rack in the center of the oven and heat the oven to 475°F. In a large bowl, gently toss the grape clusters, 2 tsp. of the honey, the oil, and the salt. Spread the grapes on a large rimmed baking sheet in a single layer and roast, flipping halfway through, until collapsed, juicy, and somewhat caramelized, about 15 minutes.

2. Meanwhile, in a medium bowl, stir the mascarpone, rum, orange zest, and the remaining 2 tsp. honey.

3. Transfer the roasted grapes to serving dishes and serve warm, with a dollop of the sweetened mascarpone. *—Liz Pearson*

PER SERVING: 370 CALORIES | 5G PROTEIN | 28G CARB | 27G TOTAL FAT | 14G SAT FAT | 8G MONO FAT | 1G POLY FAT | 70MG CHOL | 330MG SODIUM | 1G FIBER

peach and blueberry galette

SERVES 8 TO 10

FOR THE CRUST

- 6¾ oz. (1½ cups) unbleached all-purpose flour; more for rolling
- 1 Tbs. granulated sugar
- ½ tsp. table salt
- 5½ oz. (11 Tbs.) unsalted butter, chilled and cut into ½-inch dice
- 1 large egg yolk
- 3 Tbs. whole milk

FOR THE FILLING

- 1 lb. peaches, peeled and cut into ½-inch slices (about 2 cups)
- ¾ lb. blueberries, rinsed and picked through (about 2 cups)
- ¼ cup light muscovado sugar or light brown sugar
- 2 Tbs. unbleached all-purpose flour
- ¼ tsp. ground cinnamon
- Pinch of table salt
- 1 large egg, beaten
- 2 Tbs. demerara sugar

- Vanilla ice cream (optional)
- Crème fraîche (optional)

This rustic fruit tart is the perfect vehicle for ripe summer blueberries and peaches. The crust is freeform—it just gets folded over the filling and then baked. Serve warm with a scoop of vanilla ice cream or a dollop of crème fraîche.

MAKE THE DOUGH

1. Combine the flour, sugar, and salt in a stand mixer fitted with a paddle attachment at low speed. Add the butter to the flour. Mix until the flour is no longer white and holds together when you clump it with your fingers, 1 to 2 minutes. If there are still lumps of butter larger than the size of peas, break them up with your fingers.

2. In a small bowl, beat the egg yolk and milk, and add to the flour mixture. Mix on low speed just until the dough comes together, about 15 seconds; the dough will be somewhat soft. Turn the dough out onto a sheet of plastic wrap, press it into a flat disk, wrap it in the plastic, and let it rest in the refrigerator for 15 to 20 minutes before rolling out.

3. Meanwhile, position a rack in the center of the oven and heat the oven to 350°F. Line a large rimmed baking sheet with parchment paper.

MAKE THE FILLING AND ROLL OUT THE DOUGH

1. In a medium bowl, toss the peaches and blueberries with the muscovado sugar, flour, cinnamon, and salt.

2. Lightly flour a large work surface and roll out the dough to a 12- to 13-inch round. Transfer to the prepared baking sheet. Arrange the fruit in the center of the dough, leaving about 1½ inches of space around the perimeter of the dough empty. Fold the outside edge of the dough over the fruit, making occasional pleats. Brush the crust with the egg. Sprinkle the demerara sugar evenly over the dough and fruit.

3. Bake the galette until the crust turns a light brown and the filling bubbles, about 50 minutes. Let cool for 10 minutes, then cut into wedges and serve warm, topped with ice cream or crème fraîche if desired. *—Tony Rosenfeld*

raspberry and blackberry mousse

MAKES 5 TO 5½ CUPS;
SERVES 4 TO 6

12	oz. raspberries, rinsed and drained
6	oz. blackberries, rinsed and drained
¾	cup granulated sugar
1	tsp. fresh lemon juice
	Pinch of kosher salt
3	large eggs, separated
1¾	tsp. unflavored gelatin
	Pinch of cream of tartar
½	cup whipping cream
	Whole berries and mint leaves, for garnish (optional)

This cool, luscious dessert is the perfect end to a summer dinner party. If you can't find ripe berries, don't use unripe, out-of-season fruit. Instead, look for individually quick frozen (IQF) berries, and use the same amounts.

1. In a food processor, combine the raspberries, blackberries, ¼ cup of the sugar, the lemon juice, and salt. Purée until smooth. Pass the purée through a fine-mesh sieve; discard the contents of the sieve. Set the purée aside.

2. Choose a medium stainless-steel bowl that can rest just inside a medium saucepan. Pour about 1 inch of water in the saucepan and bring to a boil. Fill a large bowl with ice water; set aside.

3. Put the egg yolks, ¼ cup of the sugar, and ½ cup of the berry purée in the medium bowl. When the water in the saucepan boils, reduce the heat to a gentle simmer and set the bowl with the berry mixture on the saucepan. Whisk until the mixture reaches 140°F on an instant-read thermometer. Turn off the heat but leave the bowl over the water and continue whisking for 3½ minutes. (If the temperature reaches 150°F, remove the bowl from the water, whisk until the temperature drops to 145°F, and then return the bowl to the water bath to continue whisking.) Remove the bowl from the saucepan, stir in the remaining purée, and set the medium bowl into the ice bath to cool. Don't pour the hot water out of the saucepan.

4. Pour ¼ cup cold water into a small heatproof custard cup; sprinkle the gelatin evenly over the water in the cup. Let sit for about 5 minutes. Set the custard cup with the gelatin in the saucepan with the hot water and stir the gelatin mixture until the gelatin melts and becomes translucent, about 2 minutes. Once the gelatin has melted, whisk it into the berry mixture. Whisk occasionally until the mixture cools to 50°F to 55°F and thickens slightly.

5. In a dry, grease-free bowl, beat the egg whites with a hand mixer (be sure the beaters are dry and grease-free, too) on low until frothy; add the cream of tartar. Increase the speed to medium high. Beat until the whites turn opaque, begin to thicken, and look foamy, 1½ minutes. Gradually beat in the remaining ¼ cup sugar. Continue beating until the whites look thick and shiny (but not dry), resemble thickly whipped cream, and form medium peaks, about 3 minutes.

6. In a separate bowl (no need to clean the beaters this time), beat the cream until soft peaks form, about 2 minutes.

7. Whisk a couple of large spoonfuls of the beaten egg whites into the berry mixture to lighten it. Pour the ice and water out of the ice bath bowl; dry the bowl. Pour the lightened berry mixture into the cold bowl.

8. Scrape the remaining egg whites and cream on top and fold gently with a rubber spatula until just combined. Spoon the mousse into individual glasses, into a 6-cup bowl, or into individual soufflé dishes. Refrigerate, covered, until firm, at least 4 hours but no longer than 24 hours.

9. Just before serving, garnish with berries and mint leaves, if you like.
–Jennifer McLagan

PER SERVING: 250 CALORIES I 5G PROTEIN I 36G CARB I 10G TOTAL FAT I 5G SAT FAT I 3G MONO FAT I 1G POLY FAT I 135MG CHOL I 65MG SODIUM I 5G FIBER

serve the mousse individually or in one big bowl

Instead of serving the mousse in goblets, try 4- to 6-oz. ramekins. Create height with a parchment collar secured with a thick rubber band, and refrigerate. Remove the collar just before garnishing and serving.

Or, put the mousse in a 6-cup bowl and garnish with a jumble of berries; to serve, scoop out individual servings.

mixed berries with vanilla bean syrup

SERVES 4 TO 6;
MAKES ⅓ CUP SYRUP

- **½ vanilla bean**
- **¼ cup granulated sugar**
- **1 pint (2 cups) raspberries**
- **1 pint (2 cups) blueberries**
- **1 pint (2 cups) blackberries**
- **½ pint (1 cup) strawberries**

Use whatever berries are freshest at your market in this sophisticated, yet simple, fruit salad.

1. Split the vanilla bean in half lengthwise with a sharp paring knife and scrape out the seeds with the back of the knife; save the empty pod for a garnish, if you like. Put the seeds in a small saucepan, along with the sugar and ¼ cup water. Bring to a simmer over medium heat, stirring occasionally, until the sugar dissolves. Reduce the heat to low and cook for 7 minutes to let the vanilla infuse. Strain through a fine-mesh sieve to remove any fibrous pieces of vanilla pod or clumps of seeds. Let cool and refrigerate until completely chilled.

2. Rinse the raspberries, blueberries, and blackberries and spread them in a single layer on a towel to dry. Hull the strawberries and cut them into quarters.

3. Just before serving, combine all the berries in a large serving bowl and pour on just enough of the vanilla syrup to lightly coat them, about 3 Tbs. Toss gently. —*Irit Ishai*

PER SERVING: 110 CALORIES | 1G PROTEIN | 28G CARB | 0.5G TOTAL FAT | 0G SAT FAT | 0G MONO FAT | 0G POLY FAT | 0MG CHOL | 0MG SODIUM | 7G FIBER

tropical mango sorbet

SERVES 6

- **4** **mangos (about 3 lb.), pitted and cut into ½-inch dice (about 4 cups)**
- **1** **medium papaya (about ¾ lb.), cut into ½-inch dice (about 1½ cups)**
- **1** **cup pineapple juice**
- **½** **cup granulated sugar**
- **¼** **cup coconut milk**
- **Finely grated zest and juice of 1 lime**

Papaya and pineapple juice build on the clean, sweet flavor of mango in this sorbet, while a splash of coconut milk smooths its texture. If papayas aren't readily available or in season, just add another mango.

Working in batches if necessary, purée all of the ingredients in a blender until smooth. Transfer the mixture to a bowl, cover, and refrigerate until cold (about 2 hours). Freeze in an ice cream machine according to the manufacturer's instructions. Transfer the sorbet to an airtight container and freeze overnight to finish setting. Take the sorbet out of the freezer and let it soften for about 5 minutes before serving. It will keep in the freezer for about 2 weeks. —*Tony Rosenfeld*

pitting mangos

To remove a mango pit, position the mango upright and cut downward using a chef's knife, parallel to the pit but slightly off center. If you feel resistance, that's the pit; move the knife farther from the center and make the slice again. Do the same for the other side, cutting downward away from the center; discard the pit. Score the flesh of the fruit almost all the way to the skin lengthwise and then widthwise in the desired size dice. Use a spoon to scoop out the diced mango.

strawberry-rhubarb cobbler with honey

SERVES 6 TO 8

FOR THE FILLING

- **1** lb. strawberries, hulled and cut into ½-inch pieces (about 2½ cups)
- **¾** lb. fresh or thawed frozen rhubarb, cut into ½-inch pieces (about 2½ cups)
- **1** large lemon, finely grated to yield ½ tsp. zest and squeezed to yield 2 Tbs. juice
- **¾** cup mild honey (like clover)
- **2** Tbs. instant tapioca
- **1** Tbs. cornstarch
- **1** Tbs. finely chopped fresh basil
- **½** tsp. kosher salt

FOR THE TOPPING

- **9** oz. (2 cups) unbleached all-purpose flour; more as needed
- **2** Tbs. granulated sugar
- **4** tsp. baking powder
- **½** tsp. kosher salt
- **3** oz. (6 Tbs.) cold unsalted butter, cut into ½-inch pieces; more, softened, for the dish
- **⅔** cup plus 1 to 2 Tbs. heavy cream
- **1** Tbs. mild honey (like clover)
- **1** Tbs. turbinado (raw) sugar
- **¼** tsp. ground cinnamon

In this rustic dessert, honey flavors both the tender biscuit topping and the sweet-tart fruit. To ensure that the filling is thickened and fully cooked, bake the cobbler until it bubbles in the center.

Position a rack in the center of the oven and heat the oven to 375°F.

MAKE THE FILLING

In a large bowl, thoroughly mix all of the filling ingredients; set aside.

MAKE THE TOPPING

In another large bowl, sift together the flour, sugar, baking powder, and salt. Using your fingers, work the cold butter into the flour until the mixture resembles coarse meal. Add ⅔ cup of the cream and mix the dough with your fingers until it just comes together (if the dough seems dry, add an additional tablespoon of cream). On a well-floured surface, roll the dough out to a 14x18-inch rectangle that's ⅛ inch thick. Using a 1¾-inch round cutter, cut the dough into approximately 50 rounds, pushing the cutter down and pulling it up without twisting it as you cut each round.

PREPARE THE COBBLER

1. Butter a shallow 2-quart dish. Transfer the filling to the dish and arrange the rounds on top, overlapping slightly. In a small bowl, combine the remaining 1 Tbs. cream with the honey and brush the mixture over the rounds. In another small bowl, combine the turbinado sugar and cinnamon and sprinkle on top.

2. Bake until the biscuits are deep golden brown on top and the filling is bubbling in the center, 20 to 25 minutes. If the biscuits brown too quickly, cover loosely with aluminum foil. Let cool for at least 20 minutes before serving. *—Ronne Day*

PER SERVING: 410 CALORIES | 4G PROTEIN | 64G CARB | 16G TOTAL FAT | 10G SAT FAT | 4.5G MONO FAT | 1G POLY FAT | 50MG CHOL | 330MG SODIUM | 3G FIBER

sweet corn cake with blueberry-lavender compote

SERVES 10 TO 12

FOR THE CAKE

- **6 oz. (¾ cup) unsalted butter,** softened at room temperature; more for the pan
- **4½ oz. (1 cup) unbleached all-purpose flour**
- **2 tsp. baking powder**
- **¼ tsp. table salt**
- **2¼ oz. (½ cup) sifted stone-ground yellow cornmeal**
- **1 cup cooked fresh corn kernels (from about 1 large ear)**
- **½ cup sour cream,** at room temperature
- **¾ cup granulated sugar**
- **3 large eggs,** at room temperature and lightly beaten

FOR THE COMPOTE

- **1 cup granulated sugar**
- **2 tsp. dried lavender**
- **1¼ cups cooked fresh corn kernels (from about 2 medium ears)**
- **1 cup blueberries**

A lavender-scented topping lends an elegant touch to this rustic cake. To cook the corn, boil it in lightly salted water until tender, 3 to 5 minutes, depending on how fresh the corn is. You can skip sifting the cornmeal if you'd like a coarser texture in the cake.

BAKE THE CAKE

1. Position a rack in the center of the oven and heat the oven to 350°F. Butter the sides and bottom of a 9x2-inch round cake pan. Fit a round of parchment in the bottom of the pan and butter that as well.

2. Sift the flour, baking powder, and salt into a medium bowl. Whisk in the cornmeal; set aside.

3. Purée the corn kernels in a food processor until smooth. Strain the purée through a fine-mesh sieve, pressing with a rubber spatula to extract the liquid; scrape any purée off the bottom of the sieve into the liquid and then discard the remaining solids. Measure ¼ cup of the strained corn liquid and transfer to a small bowl (discard any excess liquid). Stir in the sour cream.

4. In a stand mixer fitted with the paddle attachment, beat the butter and sugar on medium-high speed until fluffy, about 2 minutes. Stop and scrape the sides of the bowl. On low speed, slowly pour in the beaten eggs, mixing until incorporated and stopping midway to scrape down the sides. (The mixture will be loose and curdled-looking.)

5. On low speed, add one-third of the flour mixture and mix until just blended. Add one-third of the sour cream–corn mixture and mix until just blended. Alternate adding the remaining flour and sour cream mixtures in two additions each. Don't overmix.

6. Scrape the batter into the cake pan and spread it evenly with a spatula. Bake until the cake is golden brown and springs back when lightly pressed in the center, 30 to 35 minutes. Transfer to a rack to cool for 10 to 15 minutes. Run a knife around the edge of the pan and then gently invert the cake onto the rack, removing the pan. Remove the parchment, turn the cake right side up onto the rack, and let cool completely.

MAKE THE COMPOTE

1. Combine the sugar and ⅔ cup water in a small saucepan. Bring to a simmer over medium-high heat, stirring frequently until the sugar has dissolved completely. Remove from the heat. Add the lavender and stir to combine. Let infuse for 10 minutes, then strain the syrup into a small bowl and let cool.

2. When ready to serve the cake, stir the corn and blueberries into the syrup. Cut the cake into wedges and top each serving with about 3 Tbs. of the mixture, letting most of the syrup drain off the spoon before sprinkling the blueberries and corn over the cake.
—*Mary Ellen Driscoll*

PER SERVING: 320 CALORIES | 4G PROTEIN | 46G CARB | 15G TOTAL FAT | 9G SAT FAT | 4G MONO FAT | 1G POLY FAT | 85MG CHOL | 140MG SODIUM | 2G FIBER

chocolate pavlova with tangerine whipped cream

SERVES 8 TO 10

- **4** large egg whites, at room temperature
- **⅛** tsp. cream of tartar
- **⅛** tsp. table salt
- **1** cup plus 2 Tbs. granulated sugar
- **1½** tsp. cornstarch
- **1** Tbs. red-wine vinegar
- **¾** oz. (¼ cup) unsweetened Dutch-processed cocoa powder, sifted; more for sprinkling
- **1** cup heavy cream
- Finely grated zest of 1 tangerine (about 1¼ tsp.)
- **1½** cups fruit, such as raspberries, sliced strawberries, peeled and sliced mango, peeled and sliced kiwi, or a mix

Although it may look indulgent, this billowy chocolate dessert is surprisingly low in calories and fat. It also comes together easily.

MAKE THE MERINGUE

1. Position a rack in the center of the oven and heat the oven to 350°F. Cut a piece of parchment so that it fits flat on a baking sheet. With a pencil, draw a 9-inch circle in the center of the parchment (tracing a 9-inch cake pan works fine). Line the baking sheet with the parchment, pencil side facing down (you should still be able to see the circle).

2. With an electric hand mixer or stand mixer and the whisk attachment, whip the egg whites, cream of tartar, and salt in a large, dry bowl on medium speed until foamy, about 30 seconds. Gradually add 1 cup of the sugar and then the cornstarch and vinegar; whip on medium high until the whites hold stiff peaks and look glossy, another 3 to 5 minutes. Add the sifted cocoa powder and mix on low speed until mostly combined, 20 to 30 seconds, scraping the bowl as needed. Finish mixing the cocoa into the meringue by hand with a rubber spatula until well combined and no streaks of white remain.

SHAPE AND BAKE

1. Pile the meringue inside the circle on the parchment. Using the spatula, spread the meringue to even it out slightly—it doesn't need to align perfectly with the circle, and it shouldn't be perfectly smooth or overworked. The natural swirls and ridges give the finished meringue character.

2. Bake for 10 minutes and then reduce the heat to 300°F and bake until the meringue has puffed and cracked around its edges, another 45 to 50 minutes. Turn off the oven, prop the oven door open, and leave the meringue in the oven to cool to room temperature, at least 30 minutes. The delicate meringue won't collapse as much if it cools gradually.

ASSEMBLE AND SERVE

Just before serving, put the meringue on a serving platter. In a chilled medium stainless-steel bowl, beat the cream with the remaining 2 Tbs. sugar until it holds soft peaks. Whip in the tangerine zest, making sure it's evenly distributed. Pile the whipped cream on the meringue, spreading it almost out to the edge, and then top with the fruit and sprinkle with cocoa. To serve, slice into wedges with a serrated knife. —*Gale Gand*

PER SERVING: 200 CALORIES | 3G PROTEIN | 30G CARB | 9G TOTAL FAT | 6G SAT FAT | 3G MONO FAT | 0G POLY FAT | 35MG CHOL | 60MG SODIUM | 2G FIBER

how to make a perfect pavlova shell

Beat the egg whites until they form stiff peaks and are extremely glossy.

Use a rubber spatula to gently swirl the meringue and spread into a rough circle.

Cool the pavlova gradually. Don't worry if your pavlova collapses in the center; you're going to pile on cream and fruit anyway.

spiced buttermilk pound cake
with strawberry sauce

SERVES 8 TO 10

4 oz. (½ cup) unsalted butter, softened; more for the pan

1¼ cups granulated sugar

3 eggs, at room temperature

1 tsp. pure vanilla extract

Freshly grated zest of 1 orange

2 cups unbleached all-purpose flour

2 Tbs. cornstarch

1 tsp. baking soda

½ tsp. salt

1½ tsp. ground cardamom

½ tsp. ground cinnamon

½ tsp. ground ginger

1 scant cup buttermilk

Strawberry sauce, for serving (recipe below)

This cake is wonderful plain, but it also makes a perfect vehicle for strawberry sauce or lemon verbena sauce, a purée of mixed berries and sugar, or a vanilla-scented custard sauce.

1. Heat the oven to 350°F. Lightly butter a 5x9-inch loaf pan. Line the pan with waxed paper and butter the paper.

2. In a bowl, cream the butter, gradually adding the sugar. Add the eggs one at a time, beating until smooth and fluffy after each addition. Blend in the vanilla and zest.

3. Sift the dry ingredients into a separate bowl. Add the dry ingredients alternately with the buttermilk, beginning and ending with the dry ingredients. Mix until uniformly blended.

4. Scrape the batter into the pan and level the top. Bake until a toothpick inserted in the center of the cake comes out clean, 60 to 70 minutes.

5. Cool the cake in the pan, on a rack, for 15 minutes. Turn out of the pan and peel off the waxed paper. Finish cooling, slice, and serve with Strawberry sauce.   *—Ken Haedrich*

strawberry sauce

1 qt. ripe strawberries

3 Tbs. granulated sugar

Juice of ½ lemon

Rinse and hull the strawberries. In a food processor, purée slightly more than half of the berries, the sugar, and the lemon juice. Transfer to a bowl. Coarsely chop the remaining berries by hand and fold them into the purée.

warm berries and nectarines with mascarpone

MAKES ABOUT 4 CUPS; SERVES 3 OR 4

- **2 Tbs. granulated sugar**
- **1 tsp. ground ginger**
- **4 cups mixed berries (such as raspberries, blueberries, and blackberries)**
- **3 medium ripe nectarines, thinly sliced**
- **¼ cup mascarpone (or Greek yogurt)**

Fresh summer berries become a warm dessert or breakfast treat after a quick cook in a hot skillet. Mascarpone, an Italian-style cream cheese available in most grocery stores, is a simple creamy topping for the fruit.

In a large (12-inch) skillet, combine the sugar and ginger with ⅓ cup water and put the pan over medium-high heat. When the water comes to a boil, add the berries and nectarines and cook, stirring frequently, until the nectarines have just started to soften and the juice released from the berries has thickened slightly, 4 to 5 minutes. Let cool for a minute, and then transfer to individual serving bowls and garnish with a dollop of mascarpone. —*Dabney Gough*

PER SERVING: 250 CALORIES | 4G PROTEIN | 36G CARB | 14G TOTAL FAT | 7G SAT FAT | 3.5G MONO FAT | 0G POLY FAT | 35MG CHOL | 0MG SODIUM | 6G FIBER

blueberry cheesecake with gingersnap crust

SERVES 8 TO 10

FOR THE CRUST

- **2** cups ground gingersnap cookies (about 35 cookies)
- **3** oz. (6 Tbs.) unsalted butter, melted; more for the pan
- **2** Tbs. granulated sugar

FOR THE FILLING AND TOPPING

- **1½** lb. blueberries (about 4 cups), rinsed, dried, and picked through
- **1½** cups granulated sugar
- Finely grated zest and juice of 1 lemon
- **¼** tsp. freshly grated nutmeg
- **2** tsp. cornstarch
- **3** 8-oz. packages cream cheese, softened
- **1** cup sour cream (not low- or nonfat)
- **2** large eggs
- **2** large egg yolks
- **1** tsp. pure vanilla extract

Blueberries contrast the richness of this cheesecake and pair perfectly with the gingersnap crust. The cheesecake needs to chill for about 8 hours in the refrigerator, so you may want to make it a day ahead.

Position a rack in the center of the oven and heat the oven to 350°F. Butter a 9-inch springform pan.

PREPARE AND BAKE THE CRUST
In a medium bowl, toss the cookie crumbs with the butter and sugar. Pour into the prepared pan; use your fingers and the bottom of a flat glass to tamp down the crust so it's even on the bottom and goes an inch up the sides of the pan. Bake the crust until it browns lightly and puffs slightly, 10 to 15 minutes. Transfer to a rack to cool to room temperature.

MAKE THE FILLING
1. Combine the blueberries, ½ cup of the sugar, the lemon zest and juice, and nutmeg in a large, 12-inch sauté pan and let sit for 5 minutes so the blueberries start to release their juices. Cook over medium-high heat, shaking the pan, until the blueberries start to soften and their juices boil, 3 to 4 minutes. Whisk the cornstarch with 2 Tbs. water and stir into the blueberry mixture so it thickens. Remove from the heat and let cool to room temperature. Transfer 1½ cups of this mixture to a blender and purée. Strain the puréed mixture through a fine-mesh sieve, discard the solids, and reserve the liquid. Put the remaining blueberry mixture in an airtight container in the refrigerator.

2. Beat the cream cheese and the remaining 1 cup sugar in a stand mixer with the paddle attachment (or in a large bowl with electric beaters) on medium speed until the mixture is well combined (you may need to use a spatula to free the paddle of the cheese). Reduce to low speed and, one at a time, add the sour cream, eggs, egg yolks, puréed blueberry mixture, and vanilla, and beat until just incorporated. Pour the batter into the gingersnap crust. Wrap the bottom and sides of the springform pan in aluminum foil, making sure the foil goes about three-quarters up the sides of the pan, and then put the springform pan in a large roasting pan. Pour hot water into the roasting pan so it reaches about halfway up the sides of the springform pan.

3. Transfer the roasting pan to the oven and bake until the top of the cake sets but the center jiggles slightly when shaken, about 1 hour. Using a metal spatula and an oven mitt, remove the springform pan from the water bath, discard the foil, and transfer to a rack to cool to room temperature, about 1 hour. Refrigerate the cake uncovered until completely chilled, about 8 hours. Run a paring knife along the sides of the cake to separate it from the pan, and then unlatch and remove the sides of the springform pan. Use a metal spatula to loosen the bottom crust from the pan, and then, using two spatulas, transfer the cake to a serving plate. Spoon the refrigerated blueberries on top of the cake. Cut into slices and serve. —*Tony Rosenfeld*

ice cream with cherry caramel sauce

**SERVES 4;
MAKES 1½ CUPS SAUCE**

- **1 cup granulated sugar**
- **1 Tbs. light corn syrup**
- **Kosher salt**
- **2 cups sweet cherries, pitted and halved**
- **5 Tbs. heavy cream**
- **2 pints vanilla or pistachio ice cream**

This simple dessert hinges on the bittersweet caramel sauce. The trick is to make sure the caramel gets dark enough so that it takes on a slightly bitter edge and isn't too sweet. Once it begins to color, it will darken quickly and continue to do so even after leaving the heat, so work fast to avoid burning.

1. Combine the sugar, corn syrup, a pinch of salt, and ¼ cup water in a heavy-duty 4-quart saucepan. Cook over medium heat, whisking frequently, until the sugar is dissolved, 4 to 5 minutes. Raise the heat to high and bring to a boil, brushing down the sides of the pan with a damp pastry brush to dissolve any sugar crystals. Boil, without whisking, until the mixture begins to color. Continue to cook, swirling the pan for even caramelization, until the caramel turns dark brown, about 7 minutes.

2. Immediately remove the saucepan from the heat. Quickly add the cherries and cream—be careful, the mixture will spatter. Set the saucepan over low heat and cook, whisking constantly, until the caramel is completely fluid with no lumps, about 2 minutes. Remove the pan from the heat and whisk to cool for a couple of minutes.

3. Scoop the ice cream into bowls, top with the sauce, and serve immediately. *—Lori Longbotham*

PER SERVING: 910 CALORIES | 11G PROTEIN | 112G CARB | 47G TOTAL FAT | 26G SAT FAT | 2G MONO FAT | 0G POLY FAT | 245MG CHOL | 190MG SODIUM | 2G FIBER

mango-honey-mint sorbet

SERVES 8

- **1** or 2 large oranges, zest finely grated to yield ½ tsp. and squeezed to yield ½ cup juice

- **4** cups chopped, peeled, very ripe mango (from about 3 large)

- **½** cup mild honey (like clover)

- **2** tsp. chopped fresh mint

- **½** tsp. kosher salt

Make Ahead

The sorbet will keep in the freezer for up to 1 month. If the texture becomes icy, melt the sorbet and refreeze it in the ice cream maker.

Here, honey replaces the sugar syrup that usually sweetens sorbet, lending it a deeper flavor. Be sure to purée the sorbet mixture until completely smooth for the best texture.

1. Combine all of the ingredients with ½ cup water in a blender and purée until completely smooth. Freeze in an ice cream maker according to the manufacturer's instructions.

2. Serve immediately, or transfer to an airtight container and freeze for a firmer texture. —*Ronne Day*

PER SERVING: 120 CALORIES | 1G PROTEIN | 31G CARB | 0G TOTAL FAT | 0G SAT FAT | 0G MONO FAT | 0G POLY FAT | 0MG CHOL | 70MG SODIUM | 1G FIBER

METRIC EQUIVALENTS

LIQUID/DRY MEASURES	
U.S.	**METRIC**
¼ teaspoon	1.25 milliliters
½ teaspoon	2.5 milliliters
1 teaspoon	5 milliliters
1 tablespoon (3 teaspoons)	15 milliliters
1 fluid ounce (2 tablespoons)	30 milliliters
¼ cup	60 milliliters
⅓ cup	80 milliliters
½ cup	120 milliliters
1 cup	240 milliliters
1 pint (2 cups)	480 milliliters
1 quart (4 cups; 32 ounces)	960 milliliters
1 gallon (4 quarts)	3.84 liters
1 ounce (by weight)	28 grams
1 pound	454 grams
2.2 pounds	1 kilogram

OVEN TEMPERATURES		
°F	**GAS MARK**	**°C**
250	½	120
275	1	140
300	2	150
325	3	165
350	4	180
375	5	190
400	6	200
425	7	220
450	8	230
475	9	240
500	10	260
550	Broil	290

CONTRIBUTORS

Bruce Aidells is a chef, cookbook author, and meat and grilling expert. His Live Well network television show is called *Good Cookin' with Bruce Aidells*, and he has written 10 cookbooks.

Pam Anderson is a contributing editor to *Fine Cooking* and the author of several books, including *Cook without a Book*. She blogs weekly about food and life with daughters Maggy and Sharon on their website, www.threemanycooks.com.

Jennifer Armentrout is the editor-in-chief at *Fine Cooking*.

John Ash is the founder and chef of John Ash & Co., in Santa Rosa, California. He teaches at the Culinary Institute of America at Greystone and is also a cookbook author. His book, *John Ash: Cooking One on One*, won a James Beard award.

Jessica Bard is a food stylist, food writer, and recipe tester who teaches cooking classes at Warren Kitchen and Cutlery in Rhinebeck, New York.

Karen Barker is a pastry chef and cookbook author. She co-owns Magnolia Grill in Durham, North Carolina. She won the James Beard Outstanding Pastry Chef Award in 2003.

David Bonom is a food writer in New Jersey.

Julie Grimes Bottcher is a recipe developer and food writer.

Sarah Breckenridge is the senior web producer for finecooking.com.

Jennifer Bushman is the author of *The Kitchen Coach Cookbook* and founded the Nothing To It! Cooking School in Reno, Nevada. Her *Gourmet News Segments* are produced weekly, with syndication in five Western States. Jennifer is also the National Volunteer Culinary Spokesperson for the American Heart Association.

Lauren Chattman has written 12 cookbooks, including *Simply Great Breads* and *Cookie Swap*.

Dina Cheney attended the Culinary Arts Career program at New York's Institute of Culinary Education and has taught cooking classes throughout the New York City metro area. She's the author of *Year-Round Slow Cooker*, as well as two other cookbooks. She develops recipes for *Fine Cooking*, is a monthly columnist for *Everyday with Rachael Ray* magazine, and writes for many other food and lifestyle publications.

Ronne Day is an associate food editor and food stylist for *Fine Cooking*.

Tasha DeSerio is a cooking teacher, food writer, and caterer in Berkeley, California. Her latest book, *Salad for Dinner*, was published in 2012.

Abigail Johnson Dodge, a former pastry chef, is a widely published food writer, cooking instructor, and *Fine Cooking* contributor editor. She has also written numerous cookbooks, including *Mini Treats & Hand-Held Sweets*.

Maryellen Driscoll is a *Fine Cooking* contributing editor. She and her husband own Free Bird Farm in upstate New York.

Jane Adams Finn is an independent food writer for *The Washington Post*.

Allison Fishman is a cooking teacher, healthy living and home cooking consultant, and food writer for numerous publications.

Janet Fletcher is a Napa Valley food writer and the author of *Fresh from the Farmers' Market* and *Cheese & Wine: A Guide to Selecting, Pairing, and Enjoying*.

St. John Frizell is a food, drink, and travel writer whose work has appeared in *Oxford American, Edible Brooklyn*, and *Edible Manhattan*, as well as on epicurious.com. He is the owner of the café-bar, Fort Defiance, in the Red Hook neighborhood of Brooklyn, New York.

Gale Gand is a pastry chef, restaurateur, and cookbook author. She was recognized in 2001 as Outstanding Pastry Chef by The James Beard Foundation and Pastry Chef of the Year in 2001 by *Bon Appetit* magazine.

Dabney Gough is a Honolulu-based food writer, cookbook author, and recipe developer. Her latest cookbook is *Sweet Cream and Sugar Cones*.

Ken Haedrich is a food and travel writer, cooking teacher, and product spokesperson. He is the author of many cookbooks, including the award-winning *Home for the Holidays* and *Pie*, which was named by Amazon as the best cookbook of the year in 2011. Ken started ThePieAcademy.com to help both novice and experienced pie makers become better bakers.

Karen Hatfield has worked in the pastry kitchens at Café Boulud, Jean-Georges, and Gramercy Tavern in New York City. She and her husband are co-owners of Hatfield's restaurant in Los Angeles.

Kate Hays is the chef-owner of Dish Catering in Shelburne, Vermont. She is also a recipe tester, recipe developer, and food stylist.

Martha Holmberg is a cookbook author and food writer based in Portland, Oregon. Her latest book is *Fresh Food Nation*.

Irit Ishai is Head Pastry Chef and co-founder of Sugar Butter Flour, a well-known bakery in Sunnyvale, California.

Raghavan Iyer is the author of three cookbooks, most recently *660 Curries*.

Sara Jenkins is co-author of *Olives and Oranges: Recipes and Flavor Secrets from Italy, Spain, Cyprus, and Beyond*. She is the owner of Porchetta, a takeout restaurant in New York City.

Elizabeth Karmel is a nationally known grilling and barbecue expert and cookbook author and teacher. Her latest book is *Soaked, Slathered and Seasoned*. Elizabeth is the creator of the Grill Friends™ and Kitchen Friends™ line of outdoor cooking and kitchen tools and www.GirlsattheGrill.com. In addition, she is the executive chef of Hill Country, a Texas barbecue restaurant in New York City and an instructor at New York's Institute of Culinary Education (ICE).

Eva Katz has worked as a chef, caterer, teacher, recipe developer and tester, food stylist, and food writer. She is a member of the Program Advisory Committee at the Cambridge School of Culinary Arts in Massachusetts.

Ian Knauer worked in the *Gourmet* test kitchens until the close of the brand in late 2009. Since then, he has been a contributor to several food-related publications, including his own blog. He is also the author of *The Farm*, published in 2012.

Allison Ehri Kreitler is a *Fine Cooking* contributing editor. She has also worked as a freelance food stylist, recipe tester and developer, and writer for several national food magazines and the Food Network.

David Leite is a food writer, blog publisher, and cookbook author. His first book, *The New Portuguese Table*, won the 2010 IACP Julia Child Award.

Lori Longbotham is a chef and food writer who has written 10 cookbooks; her most recent is *Luscious Coconut Desserts*.

Deborah Madison is a cookbook author, cooking teacher, and consultant. Her most recent book is *Seasonal Fruit Desserts from Orchard, Farm, and Market*.

Jennifer McLagan is a chef, food stylist, and cookbook author; her book, *Fat: An Appreciation of a Misunderstood Ingredient*, with Recipes was named the 2009 James Beard Cookbook of the Year.

Susie Middleton is *Fine Cooking*'s editor at large, a food writer, recipe developer, and cookbook author. Her latest book is *The Fresh and Green Table*. She lives and grows her own vegetables on Martha's Vineyard, Massachusetts.

Jan Newberry has been the food and wine editor of *San Francisco Magazine* for the past 10 years and contributes regularly to *Sunset* and *Food & Wine Magazine*.

Liz Pearson worked as the kitchen director for *Saveur* magazine before moving back to her native Texas, where she's a freelance writer and recipe developer.

Melissa Pellegrino, a former assistant food editor at *Fine Cooking*, is the author of *The Italian Farmer's Table* and *The Southern Italian Farmer's Table*.

Steven Raichlen is a multi-award-winning author, journalist, television host, and novelist. His books include the international blockbusters *The Barbecue Bible* and *How to Grill* and *The New York Times*-bestselling *Planet Barbecue*.

Tony Rosenfeld, a *Fine Cooking* contributing editor, is the author of two cookbooks. He's also the co-owner of b.good, a Boston-based healthy fast food chain, and the creator of cookangel.com, a culinary troubleshooting website.

Eric Rupert is formerly executive chef at Sub-Zero and Wolf in Madison, Wisconsin.

Chris Schlesinger, a graduate of the CIA, owns multiple restaurants, including Back Eddy in Westport, Massachusetts. He is also the author of five cookbooks, including the James Beard Cookbook Award winner *The Thrill of the Grill*. Chris was the winner of the 1996 James Beard Awards Best Chef of the Northeast.

Jackie Shen is the former chef at Red Light and Chicago Cut.

Ed Shoenfeld is a Chinese-food restaurateur and expert on Chinese cuisine.

Maria Helm Sinskey is a noted chef, cookbook author, and culinary director at her family's winery, Robert Sinskey Vineyards, in Napa Valley, California. She is a frequent contributor to *Food & Wine*, *Bon Appetit*, and *Fine Cooking* magazines. Her cookbook *Family Meals* was a 2010 IACP Cookbook Award Winner. Maria's accolades include *Food & Wine Magazine's* Best New Chef 1996 and *San Francisco Magazine's* Rising Star Chef 1996.

Joanne McAllister Smart, the co-author of two Italian cookbooks with Scott Conant and *Bistro Cooking at Home* with Gordon Hamersley, is a senior editor at *Fine Cooking*.

Melissa Speck is the director of restaurant talent acquisition, administration, and research at Paragon Search and Strategies.

Stu Stein is a chef in the Pacific Northwest.

Anna Thomas, a screen writer and chef, has written many cookbooks, including *Love Soup*. She cooks and entertains in Ojai, California, and teaches a screen-writing workshop in Los Angeles.

Sue Torres is the chef at Suenos and Los Dados, both in New York City.

Annie Wayte is formerly the executive chef of Nicole's and 202 in New York City. Her first cookbook is *Keep It Seasonal: Soups, Salads, and Sandwiches*.

Bruce Weinstein, a one-time advertising creative director and a Johnson & Wales graduate, and **Mark Scarbrough**, a former professor of American literature, write and develop recipes. They have co-authored more than 15 cookbooks.

Joanne Weir is a James Beard Award-winning cookbook author, chef, cooking teacher, and television personality. Her latest book is *Joanne Weir's Cooking Confidence*, the companion book to her public television show of the same name. She is also executive chef of Copita restaurant in northern California.

Dawn Yanagihara-Mitchell is a cookbook author, food writer, and recipe developer in San Francisco, California. Her most recent book is *Waffles*.

INDEX

If you like this book, you'll love *Fine Cooking*.